Braided Threads

The United States today supports the strongest, most varied nonprofit sector in the world, an economic force of about $2 trillion, responsible for 5.4% of the nation's Gross Domestic Product in 2014, and accounting that year for 10.3% of the country's private-sector workforce. Roughly three-quarters of all households in America give to charity, with the average total donation being about $2,030 annually. Yet for all this, few Americans, and more specifically, a surprisingly small proportion of the sector's practitioners, know where the non-profit sector came from, or how it developed and came to be what we know it as today. This work is a historical overview of that sector, presented less as a chronology than as a discussion of the major influences—some legal, some social, some political—that helped shape the arena.

The core message of the book is that the developmental trajectory of non-profits has not been a straight line. Rather, its path over the years might be compared to that of a pinball, moving straight and building up momentum for a time, but then ricocheting off some event or social trend and taking off in a new direction altogether. Equally important, however, the sector is also the product of a founding genome that came out of colonial, Puritan-inspired New England and spread as that culture and its values became one of the dominant forces in American society. Knowing this history is a prerequisite for understanding and appreciating the character of this deeply influential part of American social culture.

Robert M. Penna is the author of *The Nonprofit Outcomes Toolbox*, as well as numerous articles that have appeared in such outlets as the *Stanford Social Innovations Review* and the *Huffington Post*. He served for five years as a consultant to Charity Navigator, and also as an outcomes consultant to the World Scout Bureau. He has presented before numerous nonprofit organizations and nonprofit associations across the U.S., and in Canada, Poland, Kenya, Saudi Arabia, and Australia.

A native of the Bronx, he was a staff member of the New York State Senate for thirteen years beginning in 1982, over that period holding several senior-level positions including Director of Research for the Legislative Commission on Public-Private Cooperation, and Director of Communications for the Senate Finance Committee. He graduated from Fordham University and holds a Ph.D. from Boston University. He lives in Wilmington, NC, with his wife Elise and their two dogs, Charlie and Kodie, and Chester and Henry, their cats.

Braided Threads

A Historical Overview of the American Nonprofit Sector

Robert M. Penna

Routledge
Taylor & Francis Group

LONDON AND NEW YORK

First published 2018
by Routledge
2 Park Square, Milton Park, Abingdon, Oxon OX14 4RN

and by Routledge
711 Third Avenue, New York, NY 10017

Routledge is an imprint of the Taylor & Francis Group, an informa business

British Library Cataloguing-in-Publication Data
A catalogue record for this book is available from the British Library

Library of Congress Cataloging-in-Publication Data
A catalog record for this book has been requested

ISBN: 978-0-8153-9391-7 (hbk)
ISBN: 978-0-8153-9393-1 (pbk)
ISBN: 978-1-351-18703-9 (ebk)

Typeset in Bembo
by Swales & Willis Ltd. Exeter, Devon, UK

Contents

Illustrations

Figures

Table

Acknowledgments

No work such as the one you are now reading comes about in a vacuum. The author is always indebted to others. In some cases those people are the ones who went before, those upon whose earlier work the author builds and adds his or her own contributions.

As the following pages will demonstrate, the history of the American non-profit sector is the complicated product of many events, forces, and developments over a stretch of time considerably longer than most people suspect.

Many of the numerous experts cited as sources in this work focused their attention and talents upon very specific aspects of that history, and for their scholarship I am extremely grateful. Specifically, I must acknowledge the late Peter Dobkin Hall and Robert H. Bremner, who is also, unfortunately, no longer with us. I similarly want to express my appreciation for the work of Lester Salamon, Thomas Kelley, Robert L. Beebe, Stephen J. Harrison, the late Laura B. Chisolm, and Lawrence J. Friedman and Mark D. McGarvie, and the many authors who contributed to their impressive 2002 volume, *Charity, Philanthropy and Civility in American History*. Credit for the idea that led to this volume must be given to Colin Woodard, whose analysis in *American Nations* was irreplaceable. Readers may also notice that references in these pages draw from a broad range of sources, and I wish to express my appreciation to Russell Shorto, Doug Most, and Candice Millard for their respective works, each of which made for informative and enjoyable reading and allowed me to add occasional contextual color to this effort.

I want to thank Dr. Jeff Brudney of the University of North Carolina, Wilmington, and Dr. Les Lenkowsky, Professor Emeritus in Public Affairs and Philanthropy at Indiana University, Bloomington, for their thoughts and comments upon reading early drafts of this work. They were extremely valuable.

I must also express my deep appreciation to Michael Foight, Special Collections and Digital Library Coordinator of the Falvey Memorial Library at Villanova University; Bettina Hess, Special Collections Librarian of the Joseph P. Horner Memorial Library of the German Society of Pennsylvania; and Susan Mitchem, National Archivist of the Salvation Army National Archives in Alexandria, Virginia, for their gracious assistance in helping me obtain the necessary permissions for images used in this work.

Beyond all this, however, most authors rely upon the knowledge, insights, and patience of a small group of readers, individuals who not only review and comment upon successive drafts of the work, but in many instances are the ones who also help shape the effort from its earliest stages. In my case, it was only the disciplined eye of my readers, and their sense of what helped tell the story I set out to convey and what was extraneous, that kept this work on track. Without them, it simply would not have happened.

I would therefore like to acknowledge Ken Berger, Angelo J. Mangia, and Keith Pickett, and thank each of them. Their respective contributions, coming at different times and at different points in the research and writing, were invaluable in the development of this project.

I am fortunate to count these gentlemen as friends, and am ever grateful for their unwavering patience, help, and support.

Finally, to my wife, Elise, the love of my life, without whose constant faith and support I could accomplish nothing. . .*Thank You.*

Wilmington, NC
September 2017

Introduction

A common aphorism, whose ascribed origins range from Marshall McLuhan to a cartoon caption, holds that fish don't know they're in water. *How could they?* McLuhan famously asked. *They have nothing with which to compare it.*

Taking this idea a bit further, psychologist James C. Coleman wrote that so complete is its influence, that any individual deeply immersed in his or her own culture will scarcely be aware of it as a shaping force in their lives.

This observation could easily be applied to today's American nonprofit sector.

As the first twenty years of the 21st century rapidly come to a close, the American nonprofit arena is at a crossroads, but often seems to be largely unaware of it. And yet numerous changes both internal and external to the sector strongly suggest that by 2030 it could very likely bear little resemblance to its present form, and possibly even to its present function.

While the realm of American nonprofit organizations seems today to be intensely focused on a limited number of narrowly defined immediate issues, broader, more ultimately impactful challenges are looming. It is, for example, larger than it has ever been, and continues growing at a prodigious rate. It is more varied, better organized, and better funded than any of its counterparts anywhere else on Earth. In addition to its substantial social and political influence, it holds considerable, growing, and unprecedented economic clout, responsible for 5.4% of the nation's Gross Domestic Product in 2014,[1] and accounting that year for 10.3% of the country's private-sector workforce.[2] But where will these trends lead? In an arena where a limited number of outsized entities dominate not only fund-raising but also the distribution of assets, how will ever-increased competition for resources play out? At a time when some of the demarcations traditionally separating the nonprofit from the for-profit worlds are showing a new permeability, will nonprofits discover and capitalize upon characteristics that make them better suited for the tasks at hand, or will they find themselves squeezed out by more nimble competitors?

At the same time, the universe around the sector is changing. Nonprofits in 2017 are frequently closer to and more dependent upon the government than ever before. But the politics of the era are among the most divisive in the nation's history, the fundamental national consensus fraying as Blue States and Red States seemingly have less and less in common each week. In this, the nonprofit arena, all the while contending with the contradictions inherent in its "dual identity" nature—nonprofits are private agencies, but operate largely in the public sphere; they are not-for-profit, but are required to operate in a for-profit economy; they often draw heavily on volunteers, but are expected to exhibit business-like levels of professionalism[3]—also often finds itself stranded in the No Man's Land between the two sides' respective front lines. Not only are funding streams increasingly politicized, but both the tax-exempt status and donation deductibility of a number of nonprofits are being challenged on various fronts. And as familiar boundaries between the conventionally apolitical nonprofits—the 501(c)(3)s—and their often über-political (c)(4) cousins are blurring or being questioned,[4] will that make the sector more or less vulnerable to the cultural struggles around it?

Meanwhile, for the first time ever, major financial underwriters have begun demanding that nonprofits demonstrate measurable evidence of performance. . .a challenge the sector as a whole is far from ready to meet.

At more of a ground level, it has traditionally been to the sector's advantage that roughly three-quarters of all households in America give to charity. But the developing giving patterns of the post-Baby-Boomer generations are showing signs of differing significantly from those of their forebearers, as are their work patterns, marriage and reproductive rates, and settlement patterns.

And while all this happens, technology marches on, promising to change forever the relationship between nonprofits and their donors.

Yet through all of this, the sector often seems to be blithely swimming along, completely focused upon the moment, and unaware of and unconcerned with the greater long-term challenges to its familiar environment.

Given these dynamics, the nonprofit realm effectively has two choices. It can bob along like a cork upon the waves, allowing the prevailing currents to take it where they will, or it can drop a rudder, set a sail, and be an active participant in the shaping of its own future.

But what should that future look like? Unfortunately, while some futurists foresee an expanded role for nonprofits in a decidedly altered American economy,[5] there are precious few other places to look for answers. The nonprofit arenas of the rest of the world, under-developed in many places and frequently looking to America as an example, offer few contextually workable ideas. Similarly, neither the time machine nor the crystal ball having yet been perfected, we cannot go forward to see how it will all turn out and simply aim for the best possible target. . .and lacking the familiar comic book trope of easily accessible alternate universes, there is no window through which we might peer to get a glimpse of how an array of different possibilities might look.

But we can look backward, to see how we got to where we are, to understand the forces that shaped the sector, to gain a renewed appreciation for its core *raison d'être*, and thereby to make a better-informed decision about where we wish to go.

Unfortunately, as Americans, we are frequently ill-equipped for that look into the rearview mirror, because *as* Americans, we tend to live in a culture primarily of the present. If there is any timeframe other than the "now" that at all seems important to our national psyche, it is the future. Indeed, the rejection of the old and the celebration of the new has been called the true myth of America.[6]

As a people, our timeframes tend to be short; our points of reference, fairly close at hand. We tend to deal with what is, rather than what was.

One result of this perspective is that we can be, as Irving Howe observed, notorious for our collective indifference to the past.[7]

This is not to merely rehash Santayana's warning about being doomed to repeat the errors of the past if we ignore its lessons. Things have changed too much for us to ever go backwards, and neither the missteps of yesterday nor their context are likely to recur. Rather, we should take heed of David McCullough's observation that trying to plan for the future without a sense of the past is like trying to plant cut flowers: lacking roots, they just won't take.[8]

So, while being generally free from the shackles of history may have been an overall advantage to our development as a nation, our frequently absent sense of history often leaves us at a disadvantage when it comes to understanding the forces that shaped many of the institutions that impact us.[9] It limits not only our understanding of what they do, but more importantly, *why* they do it.

But as David C. Hammack has noted, literally every question concerning American nonprofit organizations and America's nonprofit sector as a whole has a historical dimension. As it exists today, our nonprofit arena is highly complex, and we can best understand that complexity if we recognize that it is the product of a long and equally complicated history.[10]

Many Americans—not only everyday folk who, although the overwhelming number of us have frequent contact with nonprofits, rarely ever even think about the sector's existence, but also practitioners and those studying for a career in the field—know little or nothing about where it all came from. Like people standing on a dock watching a ship slowly disappear over the horizon but unable to see any farther, for most of us the limits of our vision are those described by recent memory. We tend to look at the contemporary version of the nonprofit arena and sort of make a quiet assumption that it is a fairly recent development and/or that it has essentially always been as it is today. Little thought is given to its true origins, its founding DNA, the challenges it faced, or the adaptations it made to survive. . .all of which could help inform the course we set for its future.

This said, it must also be added that the history of the nonprofit realm in America is not a simple line, one string of events running unbroken from the nation's founding until today. Instead, it is more of a braid, with distinct threads—some of them not originally focused on nonprofits at all—interweaving with one another over time. As with a braid, the end result is stronger than any one fiber would have been, but it requires unraveling and separating out those strands to make sense of the whole picture. More important, perhaps, the developmental trajectory of nonprofits also hasn't been a straight line. Rather, its path over the years might be compared to that of a pinball, moving straight and building up momentum for a time, but then ricocheting off some event or social trend and taking off in a new direction altogether. It is also worth remembering that the events that influenced and shaped our modern nonprofit arena did not take place in a neat sequential order. History always being more of a stew than a series of separately prepared and served dishes, it was not always the case that Event A was completed and done before Events B or C began or took hold.

All of these dynamics had an impact, and our nonprofit community is as much a *product* of our history as it has been an actor in our history.

And so we are going to attempt in these next pages to unravel this history, focusing on primary events or developments that combined to create the American nonprofit sector as we know it. Our thesis is that while, clearly, much has happened over the course of history involving the entities we currently know as "nonprofits," the sector as it exists today is the consequence of not only certain key national developments, specific events, and trends, but also a particular gene in its DNA, something that was there from the beginning and emerged time and again over the course of two hundred years, its influence helping to shape this spirited but often awkward arena.

In keeping with this approach, this work is offered as an overview, primarily intended to give nonprofit practitioners, and senior undergraduate and graduate students studying nonprofit management and related subjects, a basic historical context for their work. It is not intended to be an exhaustive year-by-year, or even a decade-by-decade account of the sector's history. Our purpose is not to recount the varying fortunes of the sector under this administration or that one. Rather, we set out to trace and tell the stories of the key themes and turning points, the influences that came from a variety of quarters, and how the sector's genetic heritage shaped its reaction to these shifting tides. It should also be added that while the account offered in these pages is *generally* chronological, moving overall from pre-colonial times toward today, there are places where, for the sake of context, the discussion switches back in time to give the reader a fuller appreciation of the subject being discussed. The reader is also directed to the endnotes, many of which contain informative and useful information that did not properly belong in the body of the narrative. Finally, for those wishing for more detail than may be presented here, readers are directed to Robert H. Bremner's *American Philanthropy*,[11] the many excellent works of Peter Dobkin Hall, David C. Hammack's outstanding survey article, "Nonprofit Organizations in American History,"[12] and, regarding the development of religion and its influence in America, Sydney E. Ahlstrom's *Religious History of the American People*.[13]

Lester Salamon, Director of the Johns Hopkins Center for Civil Society Studies, has repeatedly called the American nonprofit arena the "resilient sector," a tribute to its ability to change with the times and find ways to stay relevant to our national psyche and our national purpose. It is our hope that the facts and analysis offered here will help both the nonprofit practitioner and *especially* the student of nonprofit management—those who will be the sector's leaders in the years to come—reach a better understanding of the nonprofit community's core identity and evolution, so that they may help guide it to its best possible future.

Notes

1 United States Bureau of Economic Analysis.
2 Bureau of Labor Statistics. "Commissioner Announcing New Research Data on Jobs and Pay in the Nonprofit Sector." October 17, 2014. http://beta.bls.gov/labs/blogs/2014/10/17/announcing-new-research-data-on-jobs-and-pay-in-the-non-profit-sector/.
3 Salamon, L. "The Resilient Sector: The Future of Nonprofit America." *The State of Nonprofit America*. Ed. Lester M. Salamon. Third Edition. [Washington, DC: Brookings Institution, 2012] p. 3.
4 Wyland, M. "Combo Religious Freedom Executive Order May Be Headed Right at Nonprofits and Johnson Amendment." *Nonprofit Quarterly*. May 4, 2017. https://nonprofitquarterly.org/2017/05/04/combo-religious-freedom-executive order-may-be-headed-right-at-nonprofits-and-johnson-amendment/?utm_source=Daily+Newswire&utm_campaign=0721edbe48-EMAIL_CAMPAIGN_2017_05_04&utm_medium=email&utm_term=0_94063a1d17-0721edbe48-12341229.
5 McCambridge, R. "The Sustainability Prerogative: Nonprofits in the Future of Our Economy."*Nonprofit Quarterly*April25,2017.https://nonprofitquarterly.org/2017/04/25/douglas-rushkoff-non-profit-sustainability/?utm_source=Daily+Newswire&utm_campaign=b8e5375445-EMAIL_CAMPAIGN_2017_04_22&utm_medium=email&utm_term=0_94063a1d17-b8e5375445-12341229.
6 D.H. Lawrence as cited in Judis, J. "American Adam." *Insurrections of the Mind*. Ed. Franklin Foer. [New York: Harper Perennial, 2014] p. 549.
7 Howe, I. "The Value of the Canon." In Foer. p. 348.
8 McCullough, D. "Knowing History and Knowing Who We Are." *Imprimis*. Vol. 34, No. 4. (April 2005). https://imprimis.hillsdale.edu/knowing-history-and-knowing-who-we-are/.
9 Mayer, J. Letter: "Young Americans with No Sense of History." *New York Times*. April 24, 1983. www.nytimes.com/1983/04/24/opinion/l-young-americans-with-no-sense-of-history-118262.html.
10 Hammack, D.C. "Nonprofit Organizations in American History." *The American Behavioral Scientist*.Vol. 45, No. 11. (2002) p. 1638.
11 University of Chicago Press, 1960.
12 *The American Behavioral Scientist*.Vol. 45, No. 11. (2002) pp. 1638–1674.
13 Yale University Press, 1972.

Part I

1   Early roots

While the form and function of the modern American nonprofit sector were greatly influenced by events of the 20th century, that arena is not entirely a modern construct nor did it spring fully formed into being with no antecedent actions, attitudes, or cultural influences. Rather, when we look at today's nonprofit realm, what we are actually seeing is the modern reflection of an idea that is heir to literally centuries of evolving thought, perspective, and actions by both the government and individuals. . .and the origins of what we see today go back farther in time than many people might think.

The concept of *charity* appears to be nearly universal among human societies. As far back as ancient Egypt, the idea was prevalent that successful passage to the afterlife depended on a lifetime record of benevolent acts toward the suffering, giving "bread to the hungry, water to the thirsty, clothes to the naked, and even a boat to one who had none."[1] But while it existed in the ancient world of Greece and early Rome, the attitude of both civilizations toward charity was ambivalent. The Greek poet Hesiod advised that self-interest should be the guiding principle in both giving and withholding, writing that individuals should "Give to those who give to you, never to those who do not."[2]

Charity as we understand it was largely a haphazard private event in the ancient world, often spurred by the desire to gain the approval of others. It was also almost never earmarked for the most needy,[3] the more common practice being for the wealthy to subsidize great public works that were open to all.[4] Cicero took note of this, criticizing the rich he called "the prodigal," for their lavish expenditures in sponsoring feasts, gladiatorial contests, and fights with animals. Even their spending on the distribution of food, he suggested, was undertaken primarily to flaunt their wealth and win popularity. Far better and more noble in his eyes were the truly "generous," who gave money to ransom captives or those held by kidnappers, provided dowries, or paid off a friend's debts. Generosity for these purposes was, he said, appropriate. . .providing that the beneficiaries were deserving and the gifts made with care and moderation.[5]

It was not until the later Roman Empire's grain dole was established as part of the *cura annonae* that the earliest traces of an approach toward the poor we would recognize today became more regularized.[6] To appreciate this development, it is worth taking a moment to recognize the impact that two specific religious traditions had at the time.

While all the world's great religions teach the importance of compassion for the poor,[7] for our purposes we must look primarily to the traditions of Judaism and Christianity.[8] Both of these were current in the Roman Empire in the early centuries of the Common Era, and to the extent that they influenced the thinking and practice of their followers, they helped lay the European foundations of "charity" as we know it. But they also had an influence in ancient Rome itself.

Roman charity was not religiously derived, but rather was drawn from personal or civic impulses. It is also true that the Romans' notion of human worth was vastly different than not only our own, but also that of the Christians and Jews who lived in their midst. Significantly inherited from the Greeks, the Roman world view saw nothing wrong with inequality. Not only was there no objection to slavery or to the superiority of husbands and fathers over wives and children, but it was also held that what was best in life was essentially only for the few, men of stature, philosophers, the political elite. Subjugated peoples were not "citizens of Rome" and effectively had few (if any) rights, expediency being the operative determinant in most cases. The totally impoverished, the poorest of Rome's poor, would have seen little or no recognition of their even being "people," as they were both politically *and* morally inconsequential in the prevailing view of the time.[9] The concept of an essential human dignity shared by all, irrespective of station, a precept central to our perspective, was not a Roman trait.

But both Christianity and the Judaism from which it derives had a completely different understanding of things. Rooted in the notion of a relationship with God, men and women as individuals were seen in these traditions as having an inherent unalienable value.[10] The prophets, meanwhile, saw a direct and contrasting link between idolatry and injustice.

Pagan deities were often the embodiment of human impulses, reflecting many of humankind's less noble or attractive traits such as jealousy, anger, and lust. . .whereas the God of Abraham taught that the most acceptable offering was justice to our fellow human beings, that we were to treat one another fairly and compassionately.[11] Jewish tradition, which holds that the righteousness of those who give generously to the poor shall endure forever,[12] was shaped by admonishments like those found in Isaiah—"This is what I wish: sharing your bread with the hungry, sheltering the oppressed and the homeless, clothing the naked when you see them"[13]—and evolved to include the notions of *tzedakah* (the religious obligation to perform charity and philanthropic acts),[14] *chesed* (deeds of kindness), and *tikkun olam* (repairing the world), which today still find expression in the practice of *ma'aser kesafim*, or tithing to support those in need.

Christianity, from the teachings of Christ ("Amen, I say to you, whatever you did for one of these least brothers of mine, you did for me.[15] Go and sell all your possessions and give the money to the poor."[16]), through its historic focus on the poor,[17] to its various activist denominations,[18] has a long tradition of inspiring its members to share with the less fortunate.

But it was the adoption of Christianity as the state religion of the empire that truly launched events toward their modern form. During the first three centuries of the Church's existence, the practical application of charity may have been the most potent single cause of Christian success;[19] it was *so* successful, in fact, that after his conversion in 313, the emperor, Constantine, apparently saw advantages to be gained in co-opting the Church's charities,[20] which also motivated both him and Justinian to develop legal doctrines of charity.[21]

This is an important point, because Constantine achieved three things. He built upon the Judeo-Christian traditions toward the poor, and moved the needy from the fringes of a formerly pagan society to a place where their needs were, at minimum, at least recognized as existing. He put the power of the state, which had previously been all but impervious to the plight of the needy, behind a new consciousness of their condition. And, by implication, he recognized that society, and not just individuals who were so moved, had some responsibility toward the poor.

However, earliest Christianity—under which followers were obliged to love their enemies, practice good deeds, and thereby gain entrance into Heaven—saw charity, the giving of alms to the needy, as a *spiritual* rather than a social act.

The effect of charitable acts on the giver's soul was doctrinally far more significant—and therefore more important—than the effects on the body of the recipient: one gave and performed other good works as intrinsic elements of salvation under the predominant Catholic theology, not to improve the situation of the impoverished recipient. The notion of "addressing poverty" was essentially foreign to this perspective. If anything, the poor were *necessary*, if everyone else was to earn Divine Favor by showing them compassion.

This formula would essentially remain intact for the next twelve hundred years.

But then several important figures, even though acting individually, would have a combined influence that would forever change the equation. . .and irreversibly alter the course leading to our own nonprofit sector.

The Reformation, Old England, and the secularization of charity

During the Dark Ages, there were effectively neither state organs nor secular institutions in a position to provide relief for the poor and needy. Where it was undertaken at all, this role fell primarily to the Catholic Church. Catholic monasteries throughout Europe were the centers of practical charity, tending to the sick and addressing the immediate need brought to their doors.[22]

They were the primary institutional vehicles for providing aid until the dawn of the Protestant Reformation in the 1500s. The Reformation, however, brought with it a number of developments that were to eventually have a significant influence on charity in America.

The first of these was Martin Luther's break with the Catholic Church over, among other things, the role of good works.

In original Christian tradition, the *combination* of faith and good works was seen as required for salvation.[23] Reflecting the Jewish tradition they had inherited—"Cursed is he who distorts the justice due an alien, orphan, and widow"[24]—and beyond mere adherence to the Commandments,[25] among the good works a Christian was expected to undertake was having an active concern for the needy and taking steps to alleviate their plight.

"It is better to give alms than to store up gold," Scripture says, "for almsgiving. . .expiates every sin."[26] But as the story of the Good Samaritan illustrated,[27] an active concern for those in need was not to be limited to monetary contributions. A functional care for others, even those we do not know or who are alien to us, the story demonstrated, was the essential key. Moreover, the Old Testament suggested in numerous places that, as stewards of God's creation, the responsibility of the faithful extended to care of the land[28] and of animals.[29] Finally, Jesus had taught that no gesture was too small,[30] so such efforts were not reserved for the wealthy only, but rather were expected of everyone according to his or her ability.

This was the basis of Christian charity for fifteen hundred years: the faithful were called upon to do good works as a *vital facet* of their salvation. But in 1510 and the years following, Martin Luther challenged this thinking on a number of grounds, and in doing so cracked the bedrock upon which the very concept of Christian charity had been built.

Rereading Scripture, Luther came to the conclusion that the Catholic Church had lost sight of what he saw as several of the central truths of Christianity. Utilizing the concept of *sola fide*, Luther taught that salvation was attainable only through faith. Mortal humans, in other words, were powerless to *do* anything to achieve salvation. One could not earn one's way into Heaven, Luther insisted, by caring for the poor or doing other good works.[31]

In this assertion, Luther decoupled faith and good works as they had been understood to be the twin pillars of salvation for centuries.[32]

This is *not* to say, however, that Luther or other Reformers dismissed good works, or implied that the Christian needn't bother with them. They all knew full well that Scripture speaks of believers having been "created. . .for good works."[33]

But they insisted that these acts should be seen as *fruits* of salvation, not a contributing cause. Works are a fulfillment of faith, Luther explained,[34] citing St. James and reminding his listeners that faith without works, *a faith that does not love or serve*, is dead.[35]

This concept, salvation through faith alone, and not through a necessary combination of faith and good works, became a mainstay of Protestantism. Christians were still called upon to do works pleasing to God.[36] But these were to be voluntary outward manifestations of faith, expressions of living according to God's law, rather than mandatory acts needed to earn an extra set of keys to the Kingdom. The idea that "we are justified by faith alone, but not by a faith that *is* alone," in fairly short order became a pillar of the Reformation,[37] and in doing so became a crucial step in the secularization of charity. . .the next stage of which would take place in England when Henry VIII instigated his own break with the Church of Rome.[38]

Unlike theologically inspired Reformers such as Luther, Calvin, and Zwingli, Henry broke with Rome for largely personal and political purposes. He established his own church and proclaimed himself its head.[39] In doing this, he also seized all Catholic property within the realm, including the entire network of Catholic monasteries.[40] By 1539 England's entire monastic establishment had been liquidated, and, with a very few notable exceptions,[41] its vast lands transferred for money or favor to lay owners.[42]

Unfortunately for England's poorest, few of the new owners to whom Henry bequeathed these institutions abided by his command that they continue the charitable work these places had traditionally undertaken. This was a powerful blow to such a safety net for the poor as had existed in England for centuries.

Yet another seismic shift came through the doctrines of the Reformation itself. While Henry's break from Rome was much more about power than doctrine, neither Henry nor his subjects lived in isolation. . .and more than a few of his subjects had heard of *and* were being influenced by the tides of reform flowing from Zurich, Geneva, and Germany. Across the Channel, new ideas were bringing about an important alteration of the familiar religious landscape against which charity had been undertaken for fifteen hundred years.

Specifically, Calvinism formulated the idea of "the elect," and the idea that poverty could be interpreted as a sign of God's displeasure with an individual. It also placed a strong, new emphasis on self-reliance and on work. More importantly for our purposes, it became an influential part of the philosophical and theological world view that was to influence the development and evolution of American charity.

It was also during this period, however, that the concept of the "deserving poor" (and by implication, their *un*deserving opposite numbers), while absolutely not new,[43] truly began to take root,[44] and would soon find expression in England's first Poor Laws.

As early as 1349, both concentrated poverty and the concomitant concentration of beggars were becoming considerable problems in the growing communities of England. To address this seemingly intractable problem, Henry's first Poor Law (1531) demanded that local authorities identify the deserving poor within their districts, and issue them what amounted to licenses to beg. . .while those *not* local, licensed, or "deserving" were either to be sent back to where they came from, or whipped. The Law was intended to *limit the number of beggars*; **not** to provide relief to the poor.[45]

When the Law failed to appreciably lessen the number of vagrants clogging the streets and alleyways of the kingdom's cities and towns, Henry followed up with another, stronger decree, this one commanding that the "sturdy" poor be put to work. For those who were found to be legitimately "impotent," a system was established by which alms were to be placed in a common box at each parish of the Church of England and then distributed by local church authorities to those deemed truly in need. Importantly, private almsgiving was *forbidden*—a decree made easier to enforce by the Reformation's strong embrace of *sola fide*—for fear that such hand-outs would "encourage" idleness and vagrancy.[46]

And so it went, with assorted penalties imposed for poverty and vagrancy, until Elizabeth I, in 1572, introduced the then-revolutionary idea that local taxpayers should pay for the relief of the (deserving) local poor.[47] This was the first formal step since Constantine to establish the concept that charity could and should be formalized as a civic function.

However, Elizabeth's most important contribution to the Anglo-American concept of charity came in 1601, with the adoption of her Statute of Charitable Uses. This landmark legislation was intended to clear the way for private charitable efforts by legally defining, for the first time, the concept of charity and, specifically, what it included.

The Statute's frequently quoted preamble contained the following as falling within the realm of charity:

> relief of aged, impotent, and poor people. . .maintenance of sick and maimed soldiers and mariners, schools of learning, free schools, and scholars in universities. . .repair of bridges, ports, havens, causeways, churches, sea-banks, and highways, [the] education and preferment of orphans. . .houses of correction. . .[the] marriages of poor maids. . .aid and help of young tradesmen, handicraftsmen and persons decayed, [the] relief or redemption of prisoners or captives, [the] aid or ease of any poor inhabitants, and [the] setting out of soldiers.[48]

While some scholars have held that the Elizabethan Statute had merely codified a long series of previous acts and precedents,[49] it is important to recognize how Elizabeth radically expanded the concept of "charity" in these relatively few words. Yes, the traditional concern for the needy—sick and maimed soldiers and mariners, "persons decayed," and any poor inhabitants—is apparent. Significantly beyond this, however, efforts that some might think belong properly (if not entirely) in the public realm—schools; the repair of bridges, ports, causeways, sea-banks, and highways; support for houses of correction; and even the "setting out of soldiers" (costs associated with the common defense[50]) and the "redemption [ransom] of captives"—are included as available avenues for charitable donations. Finally (and importantly) several notions that today might be recognized as *social engineering* (the marriages of poor maids; aid and help to young tradesmen and handicraftsmen, and the relief or redemption of prisoners) round out this revolutionary take on charity.

***

If Martin Luther inadvertently began the secularization of charity by decoupling good works from eternal salvation, Elizabeth went farther in a number of ways that would survive to have an important impact upon the development of America's approach to charitable undertakings:

- She established the concept that the poor were a civil responsibility, and not solely an ecclesiastical one.
- She inaugurated the idea that the needy were to be cared for at public expense. Moreover, she codified the idea that, rather than being chased out of town to be someone else's problem, the poor were the responsibility of localities, which were now mandated to take on the role of providing such relief as was needed. This idea was, very significantly, later to become firmly established in Puritan New England.
- She broadened the notion of charity to encompass projects of public benefit, setting into law the theory that "charity" no longer had to be restricted to alleviating the plight of the needy, but rather could be, as in ancient Greece and Rome,[51] efforts of civic importance.
- She added to the conception of "charitable causes" efforts that could be interpreted as being socially beneficial, not aimed to alleviate the plight of individuals, but for the advancement or improvement of society as a whole.

These were *all* threads that would eventually be woven into the tapestry of American charity...

Notes

1 "Charity." *The Encyclopedia of Religion*. Ed. M. Eliade [New York: Macmillan Publishing Company, 1987] Vol. 3, pp. 222–223.
2 Bremner, R. *Giving: Charity and Philanthropy in History*. [New Brunswick, NJ: Transaction Publishers, 1994] p. 6.
3 Byrnes, W. "Ancient Roman Munificence: The Development of the Practice and Law of Charity." *Rutgers Law Review*. Vol. 57, No. 3. (2005) p. 1043. http://ssrn.com/abstract=2314731.
4 Public charity on the part of public figures also took on a more important role, the amount one donated sometimes influencing how far up the ladder of power and prestige one might go. Byrnes. p. 1058.
5 Bremner. pp. 7–8.
6 The grain dole was only available to those of limited means. See Byrnes. p. 1064.
7 Brooks, A. *Who Really Cares*. [New York: Basic Books, 2006] p. 33. In Islam, Zakah, one of the Five Pillars, and the precepts of the Quran call for assistance to the poor and the indigent as a duty of the believer. The practice of charitable giving or "*dana*" is integral to religious observance among Theravada Buddhists. For Hindus, *dana* is an important part of one's *dharma* (religious duty), often expressed within the framework of the traditional extended Hindu family, which plays the role of a welfare state. The wealth a person acquires is not for him/herself, but for the welfare of the extended family and others. One has a responsibility towards those members of one's family who cannot maintain themselves.
8 With their invasion of Spain in AD 711, the Moors brought the influence of Islam to the Iberian Peninsula. Their perspective on charity fit well with those of the

Jewish and Christian communities they conquered. See "Zakah." Islamic-Islamic. www.islamicislamic.com/zakah.htm; and "The Quran and Hadiths on the Poor and Needy: A Topical Index." Sound Vision. www.soundvision.com/info/poor/quranhadith.asp.

9 Byrnes. p. 1055.

10 Wood, J.R. "Liberal Protestant Social Action in a Period of Decline." *Faith and Philanthropy in America.* Eds R. Wuthnow and V. Hodgkinson. [San Francisco, CA: Jossey-Bass, 1990] p. 167.

11 Cahill, T. *The Gifts of the Jews.* [New York: Anchor Books, 1998] p. 222.

12 Psalm 112:9.

13 Isaiah 58:6–7.

14 Rich, T. "Tzedakah: Charity." Judaism 101. www.jewfaq.org/tzedakah.htm.

15 Matthew 25:40.

16 Matthew 19:21.

17 Huffington Post. "Pope Francis Quotes on the Poor." August 19, 2013. www.huffington post.com/2013/08/19/pope-francis-quotes-poor_n_3780816.html.

18 Woodard, C. *American Nations.* [New York: Penguin Books, 2011] p. 182.

19 Kelley, T. "Rediscovering Vulgar Charity: A Historical Analysis of America's Tangled Nonprofit Law." *Fordham Law Review.* Vol. 73, Issue 6. (2005) pp. 2437–2499. http://ir.lawnet.fordham.edu/flr/vol73/iss6/1. p. 2441.

20 McManus, W. "Stewardship and Almsgiving in the Roman Catholic Tradition." In Wuthnow and Hodgkinson. p. 129.

21 Byrnes. p. 1044.

22 Ibid.

23 James 2:14–26. Matthew 5:16; 24:10–20. Peter 1:17; 2:12.

24 Deuteronomy 27:19. "He who oppresses the poor taunts his Maker, But he who is gracious to the needy honors Him" (Proverbs 14:31). "He who mocks the poor taunts his Maker" (Proverbs 17:5).

25 Matthew 19:16–21.

26 Tobit 12:8–9.

27 Luke 10:25–37.

28 Ezekiel 34:18. "Is it not enough for you to feed on the good pasture, that you must tread down with your feet the rest of your pasture; and to drink of clear water, that you must muddy the rest of the water with your feet?"

   Jeremiah 2:7. "And I brought you into a plentiful land to enjoy its fruits and its good things. But when you came in, you defiled my land."

   Jeremiah 12:4. "How long will the land mourn and the grass of every field wither? For the evil of those who dwell in it the beasts and the birds are swept away."

   Deuteronomy 20:19. "When you besiege a city a long time...you shall not destroy its trees by swinging an axe against them."

29 Proverbs 12:10. "Whoever is righteous has regard for the life of his beast."

   Exodus 23:4–5. "If you meet your enemy's ox or his donkey wandering away, you shall surely return it to him. If you see [a] donkey...lying helpless under its load...you shall surely release it."

   Deuteronomy 22:4. "You shall not see your countryman's donkey or his ox fallen down on the way, and pay no attention to them."

30 Mark 12:41–44.

31 "All...are justified," Luther wrote, "without their own works and merits...through the redemption that is in Christ Jesus. [It] cannot be otherwise acquired or grasped by any work...or merit." Luther, M. "Smalcald Articles. Article One." *The Book of Concord: The Confessions of the Evangelical Lutheran Church.* Ed. and Trans. T.G. Tappert.

[Philadelphia, PA: Fortress Press, 1981] p. 292. It should also be noted that Luther insisted that "good works" need not be special undertakings outside of one's normal daily life. Rather, in simply going about one's daily routine, doing one's daily tasks, and keeping the Commandments, one was essentially doing "good work" in Luther's view. See Luther, M. "Large Catechism." In Tappert. pp. 380, 385, 399.

32 This perspective was further enhanced by the notion of *sola scriptura*, which held that only canonical Scripture, and not tradition or subsequent teaching, was the ultimate Christian authority. "A simple layman armed with Scripture is greater than the mightiest pope without it," Luther said. Functionally, this served to further undermine traditional Catholic teaching on good works, especially as certain giving had been tied to the sale of indulgences.

33 Eph. 2:10.

34 Plass, E.M. *What Luther Says*. [St. Louis: Concordia Publishing House, 2006] p. 1509. "Faith," Luther said, "cannot help doing good works constantly. It doesn't stop to ask if good works ought to be done, but before anyone asks, it already has done them and continues to do them without ceasing. Anyone who does not do good works in this manner is an unbeliever...Thus, it is just as impossible to separate faith and works as it is to separate heat and light from fire!" See "Luther, An Introduction to St. Paul's Letter to the Romans." *Luther's German Bible of 1522*. (Trans. by Rev. Robert E. Smith from Dr. Martin Luther's *vermischte deutsche Schriften*.) Ed. Johann K. Irmischer. Vol. 63 [Erlangen: Heyder and Zimmer, 1854] pp. 124–125.

35 James 2:17.

36 Titus 2:14; 3:1.

37 Among the denominations adhering to this idea are the following:

> **The Anglican Confession**: "We are accounted righteous before God, only for the merit of our Lord and Saviour Jesus Christ by faith, and not for our own works or deservings. Wherefore that we are justified by faith only is a most wholesome doctrine, and very full of comfort; as more largely is expressed in the Homily of Justification."
>
> Thirty-Nine Articles of Religion (1571). Article XI. Of the Justification of Man.
>
> **The Lutheran Confession**: "Our churches by common consent...teach that men cannot be justified before God by their own strength, merits, or works, but are freely justified for Christ's sake, through faith, when they believe that they are received into favor, and that their sins are forgiven for Christ's sake, who, by His death, has made satisfaction for our sins. This faith God imputes for righteousness in His sight."
>
> Augsburg Confession (1530). Article IV. Justification. See Tappert. p. 30.
>
> **Southern Baptist**: "Justification is God's gracious and full acquittal upon principles of His righteousness of all sinners who repent and believe in Christ. Justification brings the believer unto a relationship of peace and favor with God."
>
> Baptist Faith and Message (2000). Article IV, sub-article B.
>
> **Reformed Baptist**: "That those which have union with Christ, are justified from all their sins, past, present, and to come, by the blood of Christ; which justification we conceive to be a gracious and free acquittance of a guilty, sinful creature, from all sin by God, through the satisfaction that Christ hath made by his death; and this applied in the manifestation of it through faith."

First London Baptist Confession (1644). XXVIII.

United Methodist: "We believe good works are the necessary fruits of faith and follow regeneration but they do not have the virtue to remove our sins or to avert divine judgment. We believe good works, pleasing and acceptable to God in Christ, spring from a true and living faith, for through and by them faith is made evident."

Article X-Good Works. The Confession of Faith.

Non-Denominational Evangelicals: "We believe in. . .the Salvation of lost and sinful man through the shed blood of the Lord Jesus Christ by faith apart from works, and regeneration by the Holy Spirit."

World Evangelical Alliance Statement of Faith.

38 Rather than one single act, this took place over the course of a series of actions between February of 1531 and June of 1539. See History on the Net. "Henry VIII and the Break with Rome Timeline." August 14, 2014. www.historyonthenet.com/Chronology/timelinebreakrome.htm.

39 The irony was that while establishing himself as the supreme governor who would thereafter appoint bishops and otherwise control the ecclesiastical system, his new national church, while Henry lived, was in all other ways effectively Catholic. It would not be until Henry's death and the ascension to the throne of his 10-year-old son Edward VI that those reformers among the boy's council of regency began the work of moving the Church of England out of the Catholic camp and more firmly into that of the emerging Protestantism.

40 At the time, there were in excess of 800 religious houses in England with 10,000 monks, nuns, and friars. About 376 monasteries were seized and closed in 1536 alone. Ibid.

41 St. Bartholomew's Hospital, founded in 1123 and London's oldest, was not only spared the royal confiscation, but was endowed by Henry so it could continue its work. See Bremner. p. 23.

42 Ahlstrom, S.E. *A Religious History of the American People*. [New Haven, CT: Yale University Press, 1972] p. 85.

43 As early as the 300s, St. Basil the Great (329–379) distinguished between charity to the needy poor and casual giving to beggars. Those who give to the afflicted and to people truly in need, he explained, give to the Lord and will be rewarded. However, one who gives to every wanderer "casts it to a dog that is troublesome on account of his shamelessness, but not pitiable because of his need." See Bremner. p. 14.

44 It is worth noting in this regard that when Richard Hakluyt, the foremost English proponent of the colonization of North America during the reign of Elizabeth I, was making the case for a large number of ships and colonists to be sent across the Atlantic, one of his foremost arguments was that, in addition to the boost to the British economy represented by the American market—the colonies would need British goods to survive—in the colonies "the able bodied poor, the unemployed, and the idle," those considered an "altogether unprofitable" drain on the economy, could be put to work for their own and the nation's benefit. See Horn, J. *A Land as God Made It*. [New York: Basic Books, 2003] pp. 25, 285.

45 Kelley. Op. cit.

46 Ibid. p. 2447.

47 14 Eliz., c. 5 (1572) (Eng.).

48 43 Eliz., c. 4 (1601) (Eng.).

49 Hall, P.D. "A Historical Overview of Philanthropy, Voluntary Associations, and Nonprofit Organizations in the United States, 1600–2000." *The Nonprofit Sector: A Research Handbook.* Eds W.W. Powell and R. Steinberg. Second Edition [New Haven, CT: Yale University Press, 2006] p. 37.

50 For an example of how these costs were assessed and paid, see Coopers Company, London. "Historical Memoranda, Charters, Documents, and Extracts, from the Records of the Corporation and Books of the Company, 1396–1848. London, 1848." pp. 65, 103, 105, 107, 108, 109. https://books.google.com/books?id=xao KAAAAYAAJ&pg=PA108&lpg=PA108&dq=setting+out+of+soldiers&source= bl&ots=y6sqERYNJz&sig=yZ2uTb9wCsEHuB3csI1B5rSdVYA&hl=en&sa=X &ei=2_eZVJ7_N4GwggTo8YGIAw&ved=0CE8Q6AEwCg#v=onepage&q=sol diers&f=false.

51 Byrnes. pp. 1081–1082.

2 Across the pond

The colonization of America

While all of England's early North American colonies were overwhelmingly "Protestant," and while their fledgling populations brought with them various strains of Reformation thought, none was ultimately to have an impact on the American view of charity to match that of the New England Puritans and the culture of "Yankeedom" that grew in their wake and spread far beyond their original borders.[1]

This is *not* to say that other peoples and cultures within the American melting pot have not also contributed to and influenced the evolving American charitable landscape; they *have*.[2] It could be argued, for example, that the first philanthropists in the New World were the Native Americans who aided the struggling Pilgrims,[3] and the Jamestown colonists.[4] But the effect of both indigenous and later immigrant cultures on the uniquely American experiment in charity was not to be felt for decades or more, and of the first Europeans to settle in the New World, among all the Spanish, the French, and even other English subjects who came to these shores,[5] none were to establish the influential templates that came out of New England. The reason for this is that no other colonies established on these shores, not those of England, France, the Netherlands, Spain, or Sweden, were founded with the vision that animated the original footholds at Plymouth or Salem, and the settlements that later followed throughout Massachusetts and much of the region. While it is true that these colonies were not the only ones founded with a special sense of purpose—William Penn, Lord Baltimore, and Roger Williams also launched their plantations as holy experiments of one sort or another—the New England colonies were instilled with a peculiarly corporate spirit. In each of them, covenantal ideas put a curb on purely individualistic endeavors, while an underlying conception of social compact bound the people together into a commonwealth of saints joined in a common task.[6]

It was no accident that when John Winthrop led a group of English Puritans to Massachusetts Bay in 1630, he established the "model of Christian charity" that would define their colony. "We must bear one another's burdens," he told his fellow settlers. "We must not look only on our own things, but also on the things of our brethren."[7] In contrast, when Sir Thomas Gates set forth the

"Articles, Lawes, and Orders, Diune, Politique, and Martiall for the Colony in Virginia" in 1610, notably absent were the sensibilities represented by Winthrop in New England. There was no mention whatsoever of voluntary activity or of charity.[8]

But while still en route to New England on board the *Arabella*, Winthrop wrote an essay on charity which sought to apply scriptural virtues to the peculiar circumstances and challenges the colonists would face in creating their new social and political order. A number of themes which would become central to American charitable, philanthropic, and nonprofit traditions are first articulated here:

1 efforts to reconcile the problem of spiritual and political equality with economic inequality;
2 concerns about the relationship between the good of individuals and the good of the community;
3 the conception of community as a voluntary, contractual bond between individuals;
4 a focus on the particular obligations of the rich toward the poor;
5 the conception of mission as the basis for formulating specific institutional goals and objectives.[9]

Following Winthrop's thinking, not only did neighbors rely upon one another for everything from raising barns to caring for the sick, but the New Englanders also established several precedents that were to set them apart from their fellows farther to the south.

In addition to community-supported churches, they built schools supported by resources from local residents,[10] so that by the 1670s, all New England colonies except Rhode Island had passed legislation that mandated literacy for children.[11]

The other thing the early New England Puritans did was to oblige every community established in their colonies to take care of its own needy inhabitants.[12] It was every person's *duty* to be charitable to those in need.[13] Community leaders would, where necessary, determine who was truly in need, and it was up to local residents to meet those needs.[14]

But the Puritans also added another element, one that was to be particularly influential in the American nonprofit sector's later tradition of advocacy.

Under Puritan practice (if not explicit doctrine) the wants, desires, and impulses of the individual were seen to be always and properly subordinate to the needs of the community,[15] needs which were specifically defined as being in accordance with "God's will" as they interpreted it. Winthrop, for example, not only saw community as defined by the interdependence of the poor and humble on the wealthy, learned, and dependable, but importantly also viewed the civil authority of the community as the ultimate arbiter of the community's best interests and one which, in all cases, stood above the claims of individuals.[16]

Thus, their laws and their culture assumed moral authority over personal behavior and *attitudes*[17] in ways completely foreign to those developing in the live-and-let-live Dutch colony of New Amsterdam[18] or in the paternalistic, stratified Tidewater colonies and those farther south.[19]

Seeking to create and maintain a community with singular values, where the loss of personal freedom was the necessary cost of social good,[20] the theocrats of New England saw nothing wrong with establishing moral and behavioral standards, and compelling others to meet these under sanction of law. They thought themselves a Chosen People, and increasingly came to see no meaningful differences between their interests and those of the Lord.[21] As early as 1648, a New England "Platform" was adopted as the result of a regional synod, mandating that uniformity was to be enforced by local magistrates. Heresy, doctrinal disobedience, and schism were to be "restrayned & punished" by civil authority.[22]

They saw the law as a means of controlling people's sinful impulses, and emphasized the need for godly obedience in all who chose to live in the commonwealth.[23] Buttressing this perspective, they also demonstrated a singular willingness for turning the power of their religion toward secular impulses.[24]

Put another way, they viewed the power of the state as a ready and perfectly available tool to enforce not only rules establishing civil order—Thou shalt not kill; Thou shalt not steal—but those establishing moral and ethical order as well. An example of this line of thinking is to be found in Cotton Mather's *Bonifacius*. Asking how society can foster the creation of a "better sort of men,"[25] he offers advice on how to proceed. Look first, he recommends, for objectionable behaviors or attitudes that require suppression. Then, he advises, exert influence through the coercion of voluntary and neighborly associations.[26] Finally, he says, seek ways to use legislative power to enact supporting laws.[27]

This idea, that developments for the social betterment of a community could be enforced by law if not voluntarily adopted, was to become an important element in the evolution of American charity as the culture of Yankeedom spread to the lands the New Englanders later settled in over the course of the 1800s, from the Mohawk Valley and on into Ohio, through the Great Lakes region and, eventually, the Pacific Northwest.[28]

From the start, the seedling colony on Massachusetts Bay was created with the idea of being not only a model that others might follow, but the progenitor of a new society. In vast contrast to the Dutch colony at the tip of Manhattan—from the start an outpost devoted solely to commerce—or Jamestown on the banks of the Chesapeake—effectively the private preserve of a powerful corporation,[29] the rationale of which was to produce goods in demand in England and thereby supplant the country's need to import necessities from Europe or Asia[30]—the communities of New England were devoted to social betterment and a better society. This founding gene, the Puritan belief that the world could be constrained and re-formed in accordance with God's revealed will,[31] was never to be lost, and had a crucial impact on the development of the American nonprofit sector.

Early America

While familiar with the idea of associational and corporate forms of collective action, the early British colonists were slow at first to embrace them. Purely private corporations in the modern sense were virtually unknown, since colonial governments lacked the authority and legal tools to issue charters,[32] and no such entities as we recognize them today existed in America before the 1780s.[33] But this did not mean that nothing was happening that would contribute to the emergence of the forerunners of today's nonprofits. There were a number of dynamics at play. As early as 1710 Cotton Mather was urging the use of voluntary associations, even though they were in their extreme infancy, to achieve socially beneficial ends.

But there was something else going on as well: religion was, if not completely losing its hold on the population, finding its grip on that population being loosened.

In Massachusetts and Connecticut, for example, Congregationalists—the former Puritans—were insisting upon the right to be free of both ecclesiastical hierarchy and central doctrine, their individual groups of worshipers effectively becoming independent assemblies.[34] Similarly, in colonies such as Rhode Island and Pennsylvania, self-supporting and self-governing congregations enjoyed an autonomy that anticipated the status of voluntary associations of the 1800s.[35]

To again cite Mather, we also find that the idea of socially valuable actions was beginning to take on an importance quite apart from the sort of ecclesiastical grounding it might have previously had. In his *Bonifacius*, although he peppers his argument with religious references, Mather more than balances this with an unmistakable civic call for action to remediate worldly problems.

> As we have Opportunity, let us do Good unto all men. . .no man begins to be Wise, till he come to make this the Main Purpose and Pleasure of his Life. The more Good any Man dos, the more he really Lives.[36]

In the pages that follow, Mather provides an ample list of service that people might render for not only their neighbors —"Would it be too much for you, at least Once in a Week? To Think, What Neighbour is reduced into a Pinching and Painful Poverty? Or in any degree Impoverished with heavy losses?"—but strangers as well. This document, with its clearly articulated concern for the earthly travails of our fellow human beings, might very well be the beginning of what we would recognize today as the overall agenda of the nonprofit sector.

But the formative years of the American nation also saw a number of structural developments that were to have a profound impact on the shape and character of modern American charity.

Perhaps the most seismic in its long-term influence was the adoption of the Bill of Rights in 1789. The First Amendment, in preventing Congress from abridging freedom of religion, freedom of speech, and the right of assembly, profoundly altered the landscape.

Within a short period of time, the American clergy—which is to say, its *Protestant* clergy—found itself in a distinctly unfamiliar position. Whereas nine of the original thirteen colonies had state-sponsored, taxpayer supported churches at the time of the Revolution,[37] things were changing rapidly.

The Revolutionary period was, generally speaking, a time of decline for American Christianity as a whole. In many ways, the war itself began the process of decline, as partisan ministers often had to flee in the advance of opposing armies,[38] and the general population was significantly more concerned with issues of a military or political nature than they were with religion. At the same time, universal religious toleration permitted many Americans to abandon religion entirely. By 1800, it is estimated, fewer than one in five Americans belonged to any religious body,[39] and by the time of the War of 1812, church membership across the colonies had dropped so precipitously that not one person in ten or twenty was any longer church affiliated. In many churches, "membership" itself became increasingly nominal.[40]

Beyond this, the First Amendment put an abrupt end to state sponsorship, and began to further erode the role the clergy had traditionally had in the civic life of the new states. Separation of church and state meant that the good reverends could thunder from the pulpit all they wanted—to increasingly sparse congregations—but they could no longer *directly* influence laws or policy.[41]

More specifically, where the churches of colonial America had, particularly in the north, often assumed major roles in providing education,[42] those in Virginia had attended to the care of the needy,[43] and across the country had maintained important community records—*in addition to* contributing to the design of laws that reflected religious sensibilities, if not outright dictates—the novel American separation of church and state acted to remove churches from all these social functions.[44] Ultimately, the Constitution required that churches *as private institutions* had to divorce themselves from acting as, effectively, public agents.[45] The clergy was going to have to find another way to exercise influence on society.

Freedom of speech in America was also quick to find new outlets beyond the spoken or written word, and Americans, further bolstered by their now constitutionally protected right of assembly,[46] began to come together in numbers not seen before, in an array of organizations and for a range of reasons and purposes never imagined in the Old World.

As de Tocqueville noted, we Americans had a propensity to organize and do things ourselves. He wrote:

> In the United States as soon as several inhabitants have taken an opinion or an idea they wish to promote in society, they seek each other out and unite together once they have made contact[47]. . .Americans constantly form

associations. . .associations of a thousand kinds. . .to give entertainments, to found seminaries. . .to diffuse books. . .to foster some feeling [or] to inculcate some truth.[48]

This was, in many ways, an exercise of our freedom of speech.

It is also important to realize that the associations that sprang up in early America did not seek, wait for, or require an official sanction. In fact, they often came into being not only in the absence of such approval, but because citizens perceived a vacuum where the government either wasn't acting or could not act.

In this way, early Americans were putting their opinions into action, whether through the founding of new religious sects,[49] or through the formation and mobilization of associations as an exercise of their right of free speech. For political and religious dissenters, associations were often the best means available for counteracting the conservative political elites that dominated so much of public life.[50] In addition, the distribution of property and wealth in the colonies was not what it had been in Europe, and this, too, influenced developments. As Boston area minister James Walker noted:

Such is the distribution of property amongst us, and such is the nature of our government, that individuals here can never hope to rival the splendid acts of princely munificence recorded of the old and immensely rich families of other countries; neither can we expect the same degree of legislative patronage. . .Much of the good that is effected elsewhere, by private munificence or royal or legislative patronage, can be effected here only by voluntary associations. It is idle to say that it is. . .our best resource, for we have no other.[51]

Early Americans, in other words, literally had to take certain matters into their own hands.

One of the first organized efforts in the fledgling colonies had been the Scots Charitable Society, organized in Boston in 1657.[52] Benjamin Franklin had formed the colonies' first subscription library association in Philadelphia in 1731, the city's first voluntary fire company in 1736, and the city's first "volunteer militia association" in 1747.[53] The Saint Andrew's Society of New York, the first such effort in the Empire State, was founded in 1756.[54]

But it was in early post-Revolutionary New England that the idea of organized citizen action really took hold.

Informal associations, clubs, and societies had existed in the region as early as the first decade of the 18th century and spread quickly. In 1780, only about fifty charitable organizations or institutions of any kind could be counted in all of New England.[55] But by 1800, Massachusetts and Connecticut had chartered more associational corporations than all the other states combined.[56] By 1820 the region boasted approximately two thousand citizen associations.[57] These included not only marine societies, masonic lodges and mechanics' associations, but also, in an unmistakable manifestation of the region's founding principles, humane organizations, schools for the deaf, missionary and Bible associations, and peace societies.[58] "We have," wrote one commentator, "societies for everything. Scarcely a month passes in which we are not called upon to join or aid some benevolent association."[59]

However, a word needs to be added here regarding terminology and the way these entities were viewed.

The most commonly used term today, "nonprofit," did not exist in the colonial era because that distinction only came into play with the passage of the Sixteenth Amendment in 1913 and the subsequent implementation of an income tax. Similarly, our usage today of "charitable organization," with its broad understanding of encompassing all 501(c)(3) corporations is also not fully applicable.

While it is true that many of these colonial institutions resembled their modern counterparts in several important ways, there were also significant differences.

Regarding similarities, they were self-governing, with decisions made by members who often delegated power to governing boards. They had no owners or stockholders. And like modern nonprofits, they could accept donations and bequests for charitable purposes such as supporting education and poor relief.[60]

However, there were also critical differences.

Perhaps the first is that our modern usage of the term "charitable organization" did not exist, was not used, and would not have been understood back then. The term as we use it today only dates from the 1950s when the modern tax code was adopted and the 501(c)(3) category was established. The 501(c) system took a large swath of "public benefit" organizations and placed them under the (c)(3) "charitable" umbrella. But that broad brush appellation did not exist in colonial times.

Moreover, our current understanding of "charity," as being closely associated with what the colonials would have viewed as almsgiving, was not the view *they* had. Indeed, as early as the 1690s they had already distinguished between "charity" and "the dole."[61]

Rather, colonial and early post-Revolutionary Americans saw "charity" as more of an emotion, attitude, or outlook, rather than an act. One "had charity" toward one's neighbors, meaning an empathy, a general disposition toward kindness. Particularly in New England, those of the early colonial period saw "charity" in many settings that included not only family and friendships, but the broader relationships that could be found in congregations, masonic lodges, and the various ties that bound communities.[62] Additionally, it is important to recognize that in their understanding, good advice, a kind word, or encouragement during times of adversity could all express charity.[63] Even patriotism was considered as falling within the bounds of "charity."[64]

Rather than "charitable," therefore, organizations that specifically looked to ameliorate the symptoms of poverty and want—particularly after 1820—were seen as "benevolent" institutions. These not only gave alms, but also were agents of, at first, compassion and, later, social change.

Many of the other organizations formed at the time, however, entities we today would term "charitable" or "nonprofit," were of three primary types that really had nothing to do with charity.

The most popular were the Bible and Tract Associations.

Missionary support initiatives had been organized as early as the mid-1600s to assist in efforts to convert the native populations and make bibles and religious readings available to frontier communities.[65] These Bible and Tract Associations, among the first truly organized volunteer efforts of the later 1700s and early 1800s, were largely the product of Evangelical Protestants[66] who were fearful of the religiously disruptive effects of the growing cities and the expanding frontier, as well as the rising tide of Unitarianism and deism.[67] They were interested not only in preserving "traditional" religion, but also in moral reform. To that point, these efforts were seen as crucial in seeking souls for Christ, and their emissaries were also expected to enforce appropriate standards of social and moral conduct among both the natives *and* the frontier pioneers,[68] an impulse which points to a second type of organization that was extremely popular during the era.

One of the characteristics of early independence America was the establishment of moral-reform societies. Taking their cue from England, where such organizations had been operating since the mid-1700s or so, it was not long before Americans were creating such associations of their own. These were effectively of two types: those focused on *social* reconstruction, and those whose goal was *personal* regeneration.[69] And once again, New England largely led the way.

In 1789, the Providence Society for the Abolition of the Slave Trade was formed, followed in 1791 by the Connecticut Society for the Promotion of Freedom, another abolitionist group. By 1813, however, these groups had been joined by the Boston Society for the Religious and Moral Improvement of Seamen, and the Massachusetts Society for the Suppression of Intemperance. Groups of this sort became increasingly popular as the century unfolded. While missionary societies always outstripped other types of organizations, by 1817 Connecticut had thirty-two reform societies, Maine had seven, Massachusetts had thirty-eight, New Hampshire another seven, and Vermont three.[70]

The other very popular type of early-19th-century voluntary organization was the so-called "mutual association."

The concept behind the mutual association, first pioneered in England in the early 1600s, was, effectively, insurance against unexpected misfortune or calamity. Members—who had to be sponsored by existing members and vetted—paid a regular set fee into a pool that would then be used to offset the financial needs of those participants who might be struck with an illness or injury, fire, or other stroke of bad luck. In many ways, these were the forerunners of today's mutual insurance companies. One of the most popular of these at the time was, perhaps surprisingly, masonic lodges.[71] But the Freemasons were not the only ones to pursue this novel experiment.

Not only did other fraternal groups spring up, but, in a way resembling today's affinity groups, mutual associations also began to spring up, centered around a common characteristic required for membership. Marine associations soon attracted ship owners, ship's officers, and other more well-to-do individuals in some way associated with maritime trade. Mimicking this, seamen's associations, aimed at crew members and some of those of lesser stature within the maritime industries, also came into being.

As has been mentioned, the Scots Charitable Society had been founded in 1657, and existed to service the many immigrants to New England from Scotland. Meanwhile the Charitable Irish Society and the Episcopal Charitable Society looked after their own. Between 1787 and 1807, the number of these mutual associations grew fourfold.[72]

Groups with specific purposes were also organized. The Massachusetts Charitable Fire Society, formed in 1792, made emergency grants to families burned out of their homes. The same year saw the Hartford Charitable Society launched, its purpose being to provide the town's poor with emergency fuel and food. Women's associations were especially active in addressing issues they saw as particularly harmful to their gender, establishing asylums for female orphans, and funds for the relief of destitute women and elderly widows.

The Boston Dispensary, founded in 1796, offered temporary home care and medicine to "poor-but-worthy" Bostonians, and in 1802 the Massachusetts Humane Society[73] was founded, to provide useful information to new immigrants.[74] Emergency food and fuel and other aid societies were organized to assist those economically hurt by the embargo announced by President Jefferson in 1807 and the British blockade of American trade during the War of 1812.

In Philadelphia, meanwhile, the Society of the Friendly Sons of St. Patrick for the Relief of Emigrants from Ireland—which still exists[75]—was formed in 1771, initially aspiring to aid the victims of starvation and eviction in Ireland, and those in exile in America from Ireland.

This is not to say, however, that the nation as a whole rushed to embrace the idea or the existence of these groups. Many early Americans distrusted voluntary associations and feared the power of wealthy private institutions.[76] George Washington and James Madison saw private associations as posing an actual danger to both popular government and the country itself.[77] There were a number of reasons for this. These groups were seen as special interests whose views, desires, and aims did not necessarily reflect the common good. The existence of these associations also seemed somehow incompatible with democratic institutions, since it was feared that organized collectivities, operating beyond the control of the government—and especially if invested with property rights—could make some citizens "more equal" than others and thereby threaten the egalitarian foundation of the new governmental order. Critics worried that as these groups grew in size and stature, they would attract both political power and financial resources, which could tip the balance of power in their favor to the detriment of the individual citizen.[78] A common concern of the day was that, given enough time, they might even capture control of the government. They were, in fact, among the "factions" against which Washington warned in his 1796 *Farewell Address*, that caution not pertaining only to political parties.[79]

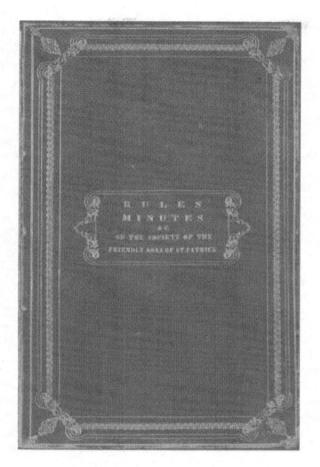

Figure 2.1 Rules & Minutes of the Friendly Sons of St. Patrick, 1771–1793. Page 41 contains the adoption of General George Washington as a member. Digital Library at Villanova University.

Reflecting these concerns, many states actively discouraged organized private charity. Having historical experience with the abuses of both the Anglican and Catholic churches in England, many colonists—and their local governments—were innately suspicious of the power of established charities.[80] There was resistance to efforts to charter these entities as corporations, and to legal reforms that would make it easier to set up and enforce charitable trusts. After independence from Britain had been secured, many states outside New England enacted laws restricting the powers of corporations, repealing sections of British common law relating to charities, and restricting the ability of citizens to give property to charities. Southern states, reflecting not only Jefferson's concerns about "un-republican" institutions, but also their own paternalistic views regarding the ordering of society, were particularly hostile to private corporations, associations, and charities. Virginia, in fact, disestablished the Anglican Church and also confiscated its assets.[81]

It is also instructive that, in spite of the fact that most people today associate it exclusively with oversight of the state's vast educational network, the Regents of the University of the State of New York was established in 1784 as a regulatory body to oversee all charitable, educational, religious, and professional organizations.[82] In the 1820s, the state enacted laws limiting the size of institutional endowments and the size of bequests that testators could leave to charity.[83]

Pennsylvania, meanwhile, not only annulled the Elizabethan Statute of Charitable Uses, but also, by declining to give its courts equity powers,[84] discouraged the establishment of charities, since without equity jurisdiction, courts could not enforce trust provisions.[85] Even Connecticut and Massachusetts, which would become the national centers for the chartering of corporations and the founding of private charities by the 1820s, were ambivalent about them in the years immediately following the Revolution. Connecticut limited the amount of property these organizations could hold, while Massachusetts declined for decades to grant its courts the equity powers needed to enforce charitable and other trusts.[86] Additionally, until the mid-1850s many state statutes, while eventually allowing for entities to incorporate for charitable purposes, did not necessarily exempt them all from state taxes.[87]

Critical to the spread of these groups, however, were a number of important developments. Perhaps the most important was early America's move away from the often ad hoc, "community" model of charity and civil engagement that had been its general model for decades.

In a pattern that was to be repeated in New York, Pennsylvania, and other colonies, as early as 1700, decades of steady population growth had effectively filled up New England's prime farming lands in the communities of eastern Massachusetts and the Connecticut River Valley, leaving only the more mountainous western part of the Bay State, Vermont, New Hampshire, and Maine's rugged terrain[88] for new settlement in the region. With little good land available to support the generation coming of age, the area faced a labor surplus. This led to the formation of a new class that included unlanded sons, day laborers, and seasonal workers, something the region had not seen before. Many of these individuals took up residence in the region's larger communities and represented an economically marginal population, men and women who worked in boom times, but had to look to the community for assistance when business and opportunities slackened.[89] By way of illustration, in 1790, Boston's almshouses held twice the number of people they'd held in an average year prior to the Revolution.[90]

By the dawn of the 19th century, the impact of growth was even more pronounced as settlement patterns, particularly in the northeast, changed yet again. Increasingly, the traditional small, familiar, self-sufficient and tight-knit villages that had once characterized the region were losing population as the often-meager land was farmed out and both the west (in those days the Ohio Valley) and developing, larger cities offered the hope of new economic opportunity. Where at an earlier time neighbor virtually always knew neighbor, a new anonymity was beginning to take hold.

More people overall, a more transient population, and the founding of new towns all contributed to the fact that it was growing more difficult to maintain the old forms of social unity.[91] In addition, growing communities also meant an increasingly visible population of poor and dependent people for whom the public was expected to take responsibility.[92] As proportionately fewer people felt tied to a certain geographic location—a town or hamlet, for example, where their parents or grandparents had settled—observers of the time noticed a distinct loosening of traditional community mores, a "moral decay," on both the frontier and in the burgeoning commercial centers. An increase in visible displays of drunkenness was noted, along with more abandoned wives, more abandoned children, more widows and elderly on their own with no support networks. . .all these presented a challenge for communities from Maine to Georgia.

Yet at the same time, overall, people felt less compelled, inclined, or bound to take care of those just passing through or whom they hardly knew, and even in New England new distinctions were being made between the acquaintance and the stranger, between the deserving and the underserving.[93] This feeling, this reluctance, however, did not mean that the needs of the orphaned, widowed, sick, or destitute went away. They still needed to be addressed.

It became increasingly clear that some new mechanism for addressing a broad range of needs was required as the familiar, neighborly community charity of the 1700s became obsolete. And the nation's emerging private organizations, particularly in New England and other parts of the north where they were by far the most numerous, appeared to many to be a likely vehicle.

A crucial facet of the development of this emerging social force was the victory these entities achieved when they ultimately won the right to incorporate. Previously, these associations, no matter what formal charters or by-laws they drew up, had no legal standing. This was a serious impediment to a good portion of their evolving agenda. The right to incorporate, until this time limited to organizations with a clearly and purely public mission—banks, turnpike and canal companies, municipalities—proved indispensable to the nation's emerging voluntary associations because it granted to them several essential abilities, such as the right to own property and enter into contracts. Corporate identity also shielded individual board members from any liability for organizational debts.

But perhaps most important of all, as corporations, these enterprises could conduct business in perpetuity, irrespective of the arrival or departure of individual members.[94] They could exist for as long as they chose to exist. . .which meant that neither their identity nor their work was dependent upon any one person or group of persons. This was a key element of their development into the institutions we know today.

Also critical to the future development of the association movement was its further secularization. Prior to the Revolution, when most of the colonies had an official religion of some sort, it was natural for charitable endeavors to be organized under the auspices of a denomination or specific congregation. However, within years of independence, this system was becoming less and less dominant.

A number of forces were at play here. The first was the disestablishment movement in the states, which began with Virginia's adoption of the Bill for Establishing Religious Freedom, in 1786. Although passage of the First Amendment in 1791 prevented the federal government from establishing any religion, the obvious loophole was that the states were not originally constrained in a similar fashion, and most of the thirteen had some form of tax-supported religion or a form of religious test for office holders.[95]

But changes in the nation's religiosity during the Revolutionary period brought this practice into growing disfavor. Although not all states with either an official, tax-supported religion or with religious tests for public office immediately rushed to adopt disestablishment—it wasn't until 1833 that Massachusetts finally eliminated its religious taxes—the die was cast. With various denominations losing their "official" status, it was only natural that they would lose some of their accustomed place as a central focus of civic life as well. It just did not seem necessary any longer to have a church or congregation be the sponsor of civic action intended to bring about civic results. The hand of God was not automatically seen as necessary to guide the work of man.

A second dynamic was the sharp increase in the number of active sects and denominations, particularly during the Second Great Awakening.

The sheer number of separate denominations openly operating and seeking converts in many places around the turn of the 19th century was leading to division and competition among early charitable efforts. Also of concern was the tendency of denominational charitable efforts to primarily (and sometimes exclusively) focus their efforts upon their co-religionists.

In reaction to this, a number of leading observers saw secular efforts, those neither affiliated with nor connected to any church, as the best agents of both unity and change. Groups like New England's Merrimack Humane Society, which drew support from across the religious spectrum and offered aid irrespective of creed, were held out as examples that ought to be emulated.[96] This is not to say that religiously affiliated efforts ended; they certainly did not and, in fact, remained a central part of both Catholic and Jewish charity, by way of just one illustration.

But recognition of the fact that religion often got in the way of otherwise laudable efforts, coupled with acceptance of the idea that purely secular organizations—groups that were both open to all and might serve all—could indeed tackle many of the challenges of the day, gave an important boost to non-religious organizations and nudged the entire voluntary association movement farther down a predominantly secular path. A "wall of separation," similar to that the new nation was adopting between church and state, became seen as increasingly useful in keeping sectarian concerns and divisions from standing in the way of necessary work.

A pivotal battle, meanwhile, was growing out of the fact that these entities were being created or incorporating under state law. At issue was whether that meant that they were subservient to state authority, existed purely at the discretion of the state, and were therefore answerable to it for what they did, which causes they took up, and what positions they espoused.

The answer came in the form of a landmark 1819 U.S. Supreme Court case, *Trustees of Dartmouth College v. Woodward*,[97] a dispute which arose when the president of Dartmouth College was deposed by its trustees, leading the New Hampshire legislature to attempt to force the college to place trustee appointment powers in the hands of the governor.

While the case and the decision it produced are important on a number of fronts, the essential benefit to philanthropies was that hereafter they were recognized as free of government control, even if they were chartered, created by, or incorporated under the laws of the state. . .and even if they were addressing essentially "public" needs. Their agendas and actions, the Court decided, were effectively "private," no matter that the goal—education, penal reform, temperance, the abolition of slavery, or the establishment of parks, zoos, or botanical gardens—was ultimately for the public benefit.[98] Perhaps most important for future generations was the Court's ruling that this freedom from government control even extended to situations where these organizations were receiving public funding. Referring to them by the archaic name "eleemosynaries,"[99] the Court stated that entities of this kind, what we recognize today as nonprofits, were free to pursue and seek support for their own visions of society.

When that "vision" included a benefit that might coincide with the public good, the Court held, donors who supported that vision did so as it was expressed by an organization's board, *not* as determined by the state, even if the two seemed to, for the moment, align with one another. Put another way, even where an organization was working to accomplish a goal also established by legislation, and even if public money were going to an organization in pursuit of that goal, it was determined that it was the *organization's* view of that goal—and not the state's—that private donors were supporting with their contributions.

Should those views diverge, the state could withdraw its money. . .but it could not force a charity or philanthropy to alter its views or methods to suit a legislatively determined definition of the public interest. The acceptance or utilization of public money by a charity, in other words, in no way diminished its independence or made it an arm of the state.[100] In recognizing the value of their role, Chief Justice John Marshall wrote that the eleemosynaries "do not fill the place which would otherwise be filled by government, but that which would otherwise remain vacant."[101]

One of the unintended consequences of the *Woodward* decision, however, was a new reality for the government. Because it could no longer dictate how private organizations would view the social tasks at hand, the government could not rely upon them to define public need; it could no longer sit back and allow these associations to be the only ones undertaking what were often essentially public responsibilities. Tasks like the education of the young and the care of the needy could no longer be left purely to private hands because, after *Woodward*, it was clear that the outcomes might not be what legislatures had in mind. The government was learning that perspective and judgments might differ, but so too could intended goals. The increasing use of associations by ever larger numbers of Americans helped to clarify the still-blurred distinctions between public and private domains of activity,[102] and after *Woodward*, it seemed that the state needed to define its priorities more clearly.[103]

But determining which priorities could not be left in private hands was only the beginning of the task, for, having done so, the government faced the reality of having to address these needs itself. . .which often meant securing the public funds necessary, and sometimes entailed creating new public offices to deal with these issues.[104] In the face of opposition to some of the required spending, however, the result was that those needs that were deemed less important, less sensitive, or less politically palatable were often left to private organizations to address as they saw fit.[105] While this did not mean that there would be a strict or impermeable demarcation between those things the government did and those the associations did, it was a crucial juncture for the development of the American nonprofit sector:

- It meant, in the most literal sense, that anything the government wasn't doing, these organizations were free to undertake. Moreover, as new needs developed or were perceived, unless and until the government decided to step in, the private organizations, the eleemosynaries, were free to act, raise and spend money, rally opinion, and, often, set the terms of the debate.
- It marked the beginning of what would ultimately become the divergent responses to social need that respectively characterize America and Europe today.
- It opened the door, by the early decades of the 1800s, to the system of "government-by-contract" we still have, whereby government monies began to flow to private organizations to achieve public ends.
- It *also* opened the door for involvement by a number of marginalized groups in American society, largely changing forever the face of our nonprofit sector.

***

Their independence assured, the country's private organizations moved into the middle and latter decades of the 19th century, with not only a new assurance, but also a new acceptance and a new sense of purpose.

For a variety of reasons, by the middle of the century the country had largely overcome its suspicion of voluntary associations,[106] and subgroups across society began to see them as an increasingly useful means of attaining their aims or protecting their interests.[107] Not only did socially excluded groups, such as women, free blacks, and immigrants, use associations to create "separate spheres" in which they could operate, exert some influence upon the larger society, and promote their interests, but artisans and laborers, as they were drawn into the industrial system, began organizing mutual benefit associations to provide social insurance and assert their political and economic rights. Similarly, farmers used associations to promote agricultural improvements and to broaden markets for their products.[108]

Following this model, the learned professions, especially medicine, law, and engineering, formed national associations to define and uphold professional standards and to promote the diffusion of knowledge. For decades, physicians and lawyers had struggled to restrict admission into their professions to educated and credentialed practitioners. To some extent, these efforts had been thwarted by populist Jacksonian state legislatures; to another degree, the expanding territories of the young nation often put self-proclaimed "professionals" beyond the reach of such authorities as might have curtailed their activities. Either way, doctors found themselves in frequent competition with quacks of every description, credentialed attorneys found themselves facing woefully unprepared young men who had succeeded in persuading increasingly politicized judges to admit them to the bar,[109] and a series of engineering disasters—the explosion of the locomotive *Best Friend of Charleston* in 1831, the 1840 collapse of a lattice bridge over rain-swollen Catskill Creek under the weight of a Canajoharie and Catskill Railroad train, and the sinking of the SS *Arctic* in 1854 among them[110]—brought new attention to the increasing demands required of professional engineers. As a result, by 1839 the American Statistical Association had been founded, followed by the American Psychiatric Association in 1844, the American Medical Association in 1847, the American Society of Civil Engineers in 1852, and the American Institute of Architects in 1857.[111]

But it was the possibilities seen by those concerned with the nation's evolving and deteriorating social conditions that had the greatest impact on the next stage of development in the nation's nascent voluntary sector.

Notes

1 Woodard. (2011) *passim.* As early as 1831, de Tocqueville recognized the role the culture of New England was to play in the American nation. "The principles of New England," he wrote, "spread at first to the neighboring states; they then passed successively to the more distant ones; and at length they imbued the whole Confederation. They now extend their influence…over the whole American world. The civilization of New England has been like a beacon lit upon a hill, which, after it has diffused its warmth around, tinges the distant horizon with its glow." See de Tocqueville, A. *Democracy in America.* Trans. Henry Reeve. [New York: Barnes and Noble, 2003] p. 15.

2 Friedman, L. "Philanthropy in America: Historicism and Its Discontents." *Charity, Philanthropy, and Civility in American History.* Eds Lawrence J. Friedman and Mark D. McGarvie. [Cambridge: Cambridge University Press, 2003] p. 6.

3 Kelley, p. 2441, Note 22.

4 Horn. pp. 68, 76.

5 In Virginia and the later southern colonies, the construction of a society premised upon the paternalistic benevolence of white, male masters of private households and estates recognized the "Christian duty" of the strong and able to care for those who were weaker (because of their gender) or less able (because of their race). In this context, "charity" was, ironically, a tool of both social control and racial subordination. See Friedman. p. 25.

6 Ahlstrom. p. 135.

7 Neuman, J. "The Distinctly American Tradition of Charity." *U.S. News & World Report.* October 18, 2010. www.usnews.com/news/articles/2010/10/18/the-distinctly-american-tradition-of-charity.

8 Hall, P.D. "Virginia and the Elizabethan Charitable Tradition." *Documentary History of Philanthropy and Voluntarism in the United States.* [Work-in-progress, Harvard University, 2017] https://www.hks.harvard.edu/fs/phall/02.%20charity%20in%20colonial%20VA.pdf.

9 Hall, P.D. (2017) "John Winthrop, 'A Modell of Christian Charity'." https://www.hks.harvard.edu/fs/phall/03.%20winthrop%2C%20Christian%20Cha.pdf.

10 This was done for at least two reasons. The first was their belief in the individual's right and duty to know Scripture. Education was essential so the masses could read the Bible for themselves. Beyond this, even though nothing in English statute required either local schoolmasters or the literacy of children, the Puritan model foresaw that, besides the Bible, people needed to be able to read in order to understand the laws of the colony. See Woodard. pp. 59, 61.

11 In 1647, Massachusetts passed a General School Law that required every town having more than fifty families to hire a teacher, and every town of more than one hundred families to establish a "grammar school." Meanwhile, just as they would resist later efforts at social reform carried out by voluntary associations, so too did the southern colonies look upon the free (public) school systems of the north as a particularly objectionable institution. See Bremner. R. *The Public Good.* [New York: Alfred A. Knopf, 1980] p. xvi.

12 Kelley, p. 2451, Note 86.

13 This is not to say, however, that the leaders of New England approved of "idleness," or thought that alms and other support ought to be given to the "unworthy poor," those who could otherwise support themselves. Famed Boston religious and civic leader Cotton Mather wrote in his 1710 *Bonifacius,* or *Essays to Do Good,* that in looking for opportunities to do good, the Christian ought to look to his neighbors. But, "If there be any Idle Persons among them, I beseech you, cure them of their Idleness; Don't nourish 'em & Harden 'em in That; but find Employment for them; Find 'em Work; Set 'em to Work; Keep 'em to Work." Only then, he advised, should such material assistance as one might want to give be offered. See Mather, C. *Essays to Do Good.* [Glasgow: Chalmers and Collins, 1825] p. 103. https://archive.org/details/essaystodogo00math.

14 Not only was this model not followed in the southern colonies, but it is instructive that in 1824, when the New York state legislature required that every county in the state build a poorhouse, and ended the residency requirements for most poor relief state-wide, the act was opposed by New York City, where the high number of poor persons who arrived from other areas would now be the responsibility of the local government. (See Institute for Children, Poverty, & Homelessness. "Poor Law of 1824." *History of Poverty & Homelessness in NYC.* http://povertyhistory.org/era/early_ny#poor-law-of-1824.) New York City, with its Dutch roots that had never

been obliterated by the British after they assumed control in the late 1600s, had a commerce-based culture markedly distinct from that of the theocracies of New England. It was never part of, and never adopted the world view of, Yankeedom. See Shorto, R. *The Island at the Center of the World*. [New York:Vintage Books, 2004] *passim*, and Woodard. pp. 65–72.

15 Massachusetts was, from the start, styled a "commonwealth," the root of which is "common weal" or, according to the *Oxford English Dictionary*, "the general good, public welfare, or prosperity of the community." See "Common weal." Definition 1. *The Compact Edition of the Oxford English Dictionary*. [Glasgow: Oxford University Press, 1971].

16 Hall. (2017) "Doing Good in the World: Cotton Mather and the Origins of Modern Philanthropy." https://www.hks.harvard.edu/fs/phall/08.%20Mather.pdf.

17 One example of the continued influence of our shared Puritan background is the effect, throughout our history, it has had on cultural norms, even in such areas as dress and outward appearance. See Weeks, L. "When Wearing Shorts Was Taboo." National Public Radio (NPR History Dept.) April 7, 2015. www.npr.org/blogs/npr-history-dept/2015/04/07/397804245/when-wearing-shorts-was-taboo?utm_source=facebook.com&utm_medium=social&utm_campaign=npr&utm_term=nprnews&utm_content=20150407.

18 Shorto. pp. 61–63.

19 Woodard. pp. 56, 87, 143.

20 Friedman. p. 25.

21 Woodard, C. *The Lobster Coast*. [New York: Penguin Books, 2004] p. 97.

22 Ahlstrom. p. 156. It was also true that, although they themselves were dissenters, no one was allowed to dissent from their view without punishment. Roger Williams ran into trouble for arguing that the local natives owned their lands and should be paid for them. He also preached the separation of church and state, asserted that civil magistrates should not punish any sort of "breach" of the Ten Commandments such as idolatry, Sabbath-breaking, false worship, or blasphemy, and that individuals should be free to follow their own convictions in religious matters. Tried for the crime of spreading "diverse, new, and dangerous opinions," he was convicted of sedition and heresy, and banished from Massachusetts.

Anne Hutchinson was a Puritan spiritual adviser and an important participant in a theological dispute that shook the infant Massachusetts Bay Colony from 1636 to 1638. Her strong religious convictions—she was an advocate of personal revelation, which called the primacy of Scripture into question—were at odds with the established Puritan clergy area, but her popularity and charisma helped create a theological schism that threatened to destroy the Puritans' religious community in New England. For this, she was eventually tried and convicted, then banished from the colony with many of her supporters. Making her way south to the present border between the Bronx and Westchester County, she attempted to start a new life there with a small band of family and friends, but she was killed in a 1643 raid by local Siwanoy natives during which every member of her party was slaughtered.

Quakers were particularly despised by the Puritan leadership for their dangerous notions of pacifism, equality, and tolerance. Captured Quakers were disfigured for future reference, having their ears cut off, their nostrils slit, or their faces branded with the letter *H* for Heretic. See Woodard. (2004) p. 101.

23 Ibid. p. 129.

24 Ibid. p. 348.

25 Although this particular line inquires specifically of sailors, throughout the work Mather implicitly suggests that "better men" are wanted and needed by society. See Hall. (2017) p. 22.

26 Hammack. p. 1642.

27 "Is there any REMARKABLE DISORDER. . .that requires our Endeavour for the Suppression of it?" Mather asks in point 1 of his advice. This he follows with point 8: "Is there any matter to be. . .moved unto the LEGISLATIVE POWER to be Enacted into a LAW for Publick Benefit?" See Hall. (2017) pp. 20–21.

28 Woodard. (2011) pp. 263–273.

29 Woodard. (2004) p. 78.

30 Horn. p. 285.

31 Ahlstrom. p. 637.

32 Hall. (2006) p. 33.

33 Hall, P.D. "Historical Perspectives on Nonprofit Organizations in the United States." Ed. D. Renz et al. *The Jossey-Bass Handbook of Nonprofit Leadership and Management.* [San Francisco, CA: Jossey-Bass, 2010] p. 5.

34 Ahlstrom. p. 143.

35 Hall. (2006) p. 33.

36 Hall, P.D. (2017) "Doing Good in the World: Cotton Mather and the Origins of Modern Philanthropy." https://www.hks.harvard.edu/fs/phall/08.%20Mather.pdf.

37 While the First Amendment required that the federal government refrain from establishing any "official" religion(s), churches established by state law not only were permitted by state constitutions of the time, but also were common. Establishment was accomplished via measures that imposed taxes on citizens to support the officially recognized church, attendance requirements, and religious oaths. In the years following the ratification of the Constitution, however, a movement to disestablish state churches made rapid progress. The two principal driving forces behind the drive to disestablish state churches in the late 18th and early 19th centuries were (1) opposition to paying taxes to support a church other than the one that an individual attended, and (2) the rapid increase in the number of competing sects and denominations.

38 While the impacts of the war were felt across the Protestant spectrum, the Anglican Church was perhaps the most impacted. Two-thirds of Virginia's Church of England rectors, by way of example, left their parishes during the war. For a time, William White was the only Anglican priest in the whole state of Pennsylvania. At the war's end, there were but five Anglican priests in New Jersey, four in Massachusetts, one in New Hampshire, and none in Rhode Island or Maine. Beyond this, already weakened by defections to various Congregationalist, Unitarian, and Methodist assemblies, the war's end further decimated many Anglican parishes as Loyalists—they were a majority in New York, New Jersey, and Georgia, and a strong presence in Virginia, Massachusetts, and Maryland—fled the victorious American governments, over seventy-thousand of them leaving the country during the war or immediately thereafter. See Ahlstrom. p. 369. Meanwhile, John Wesley's Methodists were not faring much better. Not yet a separate denomination—its formal ministers were still Anglican priests—with the Declaration of Independence all but one of Wesley's preachers left the colonies. Ahlstrom. p. 371.

39 Hall. (2006) p. 36. Also see Hammack. p. 1643.

40 Ahlstrom. pp. 364–365.

41 Another factor in this shift was the competition for souls brought on by not only the disestablishment of state-sponsored churches, but also the emergence of a variety of new sects. Ministers were increasingly obliged to please their constituencies. . .resulting in a loss of both status and power. See Ahlstrom. p. 382.

42 Harvard, Yale, Princeton, and Dartmouth, for example, were all founded as religious institutions.

43 Hall. (2006) pp. 33, 34.

44 In New York, for example, colonial poor relief had been overseen by church-wardens and vestrymen connected to the administration of the Anglican Church. After the Revolution, these ties to the church were ended; and New York City's common council adopted a plan that gave thirteen elected commissioners author-ity over the almshouse and other welfare institutions. See Institute for Children, Poverty & Homelessness. "Poor Law of 1784." *History of Poverty & Homelessness in NYC.* http://povertyhistory.org/era/early_ny#reform-of-1784. In those places where churches were supported by taxes, the tasks of levying and collecting those taxes were, in fact, often carried out by the churches themselves, acting under authority delegated to them by the government. See Hall. (2006) p. 34.

45 McGarvie, M. "The Dartmouth College Case and the Legal Design of Civil Society." In Friedman and McGarvie. p. 92.

46 Historian Leonard Levy has argued against this image of an early nation embrac-ing wholesale the idea or practice of free speech, free association, or free thought. Calling that notion "an hallucination of sentiment that ignores history," he main-tains instead that "the intolerance of community opinion. . .[was] a much. . .dreaded and active instrument of suppression." See Hammack. p. 1643.

47 de Tocqueville. p. 480.

48 de Tocqueville. p. 477.

49 The Great Awakenings, a series of at least three waves of new religious fervor, swept across the young U.S. within the first hundred years of its independence. Methodism, a denomination that did not exist at the time of the colonies' founding, grew from 58,000 adherents in 1790, to 258,000 in 1820, and 1,661,000 by 1860, growing by a factor of 28.6 in 70 years, while the total American population grew by a factor of 8. See United States Bureau of the Census. "Historical Statistics of the United States: From the Colonial Times to the Present." [Washington DC: United States Bureau of the Census, 1976] pp. 8, 392. Ideas and theologies such as deism, Mormonism, the Restoration Movement, and the Holiness Movement further splintered the nation's religious identity during the 1800s, as did the emergence of smaller congregations such as the Shakers, New Lights, the African Methodist Episcopal Church, and the in-the-nude worshiping "Adamites" of the era.

50 Hall. (2006) p. 36.

51 Bremner. (1980) p. xiii.

52 Seeley, J.R. et al. *Community Chest: A Case Study in Philanthropy.* [New Brunswick, NJ: Transition Publishers, 1989] p. 14.

53 Brands, H.W. *The First American.* [New York: Anchor Books, 2002] pp. 112–113, 135–137, 183–186.

54 Seeley et al. Op. cit.

55 Wright, C.E. *The Transformation of Charity in Post-Revolutionary New England.* [Boston, MA: Northeastern University Press, 1992] p. 5.

56 Hall. (2010) p. 7.

57 Wright. p. 52.

58 Gross, R. "Giving in America: From Charity to Philanthropy." In Friedman and McGarvie. p. 40.

59 Bremner. (1980) p. xii.

60 Hall. (2010) p. 5.

61 In 1695 Cotton Mather wrote that there is a difference between "paying the *Publick Charges* of the Place in which we live," which were "*Debts* which *Honesty* rather

than *Charity* binds us to the Payment of," and "The *Giving* of what may supply the Necessities and Relieve the Calamities of the *Indigent.*" Wright. p. 8.

62 Mather explained that "Charity [is] manifested in such *Spiritual Beneficence* as *Contributions* for the Propagation of the Gospel, *Subscriptions* toward the Education of Poor but Good *Scholars* in the University, the *Dispersion* of Bibles, and such *Temporal Beneficence* as efforts to comfort the *Sick*, to Nourish *Widows* and *Orphans*, to Redeem *Captives* and *Prisoners* and make mourning Hearts sing." Ibid.

63 Ibid. pp. 7–8

64 Ibid. p. 29.

65 And in those days, Stockbridge in the Berkshires was considered the far frontier by people living in or near Boston. New York's frontier—depending upon wars and relations with the natives—was roughly seen lying anywhere from where Rome, NY, now stands to just outside of Schenectady. See Berleth, R. *Bloody Mohawk*. [Hensonvilly, NY: Black Dome Press Corp, 2010] *passim.*

66 In the colonial context, and particularly in upstate New York and New England, this effectively meant support was drawn from Presbyterians, Methodists, Baptists, Episcopalians, Dutch Reformed believers and orthodox Congregationalist circles.

67 John Pintard, the Recording Secretary of the American Bible Society, decried the Unitarians' efforts to open a church in New York City, citing the "baleful effects of their rational system" of belief.

68 Wright. p. 83.

69 Ibid. p. 60.

70 Ibid. p. 63. In 1772, Connecticut had charitable organizations in more communities than the rest of New England combined. By 1797, even though these organizations had spread throughout the region, Connecticut still had the most. This was also the era, it should be noted, during which a number of utopian and communalist efforts were launched. Around the turn of the 19th century, by way of illustration, the Rappite "Harmony Society" was launched. By 1810, the community numbered around eight hundred members. The Shakers, founded by Mother Ann Lee in 1747, claimed twenty thousand members in five states at the height of the movement. Robert Owens, sometimes called the "Father of the Cooperative Movement," launched his New Harmony experiment, based upon concepts of moral and ethical integrity, in 1814. See Bishop, P.A. "Early American Utopias and Communalism." https://www.hccfl.edu/media/173608/ae2americancommunes.pdf.

71 By 1772 New England had over twenty-four lodges, primarily—but not exclusively—in its port cities. See Wright. p. 30.

72 Ibid. p. 52. By 1817, Connecticut had eighteen mutual associations, Maine had eleven, Massachusetts eighteen , New Hampshire twelve, Rhode Island seven, and Vermont nineteen.

73 In the 1700s, the term "humane society" did not refer, as it does today, to the care and rescuing of animals. Rather, it was applied to organized efforts to assist the poor and suffering.

74 Ibid. p. 55.

75 See the Society's webpage at www.friendlysons.com/.

76 Hall (2010). p. 7.

77 In spite of this stance, however, Washington himself was not only a Mason—he became a Master Mason at only 21 years of age—but also a member of the Society of Cincinnati, a private club founded by Henry Know for prominent former officers of the Continental Army. Membership was hereditary, passed down from one firstborn son to the next, and many in the young nation feared that the members

intended to establish themselves as a hereditary nobility on the British model. These fears were not unfounded and a Massachusetts legislative investigation ordered by John Adams concluded that the Society was "dangerous to the peace, liberty, and safety of the United States." See Woodard. (2004) p. 141.

78 Wright. pp. 113–114.

79 Hall. (2006) p. 35.

80 Byrnes, W. "Early American Distrust and Gradual Acceptance of Charitable Institutions." Byrnes' Tax & Wealth Management Blog. August 9, 2009. http:// profwilliambyrnes.com/2009/08/09/early-american-distrust-and-gradual-acceptance-of-charitable-institutions/.

81 Hall. (2006) p. 35.

82 In 1863 Massachusetts formed its own, more limited body when it established the Board of State Charities. Within a decade, ten other states had followed suit. The members of these boards generally had no administrative responsibilities and served without pay. . .making these positions not patronage attractive. Their duties were to inspect, report upon, and make recommendations for the improvement of both public welfare institutions and private ones receiving state aid or support. See Bremner, R.H. *American Philanthropy.* [Chicago, IL: University of Chicago Press; 1960] p. 95.

83 Hall. (2010) p. 7.

84 In lay terms, courts of equity, as opposed to courts of law, generally concerned matters of fairness, distribution, and redress. In *Willard v. Tayloe*, 75 U.S. 557 (1869), the Court noted that the sort of relief or judgment sought in equity cases "is not a matter of absolute right to either party; it is a matter resting in the discretion of the court, to be exercised upon a consideration of all the circumstances of each particular case."

85 Hall. (2006) p. 35.

86 Ibid.

87 Byrnes. (2009).

88 See Woodard. (2004) *passim.*

89 Wright. pp. 23–24

90 Ibid. p. 99.

91 Hall. (2010) p. 5.

92 Hall. (2006) p. 34.

93 Wright. pp. 23–25.

94 Gross. p. 42

95 During the time of the nation's founding, states imposed taxes and assessments to pay pastors and religious teachers. In Virginia, the Bill for Establishing a Provision for Teachers of the Christian Religion, introduced in 1784, would have continued the pre-Revolution practice of using general taxes to support the state's church. Vermont's legislature passed a law in 1783 that established its system of religious taxation, whereby each town established by majority vote a denomination as the town's church, which would then be supported by local taxes.

Connecticut and Massachusetts also levied taxes for the support of churches and religious schools in the late 1700s. New Hampshire went further: its religious taxes were written into its first constitution.

States also used religious oaths to establish a state church. Early constitutions, such as those of New Jersey, Georgia, South Carolina, and New Hampshire, required anyone seeking public office to profess a belief in Christianity and Protestantism. North Carolina and Pennsylvania required citizens to take strict belief oaths before holding public office, and Delaware required "all officeholders to profess belief in the Trinity and the divine inspiration of the Bible."

The fight over religious taxes sparked the disestablishment movement, and eliminating taxes was the crucial act of disestablishment in many states. Virginia passed Thomas Jefferson's Bill for Establishing Religious Freedom, on January 16, 1786. The statute disestablished the Church of England in Virginia and guaranteed freedom of religion to people of all religious faiths, including Christians of all denominations, Jews, Muslims, and Hindus. As early as 1783, Connecticut's legislature began passing laws exempting people from religious taxation, and in 1791 the Congregational state church in Connecticut was disestablished.

Massachusetts and New Hampshire took longer to repeal their religious taxes. As late as 1803, New Hampshire courts refused to grant exemptions to dissenters from religious taxes. This ended in 1819. The end of religious taxes in Massachusetts was finalized in 1833.

The U.S. Constitution eliminated religious tests for holding federal office and states eventually followed that lead. By 1793 Delaware, South Carolina, Georgia, and Vermont had completely removed religious tests from their constitutions. See Tokarev, S. "Disestablishment of State Churches in the Late Eighteenth Century and Early Nineteenth Century." *Civil Liberties.* June 6, 2012. http://uscivilliberties. org/historical-overview/3703-disestablishment-of-state-churches-in-the-late-eighteenth-century-and-early-nineteenth-century.html.

96 Wright. pp. 91–95.

97 17 U.S. 518 (1819).

98 McGarvie. *Passim.*

99 "Eleemosynary" originally meant any person or entity that was aided by, dependent upon, or the recipient of charity. By the 1800s it had come to refer—much as "a charity" does today—to an entity that existed for the relief of the poor or to carry on the "public benefit charity" recognized in Anglo-American common law.

100 McGarvie. p. 97.

101 Ibid. p. 102. A second case, *Vidal v. Girard's Executors*, 43 U.S. 2 How. 127 127 (1844), affirmed the right of not-for-profit corporations to accept bequests, further strengthening not only the basis of private philanthropy, but also the ability of these entities to act as fully independent agents even if specific actions—in this case the acceptance by the City of Philadelphia of land to be used for the building of a college—are not strictly within the scope of the direct purposes of their creation, but are collateral to them.

102 Hall. (2006) p. 38.

103 McGarvie. p. 102.

104 Regional cultural differences, however, determined the extent to which a city or state might actually do this. Generally speaking, the states and communities that inherited the cultures of Yankeedom and its allies or offshoots were the most activist in most of these areas; while areas born of the culture of the Deep South or Appalachia did the least. See Woodard. (2011) *passim.*

105 McGarvie. Op. cit.

106 Hall. (2006) p. 38. It is also worth noting that in 1835, the ten leading American benevolent societies, founded for the most part between 1810 and 1820 and fueled to a great extent by the Second Great Awakening (roughly 1790 through the 1840s), raised slightly more than $800,000 (almost $14 million in today's dollars) to fund the distribution of bibles and scriptural tracts, send missionaries to the heathen here and abroad, encourage Sunday schools, educate poor youth as Protestant clergy, and recolonize blacks in Africa. See Bremner. (1980) p. xiv.

107 Ibid.

108 Hall. (2006) p. 38.

109 Ibid. p. 41.

110 This was a period of particular devastation due to disasters associated with the nation's increased industrialization and urbanization. Philip Schaff, a scholarly Swiss immigrant, noted that at least one dark aspect of American enterprise was its all-too-frequent degeneration into both foolishness and carelessness in the pursuit of profit, which was "fearfully manifest in the countless conflagrations in cities and disasters on steamboats and railroads." Across the country portions of cities regularly went up in flames, tenement houses burned, and factories collapsed, exploded, and caught fire. A false alarm in a school in New York City in 1851 sent 1,800 children stampeding down the stairs. But under the pressure of their bodies, the insufficiently strong banister gave way and the children fell into the square around which the stairs wound. At least fifty died and the wounded lay for hours because the doors opened inward and help could not reach them as they lay piled against them.

The worst of the era's industrial disasters was the fall of the Pemberton Mill in Lawrence, Massachusetts, in 1860, which took the lives of one hundred textile workers and wounded at least as many. See Bremner. (1980) p. 8.

111 Ibid. p. 38.

Part II

3   From charity to philanthropy

The shape of charity and collective citizen action that characterized America's earliest colonial days was not destined to last. Conceived of and practiced within a fairly specific environment, changes in social structure, settlement patterns, and the composition of society itself all mandated that both would evolve as perspectives shifted under the pressure of America's evolution from thirteen nascent colonies into a growing nation.

The one-hundred-year span from roughly 1820 through the Jazz Era was possibly the most important period in the evolution of the modern American nonprofit sector. It witnessed several significant trends that shaped our current nonprofit arena. But it was also during this timeframe that the single most important development took place, the shift from charity to philanthropy.

Charity had traditionally always been personal, not only primarily springing from a sense of duty or compassion in an individual, but also mostly *aimed* at individuals, be it one person or a family in need. Philanthropy, by contrast, is something altogether different.

When most people today hear the word "philanthropy," they think of the great foundations launched by the likes of Carnegie, Rockefeller, Ford, and Vanderbilt. They think of the giving away of money in large amounts. With this in mind, most would date the birth of American philanthropy as roughly coinciding with the Gilded Age and the era of the robber barons, continuing through names like Gates and Zuckerberg today. But in this, most people would be wrong.

"Philanthropy" was actually coined as a term in the late 1600s, and came from the Greek meaning love of *humankind*; whereas "charity" comes from the Latin *caritas*, or love, as in the sense of tenderness or mercy.[1] While these concepts aren't quite two sides of the same coin, they did become the twin pillars of the practice of American benevolence, the important difference between them being that while charity engages individuals in usually concrete, *direct* acts of compassion and connection to others, philanthropy has always had broader goals and implications.

As early as 1704, the term "philanthropy" referred to "an inclination to promote the Publick Good."[2] In practice, it sought to apply reason to the solution of social problems. It aspired not so much to aid individuals, as to aid and, importantly, reform society. It focused far less on alleviating specific cases of need, than it did on the question of why the need, why certain negative circumstances, existed. It also became, as opposed to charity, institutional and abstract nearly from the beginning.[3]

By 1800, the agenda of at least some of the newly formed organizations was socially ambitious. As early as 1780, some of these socially conscious groups, particularly in New England, were pushing for significant penal reform, advocating for an end to the "brutalization" of law breakers—then subjected to such punishments as whipping, branding, shaming, and the pillory and stock—arguing instead in favor of penitentiaries where the convicted could "ponder the error of their ways." Incarceration, in this early view, was both charity and philanthropy, gentler on the offender and, through prison ministries, an avenue by which the causes of criminality might be addressed.[4] This activist gene in the sector's DNA was to color the actions and priorities of a major portion of these groups during the whole century, and continues to have a significant influence today.

But the nation was also changing, and with those changes much that had been familiar began to fade away.

While America was still an overwhelmingly rural and agrarian nation in the mid-1800s, we already had large cities that seemed to be growing by the week. Fueled in part by waves of immigrants, but also by new opportunities and an anonymity impossible to achieve in smaller, rural communities, by 1840 the population of New York City had grown to 312,710.[5] If we add to this the population of neighboring Brooklyn, then a separate city, the urbanized area surrounding New York Harbor had a population of over 350,000. Baltimore, meanwhile, boasted 102,313 residents. New Orleans had 102,193, and Philadelphia and Boston over 93,000 each.[6]

Within ten years, New York City would have 515,547 residents (and Brooklyn 96,838), Baltimore would have 169,054; Boston 163,181; Philadelphia 121,376; and New Orleans 116,375.[7]

By 1860, New York would have over 1 million residents.

Important changes in essential economic relationships were also playing a part in the shifting social dynamics. The merchant class was growing ever more wealthy *and* ever more remote from the poorer classes.[8] Early industrialization and related endeavors like the building of the railroads, mining, and large-scale timber harvesting brought with them child labor, worker mortality, wretched living conditions such as the young nation had never seen. The abuse of alcohol also took an ever-increasing toll.

Meanwhile, society, particularly in the north, embraced the relatively recent development of contract theory, which imposed a harsh new rationalism on social relationships.[9] And always lurking just over the southern horizon were the horrors of slavery, of which the rest of the nation was increasingly and uncomfortably aware.

In this environment, the personal charity of a bygone era seemed ever more impossible and impractical. It also began to be questioned. Charity was always focused on treating the symptoms of poverty and disadvantage, the hunger, the homelessness, the helplessness people might experience. In the face of growing social problems, and particularly their concentration in the burgeoning cities, however, more and more people began to wonder if charity could ever solve the issues at hand. On an ever-increasing scale, as the 1700s faded into distant memory, people began to look at the causes of some of the social evils around them and wonder if more systemic solutions were not needed.

In answer to this, the new philanthropy that emerged in the early decades of the 1800s was very distinct from traditional charity in its basic aim. Almsgiving, direct relief, was now seen as a waste of resources, because whatever was given would soon be gone. . .while the recipient's circumstances would not have changed, leading to another round of need soon to follow. More to the point, to some observers of the time it seemed clear that traditional forms of charity and almsgiving not only were inadequate to the task of alleviating misery, but might also have actually been aggravating it.[10]

Philanthropy, by contrast, was seen as an improvement upon charity because it sought to resolve the conditions it addressed,[11] and the citizens' association came to be seen as the perfect vehicle for accomplishing this lofty goal.

New players

Several segments of American society, marginalized or disenfranchised from power, took particular advantage of the opportunities presented by this evolving situation to indelibly alter not only the direction of American benevolence, but its character and mission.

As early as 1793, independent black churches in the north began to assume charitable missions within their communities. They also sought to alleviate the conditions under which so many of their race suffered, agitating for social, political, and economic rights which at the time were restricted to whites.[12] Help was also offered in the form of mutual aid and improvement societies. By 1830, in Philadelphia alone, there were over forty-five different Black Freedmen's and women's associations operating in the city and, within one year, they had paid out over $5,760—about $142,692 in today's money—in charitable benefits.[13] These organizations would continue to be vital partners in the black philanthropy movement for decades and decades to come, their aim always being to address, in a way outsiders never could, the challenges their community faced.[14] Moreover, the idea never completely faded away; strong echoes of this movement would be heard again over one hundred years later in the community-based and culturally attuned organizations that sprang out of the Civil Rights Movement and Great Society.

Two other groups that both utilized and capitalized upon the emerging philanthropic movement were women and, perhaps surprisingly, the main-stream clergy.

Stymied in many ways from undertaking a larger civic role by the mores of the day, women assumed an early leading role in organized American benevolence, using associations to create a "separate sphere" of educational, religious, and cultural activity.[15] In 1795 the first female charitable organization, the Female Society for the Relief of the Distressed, was formed in Philadelphia. Funded by its members, it pledged aid to those of any faith, irrespective of "nation or color." In 1800, Evangelical Presbyterians formed the Female Association for the Relief of Women and Children. The earliest of these efforts were strictly the creatures of the governing class. But although often underwritten financially by men, these entities were virtually always founded and run by women[16]. . .very often, the wives, daughters, or sisters of the moneyed men who comprised the civic elite. This development has been linked to the increased freedom and power that women of the American middle class were experiencing as the 19th century unfolded, and to their related claim, widely accepted throughout Victorian Era America, of possessing a morality superior to that of men. . .leaving them powerful actors in the century's developing philanthropic efforts.[17]

It was one of the ironies of history that these women, constrained in their activities by the sexism of the age, but embodying the growing bourgeois sensibilities of the time, were able to capitalize upon the popular notion of "a woman's more sensitive eye"[18] and in many cases work around the crass, cruel, unfeeling dictates of male-dominated commerce, calling attention to the high human cost of the largely male-ordered, Dickensian world in which they lived. . .even as the fruits of that world made possible their position, voice, and actions.

With amazing rapidity, the organizations these women (and their considerably fewer male allies) founded, often fueled by what has been called the "Protestant missionary impulse,"[19] cast their eyes and their attentions upon a wide range of causes.[20]

This new, largely female-led philanthropy movement tackled a broad array of social issues, ranging from penal reform and the amelioration of cruelty to animals, to measures aimed at addressing the abandonment and mistreatment of children, from the care of the sick and those labeled insane, to the treatment of reformed prostitutes. These voluntary groups opposed drunkenness, dueling, wars and imperialism, the abuse of the poor, press gangs, and injustice generally. They organized and worked to end political corruption, the slave trade, slavery itself, and the "seduction and abandonment of women."[21] In the broadest sense, their aim was to use voluntary associations to steer the nation away from not only slavery and inebriation, but also its often ill-disguised intolerance of the poor, weak, infirm, and vulnerable. Ultimately, they contributed not only to the nonprofit sector as we know it today, but to the American welfare state.

Meanwhile, largely stripped of the power to directly influence civil events by the nation's novel separation of church and state, the mainstream clergy soon found that its voice could have renewed resonance when allied with the growing female-led reform movement.[22] Working under the banner of the "Benevolent Empire," these two important segments of society worked to encourage a new moral and sympathetic social awareness through the application of a new "socially conscious philanthropy."[23] Their targets—the poverty, harshness, cruelty, crime, and suffering that largely affected the expanding and increasingly impersonal free-market capitalism of the early Republic—would, they hoped, be eliminated through forceful public attention paid to social problems.[24]

The goal of these 19th-century reformers, primarily, but not exclusively based in either the New England home of Yankeedom or lands settled in by New Englanders and influenced by their culture, was nothing less than the remaking of American society. Their "Social Gospel" viewed it as the earthly responsibility of every Christian to strive toward a just and humane society,[25] and toward this end they worked to mobilize not only their own forces, but the opinion of a largely indifferent public. Echoing the informing civil principle of the New England theocrats, their view was that the government was an essential and available tool for improving lives and constructing a better national community.[26] They also—and quite consciously—saw themselves as the vanguard that could *and would* shape the moral and political culture of the country. In place of cruel, older customs, they would establish new, more merciful ones. They would consistently push upwards, toward a better plane, the average standard of what was "right." It was no longer enough, they felt, to Christianize individuals; according to their evolving view the nation itself could and would be brought up to this standard.[27] Few of these early activists had any illusions but that they were trying to impose new views on a blind or reluctant people.[28]

Often unable, however, to win legislative approval for public initiatives to address these issues, they turned to private associational efforts in order to redesign society.[29]

Yet the line between the emerging philanthropic movement and government was not as firm as legislative reluctance to undertake large-scale social reforms might suggest, as the support for these voluntary, philanthropic associations came not only from the public,[30] but from the *public sector* as well. Notable figures like New York's Mayor DeWitt Clinton moved freely between the governmental and charitable realms, Clinton serving simultaneously as mayor of New York City[31] and as president of the Free School Society.[32]

More importantly, government began paying these philanthropic agencies to provide essentially public services: Clinton's Free School Society was funded by the city to run schools for the poor, and early in the century the New York State Legislature awarded $750—approximately $11,000 in today's money—to the Society for the Relief of Poor Widows with Small Children to support its efforts to reduce the number of destitute, female-headed families who were forced to turn to the city's almshouse. As early as 1901, Pennsylvania, California, New York, and the District of Columbia led the nation in the amounts they gave to charitable institutions for the provision of services to the poor and needy.[33]

While this was happening, the residents of the U.S. came together during the latter 1800s and formed and joined an unprecedented number of groups.

Physicians, lawyers, engineers, and other professionals organized associations to set standards, exchange information, and pressure government. Businesses organized trade associations to advocate for legislation favoring their interests. Wage earners fought for and organized trade unions to press employers to improve pay and working conditions. War veterans organized to advocate for pensions and other benefits. Advocacy groups changed with the times and now agitated for prohibition, women's suffrage, civil service, and charities reform, and other causes. The Freemasons, Odd Fellows, Knights of Columbus, and dozens of other fraternal organizations sprouted chapters in cities and towns across America.[34]

Following this model, immigrants, too, organized mutual benefit associations that offered them solidarity and provided help in times of sickness and distress. Among these immigrants, however, two groups in particular—the European Catholics and the largely Eastern European Jews—were to have substantial if differing impacts on the American chartable landscape.

New arrivals

Although they arrived in small numbers at first,[35] the Catholics and Jews who came to this country in significantly larger waves in the mid- and later 1800s and into the early 1900s were to have a profound impact on benevolence in America. One of the most significant differences between them and America's majority Protestant population was that while the Protestants largely accepted the ever-increasing secularization of charity, both the Jews and Roman Catholics retained the ethno-religious character of their respective efforts.[36]

The Catholics

Between 1820 and 1890, approximately 3.5 million Irish came to America, the overwhelming number of them Catholic. In the 1880s, 300,000 Italians arrived, followed by another 600,000 in the 1890s. By the 1920s more than 4 million had arrived, virtually all of them Catholic.

Add to these numbers those of their faith who arrived primarily from Poland and Germany, but also from across Europe and even Québec, and by 1850 Catholics comprised the nation's single largest denomination. Between 1860 and 1890, their population tripled to 7 million.

Largely marginalized because of hostility toward them on the part of nativist Protestants,[37] and (except for the Irish) often by language barriers as well, these overwhelmingly poor immigrants huddled in the nation's cities, in ghettos and tenements for the most part beyond the reach of such meager social services as existed at the time. But following these waves of immigrants were the clergy from their respective lands, and these men and women—priests, religious brothers, and nuns[38]—soon began to establish a network of charitable institutions to attend to their flock's temporal as well as spiritual needs. In addition to the schools founded by these orders, there were hospitals, foundling homes, and orphanages. They launched temperance societies and social welfare organizations. They provided direct relief in the form of food and clothing for the poor. They visited and tended to the sick and elderly in their homes.

This was to have a significant influence on the American charitable sector in a number of ways.[39] The sheer size of the Catholic population in the U.S. by the middle of the 1800s virtually dictated that its organized arm, the dioceses and archdioceses that had been created since Baltimore was named as the new nation's first in 1789, could and would have an influence upon whatever areas of civic life it turned its attentions to. Moreover, in spite of the numerous national and ethnic divisions among America's Catholics, their Church was often able to speak and act with a more unified and therefore more powerful voice than was balkanized Protestantism, in spite of the social marginalization of individual Catholics themselves.

One of the first places this potential was realized was in the sheer size and power of the Catholic charitable effort. Although mostly low-income, U.S. Roman Catholics gave millions of dollars to finance thousands of churches, schools, hospitals, sanitariums, orphanages, homes for the aged, and facilities for unwed mothers. While religious faith did profoundly influence donors' motives, so too did other values indigenous to an immigrant population. . .among them ethnicity and ethnic pride, a desire to move their Church into the mainstream of American life, and a probable determination not to be outclassed by their better-off Protestant neighbors.[40]

Raising most of their funding through contributions from the faithful, the Church hierarchy therefore enjoyed a fairly stable source of income. . .and, significantly, the facilities they created often served Catholics and non-Catholics alike.

Clustered in larger and urban areas in the East and Midwest, and in the areas of former Spanish colonization in the West and Southwest, they eventually spread their reach and the "Benevolent Empire"[41] of their institutions—not just schools, but hospitals, orphanages, and institutions created to serve the poor and indigent—across most of the nation. So broad was their reach becoming, in fact, that their presence was actually a spur to Protestant giving. "If you do not assist," wrote one Oregon correspondent in 1850, seeking good New England Protestant teachers for the youth of the rapidly settling Pacific Northwest, "the Sisters of Charity from Papal Rome will do the work!"[42]

Through the growth of their system of schools, hospitals, and orphanages, the Catholics thus contributed to the overall size and influence of the sector. They also demonstrated in a palpable and substantial way that, where the government would not act, private entities could. Finally, in many of the more urbanized parts of the country, the Catholic hierarchy came to supplant their mainline Protestant counterparts in their advocacy on behalf of the less advantaged, their influence on policy-makers, and particularly in their ability—due to the network of Catholic charitable institutions—to attract such public dollars as were available for social purposes. In many places and in many ways, Catholic charitable efforts became a primary partner of the government when it came to providing for the needy, and their influence has remained to this day.

The Jews

The Jewish contribution to the evolving mission of charity in America in the late 1800s and early 1900s was far more subtle, but no less profound. Lacking the numbers, the resources, the religious communities, and centralized hierarchy[43] of their Catholic fellow-immigrants, the Jewish émigré community was not in a position to establish a network of service entities on a scale to match what the Catholics had created.[44] But they brought with them a world view that was to have an indelible impact on the philosophical underpinnings of the sector. To appreciate the truly revolutionary nature of this attitude, it is worth taking a moment to examine the perspectives prevailing before it arrived and eventually took hold.

The New England Protestant flavor of the period's shift from charity to philanthropy, its zeal to create a better world, has already been noted. But there were several aspects of this movement that were often interpreted as less than completely benign. The first was its messianic nature.

With roots in the theocratic Puritans, the benevolent movement of the 1800s had an unmistakable missionary tone. Yes, the goal was to counter the social ills of the day, from slavery to criminality, from drunkenness to prostitution, and cruelty to women, children, and animals. But just as the Puritans saw the road to a better society as traveling unwaveringly through their theology, many of the social improvement efforts that sprang up during the period sought to imbue "Christian" values in the populations they were seeking to help, the operative theory being that if one were a good Christian, one would not fall prey to drink, loose morals, cruelty, or idleness. This tendency was only further enforced when Baptists, Methodists, and Evangelicals from the south and midlands joined these crusades.

It was not a coincidence that by the middle of the century, the American Bible Society and the American Tract Society became among the first truly national charities, their activities and influence spreading from coast to coast. Irrespective of whatever good these efforts might have done, their unmistakable underlying message was *If only you'd be more like us. . .*

This tendency only became more acute under the distinctly classist perspective of American benevolence from roughly the 1840s through the middle of the 20th century.

As early as the 1840s and 50s, the neighborhoods of the poor were not just pitied by the mostly middle-class reformers of the age, they were looked down upon, invoking repugnance, rather than compassion.[45] New York's infamous Five Points provides an illustration.[46]

In the tenements and hovels that comprised that lower Manhattan neighborhood, whole families and other groups often lived crammed into one or two dark rooms. The outhouses were too few and often overflowing. Sewage and pigs ran in the streets. The whole neighborhood just stank[47] with what one observer called "a stench that would poison cattle."[48] It was with a morbid curiosity that upper-class tourists of the day, some holding camphor-soaked kerchiefs to their noses to ward off the stench, would go "slumming" in Five Points (escorted by police!) to see if the lurid tales they'd heard about the area were true.

More importantly, however, the reformers themselves shared the view that the area was little more than an earthly approximation of Hell.

According to one Methodist reformer, Five Points was "the synonym for ignorance the most entire, for misery the most abject, for crime of the darkest dye, for degradation so deep that human nature cannot sink below it."[49]

"Every house was a brothel, and every brothel a hell," wrote Five Points missionary Lewis Pease.[50]

In 1850, *New York Tribune* reporter George Foster added, "It is no unusual thing for a mother and her two or three daughters—all, of course, prostitutes—to receive their men at the same time in the same room."[51]

While there is no denying that the conditions in Five Points and many of the nation's other slums were appalling, many viewed these areas through a middle-class filter, which contributed to their sense of dismay. Middle-class outsiders, *including* the reformers, looked at this neighborhood and others like it, teeming with activity, streets clogged with people selling food and other items, unaccustomed noises and often unfamiliar languages, and rough-and-tumble manners, and found it frightening and unnerving. They looked at it all from the outside, understanding nothing of what they were seeing, and assumed it was all bad.[52] Many, including the reformers and philanthropic missionaries to these neighborhoods, claimed that they wanted to help the poor, but what they really wanted to do was *change* the poor.

Illustration of this can be found in the Friendly Visitor Movement of the late 1800s and early 1900s. Although thought of by its initiators as a good and valid effort toward addressing poverty, it unfortunately demonstrated that the perspective held by the middle and upper classes of the era—that poverty and its impacts were largely brought on by the actions and attitudes of the poor—prevailed.

It was one of the ironies of the age that even as the dawning recognition was beginning to take hold that the disadvantaged and marginalized often labored under circumstances over which they had no control[53]—discrimination, unfair labor laws, depressed wages, and an inadequate civic infrastructure—there was still the sense that what these people were *really* lacking were middle-class values. *If only you'd be more like us* was again the underlying message.

An example of the classist perspective of these obtuse, if well-meaning, volunteers can be found in the advice given by Octavia Hill, a pioneer of England's Visitor Movement:

> You want to get to know them—to enter into their lives, their thoughts; to let them enter into some of your brightness. . .You, who know so much more than they, might help them so much. . .You might teach and refine and make them cleaner merely by going among them.[54]

This attitude not only often insulted the intended beneficiaries, many of whom resented the interference of these "busybodies" in what they thought were purely private matters,[55] but also spurred critics to argue that many of these efforts were pointless because the reformers were doing little more than simply preaching middle-class values to people who could not (or would not) adopt them.[56]

A final note pointing to the truly distinctive nature of the attitude brought to our shores by the era's Jewish immigrants can be found in the Catholic immigrant communities mentioned above.

While they might all have been Catholic, and while their bishops and cardinals were working to establish a unified *Catholic* voice and presence in America, in the minds of the teeming populations of Catholic immigrants themselves, they were Irish, Italian, German, Polish, Lithuanian, or French first. . .and they neither liked one another nor intended to worship or minister together.[57]

Thus began the pattern, still seen in many American communities today, where a Catholic church for Poles was a few blocks away from a Catholic church for the Irish, and often less than a mile or so removed from a Catholic church built for and supported by Italians. No matter their common religion, these nominally Christian immigrants brought with them all the attitudes and prejudices that had colored their native lands.

But the Jews arriving largely from Central and Eastern Europe were different. They were acutely aware, in a way virtually never shared by their Catholic fellow-immigrants, of the need for a broader social justice.[58]

Many Jews in late-19th-century Europe had endured downward socio-economic mobility as traditional Jewish economic niches were undermined by the expanding industrial capitalist system. This experience, combined with formal persecution under the Tsars—and informal discrimination virtually everywhere else—inspired many Jews to look for radical social change. Arriving in the U.S. many took manual jobs, especially in the fledgling garment industry, and experienced poverty as exploited factory labor.[59] The hunger for social justice, the seeds of which had often been planted in the socialist agitation of their native Europe, took root in this environment. This experience led to a perspective which held that, beyond the discrimination and ill treatment they experienced as *Jews*, there was something inherently wrong with a social and economic system that allowed for anyone to be subject to such exploitation and marginalization. Irrespective of a person's religion, national origin, or race, the system they found themselves living and working in in America, while it might have been an improvement upon Tsarist Russia or Poland, was, to many of these Jewish immigrants, simply wrong.

But there was more.

A scattered people for centuries, it was not their current country of residence—which, history had taught them, could change at almost any time—that gave the Jews their identity, but rather their common faith and religious culture. The diaspora had scattered them to many lands, but the commonality of their faith bound them in a way foreign to multi-national Catholicism and the broader multi-faceted Christendom. More to the point, however, they were a people who had spent a millennium or more as outsiders. The persecutions, the discrimination, the insults, expulsions, and pogroms, all had an impact. They sought not assimilation, or acculturation. What they sought in coming to these shores was simple acceptance. . .the freedom to be who they were, while still being full citizens of the new land in which they settled.[60]

While there is an ongoing debate over whether it was these historical experiences or something inherent in their theology that made Jewish immigrants sensitive to the plight of the outsider,[61] it was these two threads, their sensitivity to issues of social justice and their experience as perennial outsiders, which gave the Jewish immigrants who came to America a unique perspective on the marginalized, disenfranchised, and excluded.[62]

Within sixty short years—from the 1880s when they first arrived in large numbers, to the 1940s, when the horrors of the Holocaust unfolded and became known—the Jews in America transformed themselves from a fringe group of ethno-religious refugees to a force recognized as fighting harder than any other group in America for "the dignities and rights of all groups" in America.[63] Perhaps even more notable, it was during this latter period that American Jewish leaders developed a theory regarding the unitary character of prejudice, whereby anti-Semitism, racial, religious, and ethnic bigotry, and even the discrimination against and marginalization of the disabled were inseparable parts of the same phenomenon.[64] It is telling that by the turn of the last century the National Council of Jewish Women, founded in 1893, was already one of a number of agencies dedicated not only to Jewish causes, but also to the general advancement of human welfare and a democratic way of life.[65]

The Jewish reform vision that was to develop and eventually take its place in the larger American nonprofit movement sought out integration and inclusion for all in mainstream American life, and stood opposed to communal marginality for anyone.[66] Far from being lost, this strain of human compassion extends to this day, as, in the wake of Donald Trump's election as president, American Muslims and Jews stood together in solidarity against the fears of xenophobia, ethnic registration, and violence against their communities.[67] "If Muslims have to register, we're all going to register," said one Jewish woman.

This valuable and unique perspective, another of the "gifts of the Jews," was to have an increasing and spreading influence upon the American nonprofit sector as the 20th century unfolded.

***

Through the cumulative impact of numerous shifts in perspective and practice, it became clear that philanthropy and social reform were becoming nearly interchangeable,[68] and that both the issues upon which they focused and the remedies suggested for these problems would increasingly reflect a progressive agenda[69] and a more ideological conception of the sector.[70] American benevolence had changed forever:

- Classic charity, both as an individual action and as something that would benefit individuals, was largely becoming a thing of the past, particularly in America's burgeoning cities. Philanthropy, aimed at the root causes of human distress, was by now the norm.
- That philanthropy, moreover, was to rapidly shift toward issues of social reform, aimed not only at ameliorating poverty, but increasingly toward a broader new concept of social justice. It was in this period that the progressive, inclusive, humanitarian flavor of the sector was first cast. This perspective would only continue and expand in the following decades.
- Fueled by a missionary zeal that originated in New England but rapidly spread to the Midwest and beyond,[71] and also came to include Baptists, Methodists and Evangelicals as well as mainstream sects, this movement set out to reconstruct the country according to a Protestant vision and values. This orientation was to have a significant impact on the work of the associations from the latter half of the 1800s through the 1950s.
- Voices beyond those predominant in the mainstream would become ever more pronounced in the sector. The feminization of the movement, evident from the beginning, was to have a profound influence on the way it developed for the next hundred years. And although the sector was to remain dominated by white, Anglo-Saxon Protestants and the organizations they would found, the combined contributions of blacks, Catholics, and Jews would all help shape the sector as its development continued.

Notes

1 Kelley at Chapter 1, Note 19, this volume.
2 "Philanthropy." The Compact Edition of the *Oxford English Dictionary*. [Glasgow: Oxford University Press, 1971].
3 Gross. p. 31.
4 Friedman. p. 43.
5 In 1840 New York City was limited to just Manhattan Island, and the vast majority of its population located south of present-day 30th Street.
6 United States Census Bureau. "10 Largest Urban Places, 1840." https://www.census. gov/history/www/through_the_decades/fast_facts/1840_fast_facts.html.
7 United States Census Bureau. "10 Largest Urban Places, 1850." https://www.census. gov/history/www/through_the_decades/fast_facts/1850_fast_facts.html.
8 One of the hallmarks of the age was the fast-growing suburbs that began to spring up outside cities like Boston and New York. Linked to the central city by emerging rail or trolley links, these became havens for the well-to-do, eager to escape the burgeoning working classes that were increasingly spreading beyond their traditional slums. See Crocker, R. "From Gift to Foundation: The Philanthropic Lives of Mrs. Russell Sage." In Friedman and McGarvie. p. 204. This development was further spurred on by changes to state law that soon allowed these small satellite communities to incorporate and establish their own identities, even as Boston was annexing communities such as Roxbury, Allston, and Brighton; and New York City annexed the towns of Morrisania and West Farms in 1874, and the whole town of Westchester, half the town of Pelham, Richmond County (Staten Island), all of

Queens County, and the entire City of Brooklyn in 1897–1898. The distance of these outlying communities from the central commercial and industrial sections of the larger cities further insulated the middle and upper classes from the poor; and their exclusive (and expensive) independent nature also ensured that the poor would never live within their boundaries. See Most, D. *The Race Underground*. [New York: St. Martin's Press, 2014] *passim*, and Penna, R. "Metropolitan Political Integration: Problems, Prospects, and Promises," diss., Boston University, 1982, p. 265.

9 Friedman. p. 26.

10 Hall, P.D. "The History of Religious Philanthropy in America." In Wuthnow and Hodgkinson. p. 40.

11 Ibid. p. 39.

12 Brake, Y.H. and McMillan, Y. "Religious Basis for Charitable Giving." Learning to Give. http://learningtogive.org/papers/paper55.html.

13 Among these were the African Friendly Society of St. Thomas, founded 1795; Sons of Africa, founded 1810; Benezet Philanthropic, founded 1812; the Benevolent Sons of Zion, founded 1822; the Sons of St. Thomas, founded 1823; the Female Benevolent Society of St. Thomas, founded in 1793; the Female Benevolent Whitesonian, founded 1816; African Female Band Benevolent Society of Bethel, founded 1817; the Female Benezet Society, founded 1818; and the Daughters of Aron, founded 1819. See "Black Philanthropy and Voluntarism in the Early Republic." *Documentary History of Philanthropy and Voluntarism in America, 1600–1900*. Ed. P.D. Hall [Cambridge, MA: Harvard University Press] https://www.hks.harvard.edu/fs/phall/dochistcontents.html and http://www.hks.harvard.edu/fs/phall/05.%20Blacks.pdf.

14 Hall. (2006) p. 38.

15 Hall. (2006) pp. 38–39; Ahlstrom. p. 427.

16 Influential organizations of the time, such as the Association for Improving the Conditions of the Poor and the Charity Organization Society, all used predominantly female volunteers to organize relief and visit and aid the poor. See Institute for Children, Poverty & Homelessness. "Isabella Graham and the Society for the Relief of Poor Widows." *History of Poverty & Homelessness in NYC*. http://povertyhistory.org/era/early_ny#isabella-graham-and-the-society-for-the-relief-of-poor-widows.

17 Barker-Benfield, G.J. "The Origins of Anglo-American Sensibility." In Friedman and McGarvie. p. 81.

18 Ibid.

19 Barker-Benfield. p. 72. By the mid-1800s, the largely New-England-born egalitarian, progressive, activist strain of American Protestantism had evolved a "Social Gospel" that not only translated the quest for the Kingdom of God into the terminology of social justice, but came to influence American Catholic thought, as well as the views of American Lutherans, Methodists, and Anglican/Episcopalians, among others. The missionary zeal stemming from these roots and blossoming in the 1800s was divided, however, with more conservative sects—Baptists and Evangelicals—continuing to focus their efforts on saving souls; while more progressive, largely mainstream congregations turned that same fervor toward social reform. Significantly, this model was not welcomed in the south or on the frontier. See Gross. p. 44, and Porterfield, A. "Protestant Missionaries: Pioneers of American Philanthropy." In Friedman and McGarvie. pp. 54, 62–65.

20 It is worth taking a moment to note both the Puritan and the New England contributions to this movement. Although this crusade would eventually come to include a large number of Evangelicals and other Protestant missionaries, the inspiration of John Winthrop's "city upon a hill" and the religious world view of the Puritans

informed the reform movement undertaken by these early "philanthropists" in a way that the theology of the Anglicans and other sects never did. While Baptist, Methodist, and other Protestant denominations would eventually come to play an important part in the reformist flavor of American benevolence in the 1800s, the spark, the notion of an achievable holy commonwealth on Earth, came from the Puritans and their descendants. (See Porterfield. p. 51.) Meanwhile, it is also worth noting that during the middle of the 1800s, Boston was the intellectual capital of the abolition movement, and that Horace Mann's educational reforms and the prison and asylum reforms championed by Dorothea Dix also came out of New England. While other significant reformist efforts—women's suffrage, temperance, and the American labor movement among them—had different geographic roots, the influence of New England on 19th-century American benevolence is unmistakable.

21 Barker-Benfield. p. 72.
22 Gross. p. 40.
23 Gross. p. 43
24 Friedman. p. 26.
25 Gross. p. 65.
26 Foer, F. "The Insurrectionists." In Foer. p. xii.
27 Wood, J.R. "Liberal Protestant Social Action in a Period of Decline." In Wuthnow and Hodgkinson. pp. 166–167.
28 Ibid. p. xv.
29 Ibid; and Barker-Benfield. p. 81.
30 Gross. p. 43.
31 In addition to Clinton's terms as mayor from 1803 to 1807, from 1808 to 1810, and from 1811 to 1815, he served in the state legislature's lower house, the Assembly, in 1798; and in the state Senate from 1798 to 1802 and from 1806 to 1811. He also served as U.S. Senator from New York from February 1802 to November 1803. While serving as mayor, he organized the Historical Society of New York in 1804, and was its president. He also helped reorganize the American Academy of the Fine Arts in 1808, and served as its president between 1813 and 1817.
32 Gross. p. 41.
33 Hammack, D. Ed. *Making the Nonprofit Sector in the United States.* [Bloomington, IN: Indiana University Press, 1998]. p. 288. As early as 1788 New York State was making specific provisions for the poor. See Stuhler, L. "A Brief History of Government Charity in New York (1603–1900)." Social Welfare History Project. Virginia Commonwealth University. April 2015. http://socialwelfare.library.vcu.edu/issues/brief-history-state-charity-new-york-1603-1900/.
34 Hall. (2010) p. 12.
35 Although their presence was not to be strongly felt until the 1800s, the history of both America's Catholics and its Jews goes back literally to the earliest settlement of North America. Catholics, of course, arrived in overwhelming proportion with the French and Spanish colonizers. Within the English colonies, as early as 1610, the new colony of Virginia, needing artisans, invited and welcomed several Italian Catholic craftsmen. In 1622 Venetian glassmakers working in England were brought to Jamestown to teach and to promote their trade, bringing their Catholicism with them. By 1632 a few Italians had settled in Catholic Maryland and soon created there a haven for Italian Catholic refugees.

In 1634, Maryland recorded just fewer than 3,000 Catholics out of a population of 34,000, or around 9% of the population. In 1757, Pennsylvania had fewer than 1,400 Catholics out of a population of about 200,000. In 1785, when the newly founded United States contained nearly 4 million people, there were between

25,000–35,000 Catholics, or roughly 0.7% of the population. According to the 1790 census, while Protestant England and Ulster were the native lands of over half of the nation's population—about 69%—the 3.7% from the Irish Free State were overwhelmingly Catholic, as were most of the approximately 2% from France, and at least a portion of the 8.7% hailing from Germany, particularly those coming from Catholic Bavaria. (See United States Census Bureau. "Colonial and Pre-Federal Statistics." 2004, p. 1168. www2.census.gov/prod2/statcomp/documents/CT1970p2-13.pdf.)

During the 19th century, a new wave of immigrants from Ireland, Germany, Italy, Eastern Europe and elsewhere swelled the number of Roman Catholics. Substantial numbers of Catholics also came from French Canada during the mid-19th century and settled in New England. This influx would eventually bring increased political power for the Roman Catholic Church and a greater cultural presence, leading at the same time to a growing fear of the Catholic "menace." The Catholic Church grew through immigration, especially from Europe, Germany, and Ireland at first, and between 1890–1914 from Italy, Poland, and Eastern Europe. Beginning in the first third of the 19th century, the Church set up an elaborate infrastructure, based on diocese run by bishops appointed by the pope. Each diocese set up a network of parishes, schools, colleges, hospitals, orphanages, and other charitable institutions.

The history of the Jews in the U.S., meanwhile, has been part of the American national fabric since early colonial times. Elias Legarde (a.k.a. Legardo) was a Sephardic Jew who arrived at James City, Virginia, on the *Abigail* in 1621. Solomon Franco, a Jewish merchant, arrived in Boston in 1649. In September 1654, shortly before the Jewish New Year, twenty-three Jews from the Sephardic community in the Netherlands, coming from Recife, Brazil, then a Dutch colony, arrived in New Amsterdam. Charleston, South Carolina, has a particularly long history of Sephardic settlement, which in 1816 numbered over six hundred, then the largest Jewish population of any city in the U.S. Sephardic Dutch Jews were also among the early settlers of Newport, Savannah, Philadelphia, and Baltimore, Newport being the site of Touro Synagogue, the country's oldest surviving synagogue building. In New York City, Shearith Israel Congregation is the oldest continuous congregation, founded in 1687 and having their first synagogue erected in 1728. The current building still contains sections of the original structure.

36 Seeley et al. p. 16.

37 While much of the discrimination faced by these immigrants was on a personal level, there were also several organized groups determined to resist the spreading Catholic presence in America. Notable among these were the Know Nothings in the 1840s, the American Protective Association in the 1890s, and the Ku Klux Klan in the 1920s.

38 Numerous religious orders in Europe sent their members to America during this period. Jesuit priests from Europe (expelled from the Portuguese Empire in 1759, from France in 1764, from the Kingdom of the Two Sicilies, Malta, Parma and the Spanish Empire in 1767; disbanded in the Polish–Lithuanian Commonwealth in 1773; suppressed by Pope Clement XIV that same year; and exiled from Russia in 1820) found a new base in the U.S., where they founded many schools and colleges, such as Boston College, Fordham University, Georgetown University, and several Loyola Colleges. See McDonough, P. *Men Astutely Trained: A History of the Jesuits in the American Century*. [New York: The Free Press, 1994] *passim*. The Sisters of Mercy, founded in Dublin, sent many nuns to the U.S., where they founded primary and secondary schools, universities, and hospitals. Their numbers were further swelled by domestically founded orders, started by entrepreneurial women who saw a need and

an opportunity, and were staffed by devout women from poor families. The numbers grew rapidly, from 900 sisters in 15 communities in 1840; 50,000 in 170 orders in 1900; and 135,000 in 300 different orders by 1930. See O'Toole, J. *The Faithful: A History of Catholics in America.* [Boston, MA: Belknap Press, 2010] *passim.*

39   Hall. (2010) p. 8.

40   McManus. p. 117.

41   Hall. Op. cit.

42   Bremner. (1980) p. 15.

43   In a sense, there came to be in America as many Judaisms as there were Jews. Like so many of their Protestant counterparts—the Congregationalists, Baptists, and Quakers in particular—Jews resisted the hierarchical religious authority structures of Europe. No nationwide "chief rabbi" emerged and no religious organization wielded unchallenged authority. Instead, a spectrum of Jewish religious movements competed for adherents, each insisting that its strategy alone provided hope for American Judaism's survival. Sarna, J.D. and Golden, J. "The American Jewish Experience through the Nineteenth Century: Immigration and Acculturation." TeacherServe. National Humanities Center. http://nationalhumanitiescenter.org/tserve/nineteen/nkeyinfo/judaism.htm.

44   This is not, however, to imply that Jewish immigrants to our shores did not organize themselves into numerous groups. Particularly from about 1881 to the outbreak of World War I, Jewish self-help organizations sprang up in many American cities. The first Jewish charity group in Minnesota was the Hebrew Ladies' Benevolent Society, founded it in 1871. The Union of American Hebrew Congregations was launched in 1873, and, in Cincinnati, Hebrew Union College began its work in 1875. The National Council of Jewish Women was created in Chicago in 1893. The Albany Hebrew Tailors Association was formed in New York's capital city in 1901.

In Boston, the United Hebrew Benevolent Association sought to address the needs of Jewish newcomers. The society provided safe temporary shelter, a meal and, more importantly, it represented newcomers before immigration authorities. In New York, meanwhile, Rabbi Judah Magnes led the fight to "develop a real Jewish community," and founded the New York Kehillah. The Jewish Federation movement began in Boston in 1895. (See Finkelstein, N.H. "Jewish Communal Organizations: The Early Years." My Jewish Learning. www.myjewishlearning.com/article/jewish-communal-organizations-the-early-years/.) Between the 1820s and the Civil War, Jews laid the foundations for many charitable institutions that still endure, including Philadelphia's Albert Einstein Medical Center, New York City's Mount Sinai Hospital, the Federation of Jewish Philanthropies, the earliest Jewish-sponsored orphanages in the country, and B'nai B'rith, a network of Jewish fraternal lodges. Beginning in the 1830s, German–Jewish immigrants to America founded a network of charitable institutions outside of the synagogue, including orphan asylums, hospitals, retirement homes, settlement houses, free-loan associations, and vocational training schools. These efforts attested to the determination of American Jews to care for the chronically sick and destitute within the Jewish community. (Dalin, D. "Judaism's War on Poverty." The Hoover Institution's *Policy Review.* September 1, 1997. www.hoover.org/research/judaisms-war-poverty.)

45   Bremner, R. *From the Depths: The Discovery of Poverty in the United States.* [New York: New York University Press, 1967] p. 5.

46   Five Points was a neighborhood in Lower Manhattan, generally defined as being bound by Center Street to the west, the Bowery to the east, Canal Street to the north, and Park Row to the south.

47　Anbinder, T. as quoted in Chamberlain, T. "'Gangs of New York': Fact vs. Fiction." *National Geographic.* March 24, 2003. http://news.nationalgeographic.com/ news/2003/03/0320_030320_oscars_gangs.html.

48　Bremner. (1967) p. 6.

49　Chamberlain. Op cit.

50　Ibid.

51　Ibid.

52　Yamin, R. as quoted in Chamberlain. Op. cit.

53　Ibid.

54　Bremner. (1960) p. 100.

55　For a colorful and accurate portrayal of this general attitude see Shanon, D. *Death of a Busybody.* [New York: Doubleday Books, 1988] p. 63. "Damn rich-bitches come slumming," complains O'Hara, a central character, "handing out charity, and think because they got more money 'n me they can tell us how to live!"

56　Kelley. p. 2454.

57　This pattern was often mirrored in the western parts of the U.S. among Asian immigrants. While little distinction between Asians of differing national origins was made by racist nativists opposed to "the yellow peril" of Asian immigration, these immigrants, hailing primarily from China, Japan, and Korea (with later additions from the Philippines and the Indian subcontinent) not only failed to make common cause with one another, but also gravitated to differing kinds of labor—railroads for the Chinese and agriculture for the Japanese—rarely mingled, and failed so see themselves as suffering from the same prejudice. While all might have been viewed as "dirty Orientals" by the native white population, they saw nothing in common with one another. Within a narrower focus, those seen commonly by native Anglo-Americans as "Italians" generally saw themselves as nothing of the sort, as both class and regional distinctions were far more important to them in an era when the unified country of "Italy" did not even exist.

58　Cahill. p. 252.

59　Many within this population began to see themselves for the first time as proletarians, members of the industrial working class. These were the seeds of Jewish socialism in America, and it has often been argued that the liberalism that American Jews exhibit to this day descends partly from this socialist legacy. See Soyer, D. "Jewish Socialism in the United States, 1880–1920: The Birth and Growth of American Jewish Socialism." My Jewish Learning. www.myjewishlearning.com/ article/jewish-socialism-in-the-united-states-1880-1920/2/.

60　Svonkin, S. *Jews Against Prejudice.* [New York: Columbia University Press, 1997] p. 6.

61　Ibid. pp. 6–7.

62　Ibid. p. 7.

63　Ibid. pp. 11, 17.

64　In 1947, Stephen S. Wise, president of the American Jewish Congress, told the members of a U.S. Senate subcommittee considering federal fair employment legislation, "We regard ethnic discrimination, whether directed against Jews, Negros, Chinese, Mexicans, or any other group, as a single and indivisible problem and one of the most urgent problems of democratic society." Svonkin. p. 18.

65　Organized Jewish philanthropy was already well established in the America of the 1800s. The Hebrew Benevolent Society in New York and the United Hebrew Beneficial Society in Philadelphia were both founded in 1822. The Philadelphia Hebrew Sunday School Society (1838), followed by the Hebrew Education Society (1849), established schools that served mainly the poor. In New York, Mount Sinai Hospital opened its doors in 1852. Jewish welfare agencies had joined in

Philadelphia in 1870 and in New York in 1874 to form the United Jewish Charities. The Montefiore Home for Chronic Invalids in New York City was founded in 1884 by Jewish philanthropists who wanted to do something for patients whom other hospitals of the day would not help. See Bremner. (1960) p. 98; The Jewish Virtual Library. "Charity (Tzedakah): Charity Throughout Jewish History." www. jewishvirtuallibrary.org/charity-throughout-jewish-history#4; and Montefiore Health Systems. "History and Milestones." www.montefiore.org/history-and-milestones.

66 Friedman. p. 11.

67 Goodstein, L. "Both Feeling Threatened, American Muslims and Jews Join Hands." *New York Times*. December 5, 2016. www.nytimes.com/2016/12/05/us/muslim-jewish-alliance-after-trump.html.

68 Barker-Benfield. p. 73.

69 Unfortunately, not all of the groups arising out of this era were either progressive or benign. Reconstruction in the south showed some of the darker possibilities of voluntary associations, as embittered southerners organized groups like the Ku Klux Klan to terrorize blacks and the northern volunteers who were helping them. Hall. (2010) p. 10.

70 Salamon, L. *The Resilient Sector Revisited*. Second Ed. [Washington, DC: Brookings Institution Press, 2015] p. 14.

71 This model continued to be resisted in the south, both before the Civil War and afterwards. Landed gentry not only preferred personal actions to organized efforts, but also were not enamored of the social reform flavor unmistakable in the efforts of northern organizations. In both the south and on the frontier, meanwhile, common people came to strongly resent the "New England Rat," a figure widely derided as an interloper "in one hand holding a Bible and the other open for donations." See Freidman. p. 44.

4 Abstract philanthropy

Professionalization and the business of benevolence

Growing out of both the shift from charity to philanthropy and its philosophical underpinnings, additional trends emerged in the latter decades of the 1800s which contributed to the evolution of the modern nonprofit sector.

Organized benevolence

The shift from personal charity to larger-scale philanthropy meant, among other things, the organization of benevolence.

The period from about 1870 to 1920 saw benevolence move more and more away from a model whereby people in need intersected with individuals acting upon personal impulse, and more and more toward a model where they all interacted with organizations. Increasingly, people of means gave to organizations or associations whose mission was not only the care of the poor, but also the application of a new approach called "social work," specifically intended to get at the root causes of poverty, inequality, and the myriad issues—alcohol abuse, domestic violence, children born out of wedlock and abandoned—that plagued the lower economic classes.

These groups mobilized members, resources, and public attention, and set out to organize endeavors aimed at the problem they intended to address.[1] Increasingly, as the 19th century progressed, efforts on behalf of the poor and marginalized, efforts toward social change, were the work of these entities. Individuals played their part by working for or through these entities. But by the middle of the century, the larger associations, a number of them already national in scope, had also "rationalized" the business of benevolence and introduced America to modern bureaucracy.[2]

Importantly, while this was happening on the delivery side, a significant related development was unfolding on the funding side of the fence.

As the scale of what was being attempted by these associations became clearer, and as the idea was accepted that the old charity was no longer either sufficient or desirable, the need for a more systematic approach took hold. Called *scientific philanthropy*, it saw facts and theories of social change as both necessary and preferred to the personal and often ad hoc charity of the past. In the eyes of the post-Civil-War reformers, changes in the nation's approach to charity were long overdue. It was time, they insisted, for the charitable impulse to become disciplined, for the head to triumph over the heart, and for a "machinery of benevolence" to be engineered and understood.[3] This new generation of philanthropists espoused an "ecological" view of poverty and social injustice, a perspective which held that all social problems had environmental causes and could be solved by well-trained experts armed with the facts.[4] Their approach was to study the problems they faced in an effort to arrive at "scientific" solutions, believing that if only enough facts were unearthed, if only the true root causes were discovered, then logical solutions and policies would also become evident.[5]

While this movement effected a façade of efficiency, there was about it also the unmistakable scent of the age-old obsession with the predations of the "unworthy" poor. Many of these reformers were quite unabashed about their desire to discover, construct, and employ a system whereby "the idleness and begging. . .encouraged [by existing charitable approaches], may be suppressed, and *worthy self-respecting poverty* be discovered and relieved at the smallest cost"[6] (emphasis added).

In practical application, this led to the creation of charity organization societies throughout the 1870s and 1880s. The purpose of these entities was *not* the granting of relief to the needy. Quite the opposite, the founders of these agencies believed that there were already too many agencies giving alms and used clothing to the poor. Their idea, instead, was to promote cooperation and higher standards of efficiency among relief-giving agencies. They acted, in effect, as clearinghouses and bureaus of information, maintaining registries of those seeking relief, as well as detailed records of how their cases were handled by the participating agencies. They also undertook investigations of the "worthiness" of cases, seeking persons deemed "helpable."

It was a ponderous approach and daunting work.

Several developments followed from this line of thinking.

The first was the emerging professionalization of these efforts.

It is one of history's ironies that at just about the point when the organizations behind these efforts were coming to be collectively known as *voluntary associations*, a name which stuck through the 1950s, professionals working for these organizations were already making careers out of dependent care. Theirs was a self-consciously modern, empirical approach, increasingly based upon what would eventually come to be called "casework," and which would eventually completely supplant what was seen as the emotional and disorganized efforts of charity volunteers.[7] Moreover, as various populations in need— including those labeled insane, prisoners, unwed mothers, and "the disorderly poor"—became the focus for these early social workers, they progressively began to squeeze out and displace the well-meaning volunteers who had preceded them, derided by some at the time as primarily "spinsters and society ladies" for whom the *idea* of charity had a primary emotional appeal.[8]

But it was also becoming clear that in order to accomplish the lofty new goals of scientific philanthropy, *resources* were needed. In the face of this, however, reformers encountered a number of obstacles. . .and one major roadblock was the enduring public skepticism of big government in many parts of the country. The fact was that by the latter decades of the 1800s, both the federal and the state governments were viewed by many as little more than the tools of the corporations and the trusts. Adding to this perspective was the government's uneven and spotty record in taking up certain public responsibilities.[9] The government's actual interest in the kinds of far-reaching systemic social changes many of the reformers espoused was viewed with skepticism, at best.

Vast portions of the country remained overwhelmingly rural, and the opinion in these areas was that the public relief systems found in most cities were little more than patronage tools for the political machines.[10]

The economic battles of the time, with the unemployed, farmers, and strikers battling their class enemies (and often the police) in the streets,[11] also played a part, moving state and local governments in many parts of the country to rethink policies toward the poor, in some cases adopting tougher policies.

The Panic of 1873–1878 provides an illustration of the sharp differences of opinion that existed regarding the question of how to address those in need, and brought the battle lines of the debate into sharp relief.

In a harbinger of worse things to come half a century later, the impact of that economic reversal was akin to those of a nationwide natural disaster.[12] The care of the "dependent classes" (as they were then called), a challenge in normal times, became an even more serious problem as the number of people needing and wanting assistance vastly increased. Into the breech stepped a wide variety of players launching a wide variety of efforts. Private citizens, the older charitable organizations, and even some public authorities responded by setting up soup kitchens, bread lines, and free lodging houses. Free food and coal were distributed to the poor in their homes. Under the circumstances, little attention was paid to the investigation of need, tests of destitution, safeguards against fraud, or an examination of "underlying causes."

All of this, of course, horrified the advocates of a more modern and systematic response to need. It was maddening for them to witness what they saw as the "excesses of kindly, but mistaken charity." They deplored the "profuse and chaotic" distribution of private charitable aid to the "clamorous and impudent." Such untethered aid, many felt, was not only going to imposters, but also having an overall negative effect on the laboring classes by harming both their character and their willingness to work.[13]

Perhaps worse still in the eyes of many, "corrupt municipal officials and politicians"—always an easy target, as there were so many of them from Brooklyn to San Francisco—were profiting politically from the largess, buying votes and partisan loyalty through the distribution of aid.

This was not simply a classist debate, for there were those of differing means on both sides of the argument.

Meanwhile, the public relief of poverty was suspended altogether in New York City for a time, and all of this tumult polarized popular (as in, *middle class*) opinion.[14] In sum, there was no broad consensus behind a meaningful public investment in the existing mechanisms for changing the conditions or the prospects of the poor or of the laboring classes living on the margins of poverty.

What was needed was a new mechanism for funding the vast social enterprises the reformers foresaw, something that would end the chaos, and organize the developing philanthropy along modern, logical lines, immunize it against the maudlin, personal, and emotion-laden decision-making that characterized existing charitable efforts, and insulate it from the political calculations that often impacted public relief efforts of the day.

In the meantime, so eager for financial support was the ballooning number of "charities" across the country that the earliest philanthropists found themselves besieged. Not only were they buried under the more traditional individual requests for assistance—letters and telegrams from desperate people arguing that their cases were each unique and worthy of a wealthy person's direct financial intervention—but increasingly they were also inundated by literally "thousands of [requests] from institutions. There were appeals from schools and colleges, churches, hospitals, and every kind of religious, cultural, and charitable association."[15] On behalf of the disadvantaged, organizations mounted publicity campaigns calling the attention of potential donors to the plights of newsboys, working girls, distressed immigrants, tenement dwellers, southern mountain children, and a broad variety of others in need. These were also the years when the Boy Scouts, Girl Scouts, Campfire Girls, National Tuberculosis Association, American Cancer Society, Lighthouse, National Association for the Advancement of Colored People , National Urban League, and hundreds of other organizations and leagues for the betterment of society came into being. . .and all were seeking donations.[16] After 1914, the situation was made even more complicated by the need to relieve those suffering from the war in Europe.[17]

As just one illustration of the pressure to give brought by the charitable entities of the day, John D. Rockefeller, in spite of his reputation for being ruthless in business, personally considered and carefully weighed the thousands of begging letters that poured into his offices.[18]

It was a system bound to collapse under its own weight and the dawning realization was that if philanthropy was now to be "scientific," so, too, should be its funding.[19] The newly emerging grant-making foundations seemed to be the answer.

The first charitable foundation in the U.S. had been the Peabody Fund, founded in 1867 for the purpose of promoting "intellectual, moral, and industrial education in the most destitute portion of the Southern States." Its main purpose was to aid elementary education by strengthening existing schools. It did not, however, benefit freed slaves. That challenge was taken up by the Slater Fund, established in 1882, to aid in the "uplifting" of the recently emancipated black slave population in the south. But the model was not at first widely copied. Prior to 1900, only twenty-six entities we would recognize as "foundations" existed in the U.S. By 1929 there were about one hundred and fifty.[20]

Through the end of the 1800s and the early decades of the 1900s, however, their number continued to grow, their ranks swollen by the organizations founded by Mrs. Russell Sage (1907), Carnegie (1911), Rockefeller (1913), Duke (1924), Kresge (1924), and Ford (1936).

The thinking behind these efforts was that to be "scientific," giving had to move away from the "retail" model, and become more "wholesale," and so these organizations moved away from distributive charity and toward "grant-making," their investments (and their considerable wealth) going to organizations, and not people. There were two ideas that animated this approach. The first was that these recipient organizations, through their volunteers and the professionals they increasingly hired, would help the afflicted by addressing the causes and conditions of their affliction. The purpose was not the transfer of wealth from the rich to the poor, but rather the transfer of resources—knowledge and expertise, in particular—in an effort to ameliorate the conditions under which the poor labored. The second idea, once again echoing the change-the-world impulse of the sector's early days, was captured in a slogan used by Andrew Carnegie: "Systemic change through systemic philanthropy."[21]

The goal of these "scientific" reformers was nothing less than a broad-scale change in American society—the *systemic change* of which Carnegie spoke—accomplished through a "systemic"—as in "organized"—approach to giving.

More important, these entities took on the corporate/business organization model as their guide, with boards of trustees, public charters, annual reports, and managerial staff.[22]

Not everyone was impressed with this new model, however. The new "bureaucratic charity" had, many felt, destroyed the essential relationship between the helper and the helped that had not just existed under the older, more personal model, but which had been its emotional heart. For many observers of the time, the new philanthropy—organized, institutional, and monied—was little different than the big businesses that had emerged during the era, dehumanizing in its impersonal approach, even more offensive than the classist Friendly Visitors had been in its efforts to reduce people to factors in an equation. Worse still, some maintained, the foundations and the associations they supported had reduced charity to a cold impersonal monetary exchange, the individual donation now merely paying a bill of conscience.[23]

In addition to this, throughout this period the new "scientific" approach to philanthropy threatened to take on a distinctly Darwinian perspective.

Social Darwinism and the battle for the soul of philanthropy

The increasing professionalism of the field had led to the creation of a cadre of highly trained, university-based specialists who were fast becoming a cornerstone of the developing arena of social work. But although they might have employed a rhetoric of benevolence, the "scientific" approach they and several of their wealthy allies advocated seemed to be anything but humanitarian.[24]

The old English notion of the "worthy" and "unworthy" poor still had considerable currency in the America of the mid- to later 1800s and into the early 1900s. Whether an echo of a harsh founding Calvinism or, later, of Herbert Spencer's insistence that humanitarian impulses could not be allowed to interfere with the "natural" law mandating the survival of the fittest, by the 1850s there were calls by some for laws that would prevent the "spreading curse of race deterioration."[25] In this, what was meant was not only the "white race" by implication, but more directly the human race itself. There existed among some a contempt not only for the "unfit"— "the most misshapen, physically and morally"—but also for those who would care for them.[26]

Andrew Carnegie wrote, "It were better for mankind that the millions of the rich were thrown into the sea than so spent as to encourage the slothful, the drunken, [and] the unworthy."[27]

For a variety of reasons, by the second half of the century voluntary charitable efforts had become so ubiquitous that even the traditional reformers had begun to worry about inefficiency, duplication, and waste. Their critics, meanwhile, saw the vast number of charitable efforts as "lavish, uninformed, and aimless," and believed that rather than helping the situation they made it worse by "encouraging pauperism and imposture."[28]

None of this, of course, took place in a vacuum, and the larger social issues of the period—increased immigration, labor unrest, urbanization, industrialization, and a nativist backlash against not only foreign-born labor, but also the presence of former slaves in the labor market—impacted both opinions and the debate. It is telling that the State Charities Aid Association, a group formed after the Civil War to make "scientific" recommendations on how to best manage poor houses and similar facilities, opposed public relief as "undermining the self-respect of recipients, fostering a spirit of dependence opposed to self-support, and *interfering with the laws governing wage and labor*"[29] (emphasis added).

More to the point, if the new "scientific" approach was to be proven a success, subjectively defined *needs*, the stuff of the old charity, had to be replaced with a new calculus of *eligibility* of individuals for assistance: were they potentially good investment vehicles?[30] Not everyone, the new thinking went, could or should be the object of ameliorative efforts. Once again, the old question appeared: were they "worthy," or not?

The traction gained by proponents of the new "scientific" approach could be largely explained by the fact that for all the efforts being expended upon the poor—and "poverty" was not the only challenge they faced, nor the only characteristic of their condition that the middle and upper classes found appalling—conditions were worsening. Their sheer and growing numbers, exacerbated by their often foreign origins and increased concentration in squalid urban slums, meant that the needy were no longer viewed as they had once been in simpler times. These were no longer neighbors, members of the community who had fallen on hard times or had a run of bad luck. They were in many ways not only complete strangers, but "others," unknowable, often incomprehensible, and, to many, clearly wanting in the sort of moral fiber and self-reliance upon which the upper classes staked their claim to superiority.

New approaches to addressing the "problems" of the underclasses, therefore, even if they tended to dehumanize the victims and reduce them to factors in some sort of equation, met little resistance among significant portions of society; because in large measure those victims had already lost the connections to the larger society around them that would have allowed them to be viewed as *people*, and not simply a problem.

Social concerns beyond just poverty were becoming entangled in the debate, and it was becoming ever more apparent that some sort of clarifying understanding, not only of the place of charity in American life, but also regarding the means by which it would be carried out, was needed. In the face of the new "scientific" approach to addressing poverty and need, it appeared as though the essential spark of human concern was in danger of being supplanted by a sterile perspective more based upon what we'd today recognize as "social policy." Where this would leave the nation's voluntary charities and their organizational allies was an open question.

Into this breech, however, stepped a new generation of mostly Protestant clergy, specifically those who entered the pulpits in the turbulent period between 1873 and 1893. Looking at the social disorder around them, they saw a distinctly spiritual challenge: if charity itself was being rethought, so too had to be their theology.

Swimming against both the tide of the times and the historic tide of increased secularization of social reform and charitable/philanthropic efforts, these men came to the position that the moralistic pronouncements of the Social Darwinists and their allies in the "scientific philanthropy" community simply did not apply to the immediate realities of human suffering. Evidence of wholesale changes in society was undeniable and all around them as the Industrial Age expanded its reach and influence. In the face of this, these resurgent voices insisted, dismissively blaming the poor for their poverty in an economy in which human destinies could already be profoundly impacted by technological change and global markets was not only unfair, but simply did not make sense. Moreover, it was a waste of time and energy, because "explaining" the causes of poverty in "scientific" terms and formulating far-reaching programs for its eradication[31] did nothing to alleviate the hunger, fear, and humiliation of those actually and immediately suffering its effects.[32]

But most profoundly, this dissenting view saw the doctrines of Social Darwinism and scientific philanthropy as unsupported by and incompatible with the lessons of Christian scripture. The Good Samaritan, they noted, did not stop to assess the "eligibility" or worthiness of the man by the side of the road.[33] True brotherly love did not trifle with questions of "fitness." Rather, it *acted* in compassion.

The unavoidable consequence of this view was a renewed conviction among some, one that echoed the perspective of the old New England Puritans, that one's belief and one's work in the world could not be separated, that true Christian charity demanded that there had to be more than simply the economic provision of services and interventions. Philanthropy, the love of humankind, ultimately needed to be leavened with "charity" in its original sense: love, tenderness, and mercy.

But while the young ministers who preached this Social Gospel were fighting the current of "science," the lure of "efficiency," and the "logic" of Social Darwinism, there was an undertow that was also working against them, an evolution in American religion itself which made it that much more difficult for their message to gain the purchase it needed to prevail.

A new kind of religion

While additions to the American population had somewhat changed its overall complexion—particularly with the arrival of Catholics and Jews—the fact was that throughout the 1800s the U.S. was still quite overwhelmingly a Protestant country. Moreover, while religious practice and affiliation had waned during the Revolutionary period, the Second Great Awakening, a predominantly 19th-century period of religious revival that lasted almost sixty years and during which the Baptists and Methodists became major denominations,[34] had recharged and brought a new life to American Protestantism.

But that Protestantism had changed.

Although there were Quakers in Pennsylvania, some Catholics in Maryland, a significant number of Dutch Reformed believers in New York, and smatterings of Anabaptists, Lutherans, and others to be found here and there in the pre-independence colonies, at its founding the predominant religious traditions in our country were the Anglicans—a majority in virtually every colony south of New England—and those who had dissented against Henry's Church of England, the Puritans of New England. The Anglicans were still largely Catholic in much of their dogma, and the early Calvinistic Puritans had dogma of their own and enforced it by law.

But this situation had begun to change even prior to the Revolution. Before the 1600s had ended, the Puritans had for the most part become Congregationalists, and in doing so rejected any authority above the local assembly of believers. Although they represented the official state religion—their ministers, churches, and other institutions supported by taxes levied on the entire population irrespective of any individual's actual faith—differences in belief, small at first but later broadening, began to distinguish even neighboring Congregationalist assemblies in New England. Due to a variety of forces, by 1700 the more "practical" side of the Puritan heritage—commitment to useful labor, the concern for lawful government, the passion for learning, and the sense of civic responsibility—was becoming ever more prominent, even while actual religious zeal was flagging under the pressures of the emerging modernity of the time.[35]

Influenced by, among other things, the "new thinking" that came out of the Age of Reason and the more robust Age of Enlightenment (approximately

1715–1789), cracks began to appear in the façade of Protestant dogma as people began to seek more simplicity and a "reasonableness" in their religion.[36] It was not that the era's foremost thinkers and writers rejected the idea of God outright; rather they and those influenced by them began a process, reminiscent of the Reformation itself, of trying to identify and separate the wheat of truth from the chaff of accrued and ossifying tradition.

One result of this was the emergence of a far less mystical, far more populist, and, some might say, far more *useful* kind of religion in America. By the early decades of the 1700s, such perspectives as deism—which attracted several notable leaders of the colonies' rebellion[37]—Unitarianism, and Universalism had begun to chip away at the hold the older, more traditional theologies had enjoyed on the American population.[38] Doctrines were jettisoned,[39] formal religious hierarchy was frequently dispensed with,[40] and the "good works" that had at one time been seen as indelibly stamped with sacred purpose began to take on a social value of their own.[41] There seemed to be less and less need to fall back upon religious tradition or scripture,[42] ecclesiastical reasoning, or worldly interpretations of God's will to build a valid and compelling case for social change.[43] Thanks to the constitutional separation of church and state and subsequent disestablishment of such state churches as had existed, the possibility of imposing "God's will" on the nation as a whole was becoming increasingly problematic.[44] In this atmosphere, the "Social Gospel," while definitely not without influence, was fighting an uphill battle against not only the proponents of a "scientific" approach to the social issues of the day, but the general march of society as well.

These two perspectives, the "scientific" and organizational/institutionalist on the one hand, and the resurgent "Christian" and "caring" on the other, fought for supremacy throughout the closing decades of the 1800s and into the early 20th century. Ultimately, however, even though the reaction to the rise of fascism and its inhuman excesses cast the entire notion of Social Darwinism into the dustbin of history, the die was largely cast in favor of the secular and "wholesale" approach to poverty favored by the growing cadre of social work professionals who largely eschewed denominational identification, sanction, or justification for their work.[45]

Instead, by the 1920s, this work was increasingly being carried out within a framework of bureaucracies, and social service agencies had supplanted personal and religious commitment as the basis of charitable activity.[46] By the 1930s it was clear that the religious spirit of the past had been substantially replaced by fact-finding, and that "experts" would thereafter lead the work of finding technical solutions to complex social problems. Human compassion, religious commitment, and their role in inspiring volunteers would continue to be important, but they would never again lead. Things had simply changed too much, and would continue to change as the government came to play an ever-larger part in the effort to confront society's most vexing challenges.

***

The developments that marked the period from the latter part of the 19th century into the early decades of the 20th were crucial for the development of the nonprofit sector as we know it today. They:

1 sanitized the business of charity for the middle and upper classes by removing virtually any prospects, other than those that might have been voluntarily assumed, for dealing directly with those in need. This was "charity at a remove," the donor completely insulated from the harsh realities of the unseen intended recipients. Personal charity was hereby reduced to essentially a financial exchange, whereby one could deal with one's own class, make a donation, and be content in the fact that one had done one's part.

2 led to another change that was to have significant impacts through the following decades. The intermediary organizations not only became the conduit to the needy for resources from the more fortunate, but they also became the primary source for donors of information *about* the needy. As the gulf between benefactor and beneficiary became ever wider, the associations became the arbiters of reality for both.

3 planted the seeds—which would germinate in the 1920s, bloom during the Depression, and bear fruit by the second half of the century—of the movement that would spell the end of the era when these organizations could accurately be said to comprise "the voluntary sector." Credentialed specialists, including social workers, casework managers, and therapists would, in the future, be taking the place of the volunteers, the "friendly visitors," and others who had worked on behalf of the less fortunate for almost one hundred years.

4 directly led to the "business" of charity we currently know today.

The issue of taxation

While local associations were evolving into eleemosynaries, and then philanthropic organizations, charities, and eventually into today's "nonprofits," another important development was slowly taking place that would fix the place of these entities in law. This was the evolution of their tax status.

In colonial America, not only was church property not taxed, but such tax revenues as were raised from other sources were in part used, as they had been in England, for the support of the various colonies' official churches. With independence and the passage of the First Amendment, the former practice stayed in place, even as the latter disappeared. This exemption was extended over time to schools, colleges, libraries, and other public benefit entities. While different states approached the issue from different perspectives, New York State provides a general example of approaches that were favorable to the development of private eleemosynary organizations.

The earliest general exemption from taxation in New York State, included in a 1799 law entitled "An act for the assessment and collection of taxes," provided that:

no house or land belonging to. . .any church or place of public worship, or any personal property belonging to any ordained minister of the gospel, nor any college or incorporated academy, nor any school house, court house, [jail], alms house, or property belonging to any incorporated library, shall be taxed by virtue of this act.[47]

In 1823 the law was amended to exempt "real estate belonging to. . .any college or incorporated academy. . .any building for public worship, school house. . .alms-house, house of industry, and all the real and personal property belonging thereto. . .[and] the property belonging to any public library."

In 1828, this was again changed to include "[every] building erected for the use of a college, incorporated academy, or other seminary of learning; every building for public worship; every school house. . .and the several lots whereon such buildings are situated." Also exempted were "every poor-house, alms-house, house of industry, and every house belonging to a company incorporated for the reformation of offenders, the real and personal property belonging to, or connected with the same," and the "real and personal property of every public library."

The statute remained substantially the same until 1893, primarily because the more common method of tax exemption in New York at the time was through enactment of special legislation, and between 1828 and 1896 an estimated one hundred such supplemental acts were passed extending the exemptions. It is worth noting here that the New York courts held that property had to be owned by a *corporation* to qualify for the exemption.[48]

In 1893 the phrase "moral and mental improvement of men and women" was added to extend the exemption to the Young Men's Christian Association (YMCA) after the organization had lost its bid for tax immunity in an 1889 court case. In spite of the YMCA's having lost the case, the court wrote that "associations of this character are so useful and so deserving of encouragement and support" that they ought to be exempt.[49] This thinking was to influence future legislation in New York and other states in coming years.

This is reflected in New York's 1896 rewriting of the law to include:

real property of a corporation or association *organized exclusively for the moral or mental improvement of men or women*, or for religious, bible, tract, charitable, benevolent, missionary, hospital, infirmary, educational, scientific, literary, library, patriotic, historical or cemetery purposes, or for the enforcement of laws relating to children or animals, or for two or more of such purposes, and used exclusively for carrying out thereupon one or more of such purposes (emphasis added).[50]

Several new categories of exempt property appeared in this version, including those for tract, charitable, benevolent, missionary, hospital, infirmary, educational, scientific, literary, patriotic, and historical or cemetery purposes, as well as those utilized for the enforcement of laws relating to children or animals.

By 1980, the law had been expanded to include not only all the 1896 categories, but also public playgrounds, and properties owned by scientific, literary, bar association, and medical societies.

In neighboring Massachusetts, the 1874 charities statute extended property-tax exemption to any "educational, charitable, benevolent or religious purpose" including "any antiquarian, historical, literary, scientific, medical, artistic, monumental or musical" purpose; to "any missionary enterprise" with either foreign or domestic objects; to organizations "encouraging athletic exercises and yachting"; to libraries and reading rooms; and to "societies of Freemasons, Odd Fellows, Knights of Pythias and other charitable or social bodies of a like character and purpose."[51] Even today, one of the Bay State's applications for a property-tax exemption lists organizations of a literary, benevolent, charitable, scientific, or temperance nature as eligible. . .and this only hints at the array of eligible entities in the Commonwealth.[52]

From these two examples we can see that the list of exempt properties, and more importantly of types of organizations owning those properties, was expanding. The broad palate of nonprofits was growing. . .and with it the kinds of organizations considered tax-exempt. This said, however, it also should be noted that not all jurisdictions followed the early examples of New York and Massachusetts in the broad inclusion of entities that would be considered tax-exempt.

Pennsylvania's 19th-century charities statute, by way of illustration, required that such entities advance a charitable purpose, donate or render gratuitously a substantial portion of its services (limiting a charity's ability to charge fees), benefit a substantial and indefinite class or persons who are legitimate subjects of charity, relieve government of some of its burdens, and operate entirely free of private profit motives. Clearly, a good number of the kinds of entities designated as tax-exempt under New York and Massachusetts law would not have been regarded as such in Pennsylvania.[53]

Still, recalling the thinking in the YMCA case, where the court said that associations of its character are useful and deserving of encouragement and support, in 1970 Chief Justice Warren Burger wrote that there exists a broad category of associations having many common features, a chief one being that all are dedicated to social betterment. Two points derive from Chief Justice Burger's words.

The first is that a direct echo of Elizabeth I's thinking in her 1601 Statute of Charitable Uses can be heard in the opinion articulated by Chief Justice Burger. The notion that undertakings of *public good* were to be encouraged and also supported by the state had not simply survived for almost 370 years, but had flourished.[54]

The second is that the real-world application of this perspective meant that, as well as churches, museums, hospitals, libraries, charitable organizations, professional associations, and the like—all nonprofit, and all having a beneficial and stabilizing influence on community life—were to be encouraged by being treated specially in the tax laws.[55] This "special treatment" was the exemption from most taxes.

The question of *which* taxes, however, has had a different answer through time.

From the founding of the nation through the 1800s, most taxes were levied by the state. Such local taxes as existed—primarily in the north—were on property. In effect, this meant that the tax exemption enjoyed by the eleemosynaries, associations, philanthropic organizations, and charities of the day was associated primarily with such properties as they owned. Even so, it was a significant financial benefit for any of these organizations to be free from paying that tax, and the exemption contributed to their sustainability and growth.

The federal government's taxation, by contrast, was minimal for individuals and many types of business, the largest portion of government revenue coming from sources such as customs duties. In 1881, for example, the customs duty was the single largest source of federal revenue, and 90% of it came from duties collected at the New York Customs House.[56] It was not until the imposition of broad federal taxation of income that the federal tax exemption became a factor.

The federal entry into this territory comprised three steps. The first was an exemption granted to organizations operating for charitable purposes. The second were the stipulations that these entities operate on a nonprofit basis and be free of private inurement, and that no profits or dividends issuing from them would go to any individuals. Finally, an income tax deduction for contributions, designed to encourage charitable giving, was developed.[57]

The Wilson-Gorman Tariff Act of 1894, one of the earliest federal references to the tax-exempt status, established the requirement that eligible organizations operate for charitable purposes. While establishing a flat 2% tax on corporate income, the Act stated "nothing herein contained shall apply to. . .corporations, companies, or associations organized and conducted solely for charitable, religious, or educational purposes, including fraternal beneficiary associations." Though the law was declared unconstitutional by the Supreme Court in 1895, the exemption language contained in the Act would provide the cornerstone for tax legislation involving charitable organizations for the next century.[58]

The Revenue Act of 1909 mirrored and expanded the language from the 1894 Act. Under this statute, tax exemption was granted to "any corporation or association organized and operated exclusively for religious, charitable, or educational purposes, no part of the net income of which inures to the benefit of any private stockholder or individual." This important addition set forth the idea that tax-exempt charitable organizations should be not-for-profit.[59]

The passage of the Sixteenth Amendment gave Congress the power to levy an income tax. The subsequent Revenue Act of 1913 established the modern federal income tax system. For charitable organizations, the Act used identical language as that found in the Tariff Acts of 1894 and 1909 with regard to charitable purpose and private inurement. The Revenue Act of 1917 established, for the first time, an individual income tax deduction for contributions made to tax-exempt charitable organizations. This deduction was conceived as a way to encourage charitable contributions at a time when income tax rates were rising in order to fund World War I. One year later, the Revenue Act of 1918 stipulated that charitable bequests were entitled to a similar deduction on estate tax returns. Finally, corporations were able to claim the charitable deduction beginning in 1936.

Several adjustments would be made to these regulations over the years:

- The federal Form 990 was introduced as a two-page form with only three yes/no questions in 1943;[60] and filing for certain organizations was made mandatory by the Revenue Act of the same year.
- The exemption from taxes accruing from commercial activities undertaken by a nonprofit—so long as those profits were used for exempt purposes—was enacted in 1950.
- The modern tax code, with its Section 501(c) was introduced in 1954.
- The Revenue Act of 1964 raised the limitation on deduction for donations to public charities from 20% in most cases to 30% of adjusted gross income.
- Sweeping reforms were enacted 1969, including private foundation rules, which covered a minimum charitable payout requirement and a 4% excise tax on net investment income. It also raised the limitation on the deduction for donations to operating private foundations and public charities to 50% of adjusted gross income.[61]

But in the federal actions of 1894–1936, the basics were established, and this all had several significant impacts on the voluntary sector of the day. The first was to establish, as a *federal* model, a tax deduction for charities. No matter what the various states might do in the future, the federal government had at long last set a standard. The second was that the federal exemption went beyond the traditional exemptions on property tax as enacted by the states and localities, and covered income as well. Moreover, even though the federal tax exemption did not specifically cover sales taxes, and while several states have an *official* policy that nonprofits don't have a blanket exemption from sales and use taxes,[62] in practice most need only show their federal tax-exempt certificate to have the tax waived.

Combined, this relief from most taxes represents a tremendous boon to nonprofits. When the incentive represented by the tax deduction on charitable donations is added—even though for most people that deduction is not a primary motivator in their giving—it becomes clear that the tax policies of the U.S. have had a marked positive and enabling influence on the growth of the American nonprofit sector.

Notes

1 This last part, however, was not always successful in actually getting off the ground. It was the experience of many of the early reformers that it was far easier to identify a need, rally support for a position, organize, and agree upon a constitution and by-laws than it was to take effective action. The problem for a good number of these groups

and their members was that while they sincerely wanted to play the role of Samaritan, they did not actually know what that entailed. They might have had a "goal"—moral restoration, an end to the conditions of poverty, the "redemption" of prostitutes—but many did not actually have a program. Indeed, one group, the New Haven Moral Society, dissolved itself after only two meetings upon coming to the conclusion that, noble intentions aside, it had no useful purpose to serve. See Wright. pp. 96, 100, 109.

2 Gross. p. 43.
3 Bremner. (1960) p. 90.
4 Ibid. p. 211.
5 Sealander, J. "Curing Evils at their Source: The Arrival of Scientific Giving." In Friedman and McGarvie. p. 228.
6 Bremner. (1960) p. 98.
7 Crocker. p. 212.
8 Ibid. p. 205. Interestingly, the older organized charities, in no small measure because of the significant number of women who had been among their founders, were now seen as "feminized" and "sentimental," and contrasted unfavorably with the ruddy, masculine precepts of (increasingly male dominated) "scientific charity." See Crocker. p. 206.
9 For a variety of historical, cultural, and economic reasons, government in the Northeast and Midwest was much more likely than its counterparts in other regions of the country to take on a number of what we might today call "social responsibilities." See Woodard. (2011) *passim*.
10 Morris, A.J. *The Limits of Volunteerism.* [Cambridge: Cambridge University Press, 2009] p. xxxiii.
11 Within just a 14-year period from 1874 to 1887 there were numerous incidents of civil unrest around the country as workers, farmers, anarchists, and others battled the entrenched power of the banks and corporations, which usually had the government on their side. Even a brief list of these events would include the January 1874 Tompkins Square Riot in New York City, which occurred as unemployed workers demonstrated and a detachment of mounted police charged into the crowd, beating men, women, and children indiscriminately with billy clubs and leaving hundreds of casualties in their wake. The Baltimore Ohio railroad strike of 1877 caused a series of riots that spread to such cities as Baltimore, Pittsburgh, Chicago, and St. Louis. The outburst of violence in Baltimore lasted four days and cost fifty lives. In July of that same year a general strike halted the movement of American railroads. In the following days, strike riots spread across the U.S. The next week, federal troops were called out to force an end to the nationwide strike. At the "Battle of the Viaduct" in the Pilsen neighborhood of Chicago, violence between protesting workers and federal troops killed thirty workers and wounded over one hundred. In 1885, ten coal-mining activists known as the "Molly Maguires" were hanged after being convicted of murder and other violence in the Coal Wars in Pennsylvania.

The Bay View Tragedy took place in May 1886, when about two thousand Polish workers walked off their jobs and gathered at St. Stanislaus Church in Milwaukee, Wisconsin, angrily denouncing the ten-hour workday. The protesters marched through the city, calling on other workers to join them. All but one factory was closed down as sixteen thousand protesters gathered at Rolling Mills. Wisconsin's Governor Jeremiah Rusk called the state militia, which camped out at the mill while workers slept in nearby fields. On the morning of May 5th, as protesters chanted for the eight-hour workday, the commander of the militia ordered his men to shoot into the crowd, some of whom were carrying sticks, bricks, and scythes, leaving seven dead at the scene, including a 13-year-old boy. Eight more would die within twenty-four hours.

And in November 1887, in Thibodaux, Louisiana, a local militia, aided by bands of "prominent citizens," shot at least thirty-five unarmed black sugar workers striking to gain a dollar-per-day wage, and lynched two strike leaders. Between 1851 and 1949, there were at least 133 incidents of civil unrest tied to labor, farm, or ethnic activism in the U.S.

12 Just as one example, the September 18, 1873 failure of the Jay Cooke bank, a major player in the American banking establishment, set off a chain reaction of bank failures and temporarily closed the New York stock market. Factories began to lay off workers as the U.S. slipped into depression. The effects of the panic were quickly felt in New York, and more slowly in Chicago, Virginia City, Nevada, and San Francisco.

The New York Stock Exchange closed for ten days starting on September 20th. By November some fifty-five of the nation's railroads had failed, and another sixty went bankrupt within a year. Bank reserves in New York City plummeted during September and October 1873 from US$50 million to $17 million. Construction of new rail lines, formerly one of the backbones of the economy, plummeted from 7,500 miles (12,070 km) of track in 1872 to just 1,600 miles (2,575 km) in 1875. Eighteen thousand businesses failed between 1873 and 1875. Unemployment peaked in 1878 at 8.25%. Building construction was halted, wages were cut, real estate values fell and corporate profits vanished.

13 Bremner. (1960) pp. 96–97.

14 Crocker. p. 204.

15 Ibid. p. 207.

16 Bremner. (1960) pp. 122–123.

17 In addition to the prodigious humanitarian aid it provided during the war, in its aftermath American philanthropy almost single-handedly undertook the task of feeding and caring for millions of European children left orphaned, disabled, homeless, and undernourished by the carnage. Ibid. pp. 129–135.

18 Hall. (2010) p. 13.

19 Sealander. p. 218.

20 Today, by contrast, there are 93,126.

21 Fleishman, J. *The Foundation: A Great American Secret.* [New York: Public Affairs, 2007] p. 26.

22 Not all of the early foundations of the era, however, followed this model. Many were established as community foundations and community chests, still engaged in distributive charity, or helping to coordinate aid to the poor within their cities. Still others were founded with very specific targets in mind, such as aiding Swedish teachers, establishing homes for aged missionaries, giving vocational training to white orphan boys from Pennsylvania, or educating freed southern blacks in the agricultural or mechanical trades. See Sealander. p. 223.

23 Gross. p. 46.

24 Hall. (1990) p. 46.

25 Ibid. p. 49.

26 Ibid. p. 48.

27 Ibid. p. 41.

28 Ibid. p. 43.

29 Ibid. p. 45.

30 Ibid. p. 42.

31 In this context, programs for the removal of indigenous children from their parents and their placement in institutions or white foster homes in order to "civilize the savage," a practice common in the U.S., Canada, and Australia from the latter 1800s through the mid-1900s, come to mind.

32 Hall. (1990) p. 51.

33 Luke 10:25–37.

34 This period was also either accompanied or soon followed by the emergence of such alternatives as Adventism, Mormonism, the Jehovah's Witnesses, and Christian Science.

35 Historian Conrad E. Wright has argued that New England Evangelicals intentionally gave up the effort to create small, closed, perfected communities in favor of more narrowly targeted reform and service-provision efforts. See Hammack. (2002) p. 1645.

36 Ahlstrom. p. 374.

37 Among the New England deists of the period were John Adams, Ethan Allen, and John Quincy Adams. George Washington and James Madison were said to be among the Virginia contingent. One of Thomas Paine's most popular works, *The Age of Reason*, was a treatise on behalf of deist beliefs designed to explicitly appeal to ordinary people, using direct language familiar to the laboring classes.

 Peripatetic polymath Benjamin Franklin initially gravitated toward the mechanistic approach of deism. Reading a book intended to refute deist positions, Franklin found that "the arguments of the deists appeared to me much stronger than the refutation." The effects of deism, however, later repelled him. He blamed it for the "perversion" of his friends John Collins and James Ralph, and believed it contributed to his abandonment of his betrothal to Deborah Read. "I suspect," he wrote, "that this doctrine, though it might be true, [is] not very useful." (Brands. p. 94.)

 As for Thomas Jefferson, while he is often counted among the deists of the period, he explicitly refused to ever discuss his religious opinions, although he was accused of being a deist and worse when he led the fight for the disestablishment of Anglicanism in Virginia. Many, however, hold that his "Jefferson's Bible," a work in which he stripped away from the gospels all references to the supernatural, stands as evidence of his actual beliefs. (Rubenstein, H. and Clark Smith, B. "History of the Jefferson Bible." *The Life and Morals of Jesus of Nazareth Extracted Textually from the Gospels in Greek, Latin, French & English.* By Thomas Jefferson. Smithsonian Edition. [Washington, DC: Smithsonian Books, 2011] pp. 12–13, 15 and *passim*.

38 The New England Congregationalists, by way of example, in spite of being the religious and social heirs of the founding Puritans, found it impossible to stem the tide by which virtually all nominally Congregationalist churches in the Commonwealth became, in fact, Unitarian. Ironically, however, it was not a Congregationalist church, but Boston's King's Chapel, an Anglican parish, that became the first officially Unitarian church in America when, in 1785, under the influence of lay minister James Freeman, all references to the Trinity were taken out of its *Common Book of Prayer*. Before long, twelve of the fourteen Congregationalist churches in Boston had become Unitarian. Avowed Universalist Henry Ware was elected as the Hollis Professor of Theology at Harvard in 1805, and theological liberal Samuel Webber to the presidency of the college two years later. In short order, the Harvard Divinity School soon shifted its curriculum to teach Unitarian theology. This began around a period of Unitarian control of Harvard that lasted well into the last century. It is telling that today Massachusetts hosts 142 Unitarian/Universalist congregations, by far the most of any state in the Union.

39 Deism centers on the concept that God does not interfere directly with the world. The Supreme Being, in the deist perspective, set the universe in motion, but thereafter stepped back from human affairs, ruling, if at all, from long ago and far away. (See Ahlstrom. p. 358). The Unitarians began by rejecting the Trinity…and went on to essentially discard any standard dogma whatsoever. The divinity of Christ,

the essential sinfulness of man, the atonement and numerous other key beliefs of Christianity were all eventually dismissed as unreasonable. (According to the website of the Unitarian Universalist Association, "We have no shared creed. Our shared covenant...supports the free and responsible search for truth and meaning." See Unitarian Universalist Association. "What We Believe." www.uua.org/beliefs/what-we-believe.) The Universalists rejected the idea of eternal damnation for anyone as antithetical to the concept of a loving and merciful God. Quite to the contrary, according to their reading of Scripture, salvation truly is universal, and everyone will eventually be saved. For their part, the Baptists offered no creeds but the Bible itself, and appealed to people on the basis of four simple principles: separation of church and state, church democracy, simple worship services, and freedom of conscience (Whalen, William J. *Separated Brethren*. Second Revised Edition. [Milwaukee: The Bruce Publishing Company, 1968] p. 65.)

40 The Baptists and Methodists both relied heavily upon often little-trained or untrained lay preachers to spread the word. For the Baptists, most important to their success was their reliance on the farmer-preacher instead of a frocked formal clergy. This incredibly effective figure often came from the same area in which he preached. Typically of humble rural origins, he was most likely in an area where schools were non-existent, and hopes of "higher education" unheard of. He himself had probably been converted by the visit(s) of an itinerant preacher and had been "awakened," "born again," and probably baptized. Feeling the call himself, he would, with little or no training, begin preaching on his own, frequently gathering a congregation to himself and being "ordained" as their minister. Since any home, barn, or clearing would suffice for his purposes, the poverty of the area was no impediment to his work (Ahlstrom. p. 323).

As for the Methodists, one of the most famous Wesleyan surrogates Robert Strawbridge actually ordained himself. Wesley eventually came to believe that the New Testament evidence did not leave the power of ordination to the priesthood in the hands of bishops alone, but that other priests could perform an ordination. In 1784, he ordained preachers for Scotland and England and America, assigning to them the power not only to ordain, but to administer the sacraments, something the lay preachers had not been doing. (See Sweet, W.W. *The Story of Religion in America*. Third Edition. [New York: Harper Row, 1950] p. 153.) This action was a major reason for Methodism's final split from the Church of England after Wesley's death. Meanwhile, until 1960 when the Earlham School of Religion was opened as a Friends' seminary, the Quakers had for centuries done away with all formally ordained clergy.

41 This shift in attitude was not limited to the nation's Christians. Even among Jews it was noted that "social welfare became secularized and impersonal; a sense of civic duty largely replaced an awareness of the Divine Commandment." See Jewish Virtual Library at Chapter 3, Note 65, this volume.

42 This was particularly true of the divisive issue of slavery, as partisans of both sides in the debate were able to find support for their arguments in Scripture.

43 This was amply illustrated by the Quaker's 1688 Germantown Petition against slavery, which relied entirely upon the Golden Rule for the weight of its argument. Containing absolutely no references to Jesus or God, the petition argued that every human, regardless of belief, color, or ethnicity, has rights that should not be violated. As they themselves had been horribly persecuted in both England and America, the Germantown Quakers saw a fundamental similarity between their right to be free from persecution on account of their beliefs, and the right of others to be free from being forced to work against their will. The only religious reference made, in fact,

was when the petitioners asked their fellow Friends how "Christians" could buy and sell people like cattle, with husbands and wives, and parents and children being separated in the process. They rested their entire case, not on Scripture or a Godly command, but on the idea of treating other people as we ourselves would want to be treated: a powerful argument for social justice that needed no divine embellishment.

44 Hammack. (2002) p. 1645.
45 Among the new professionals who emerged during this period were the fund-raisers, whose business it was to mobilize local people, money, and ideas to secure an ever-increasing flow of revenue. Whereas the also increasingly professional caseworkers and other social work professionals were paid notoriously poorly, the fund-raisers were from the start handsomely rewarded. Even then being paid a pro-portion of the dollars raised, the new calling was attractive enough that by the end of the 1920s there were twenty professional fund-raising firms in New York City alone. See Bremner. (1960) p. 140; Seeley. p. 20.
46 Hall. (1990) p. 54.
47 1799 N.Y. Laws ch. 72, § 32. See Beebe, R. and Harrison, S. "A Law in Search of a Policy: A History of New York's Real Property Tax-Exemption for Nonprofit Organizations." *Fordham Urban Law Journal*. Vol. 9, Issue 3, Article 2. (1980) p. 537.
48 Beebe and Harrison. p. 538.
49 *YMCA v. Mayor of New York*, 113 N.Y. 187, 190, 21 N.E. 86, 87 (1889).
50 N.Y. Tax Law § 4(7) (1896).
51 Under the law, trustees who managed charitable funds were also permitted broad authority in financial management and protected from claims by donors and ben-eficiaries. See Hall. (2006) p. 37.
52 Commonwealth of Massachusetts. Application for Statutory Exemption. Form 1B-3. In Massachusetts at present, nonprofit corporations eligible for a tax exemp-tion include those entities organized for the following purposes: "(1) any civic, educational, charitable, benevolent or religious purpose; (2) the prosecution of any antiquarian, historical, literary, scientific, medical, chiropractic, artistic, monu-mental or musical purpose; (3) for establishing and maintaining libraries; (4) for supporting any missionary enterprise having for its object the dissemination of religious or educational instruction in foreign countries; (5) for promoting tem-perance or morality in the Commonwealth; (6) for fostering, encouraging, or engaging in athletic exercises or yachting; (7) for encouraging the raising of choice breeds of domestic animals and poultry; (8) for the association and accommo-dation of societies of Free Masons, Odd Fellows, Knights of Pythias or other charitable or social bodies of like character and purpose; (9) for the establishment and maintenance or places for reading rooms, libraries, or social meetings; (10) for establishing boards of trade, chambers of commerce and bodies of like nature; (11) for providing nonprofit credit counseling services; (12) encouraging agricul-ture or horticulture; for improving and ornamenting the streets and public squares of any city or town by planting and cultivating ornamental trees therein and also otherwise improving the physical aspects of such city or town and furthering the recreation and enjoyment of the inhabitants thereof; (13) for the purpose of purchasing, holding, preserving and maintaining burial grounds; and (14) the pur-pose of forming self-insured workers compensation groups." See Secretary of the Commonwealth. "Nonprofit Corporation Information." www.sec.state.ma.us/cor/corpweb/cornp/npinf.htm.
53 Hall. (2006) p. 37.
54 It should be noted, however, that not all manifestations of private associations did, in fact, promote the "public good." Just as the Ku Klux Klan, a private "voluntary

association," disenfranchised, terrorized, and murdered blacks, segments of the nation's upper class sought to exercise their power through the private institutions that were becoming increasingly central to the nation's development. By the middle of the 19th century, such metropolitan centers as Boston, New York, and Philadelphia boasted constellations of cultural, educational, and charitable institutions tightly linked by interlocking boards of directors. These not only enabled moneyed elites to extend their cultural and political influence but also, to the extent that institutional endowments were among the largest capital pools of the period, served as arenas for collective economic decision-making. It was no accident that Massachusetts, whose charity-friendly laws permitted such institutions as Harvard and the Massachusetts General Hospital to accumulate very substantial endowments, became an early center of investment banking, based on the strategic investment of these funds in the textile industry and western railroads. See Hall. (2006) p. 38.

55 *Walz v. Tax Commission*, 397 U.S. 664 (1970) at 672–74.

56 Millard, C. *Destiny of the Republic.* [New York: Doubleday, 2011] p. 109.

57 Arnsberger, P. et al. "A History of the Tax-Exempt Sector: An SOI Perspective." *Statistics of Income Bulletin.* (Winter 2008) p. 106. https://www.irs.gov/pub/irs-soi/tehistory.pdf.

58 Ibid. p. 107.

59 Ibid.

60 In 1941 Form 990 contained three yes/no questions, an income statement, and a balance sheet, although some line items required attached schedules. By 1947, the form (including instructions) had reached four pages, although some portions applied only to certain types of organizations such as farmers' cooperatives. The required financial information was far more extensive than that of the first 990. In 1976, Form 990 itself consisted of two pages plus three and one-half pages of instructions. Schedule A consisted of four pages plus four pages of instructions. As of 2000, the form was up to six pages for the 990 itself, six pages for Schedule A, at least two pages for Schedule B (including instructions), and a separate forty-two-page instruction book. National Center for Charitable Statistics. "What is the Form 990? What is its history?" June 21, 2009. http://nccsweb.urban.org/knowledgebase/detail.php?linkID=106&category=13&xrefID=3481. Until 1969 annual reports to the Internal Revenue Service were required only of private foundations; after that all charitable organizations except churches were subject to the reporting requirement. See Fremont-Smith, M. "Trends in Accountability and Regulation of Nonprofits." *The Future of the Nonprofit Sector.* Ed. V. Hodgkinson, et al. [San Francisco: Jossey-Bass, 1989] p. 77.

61 Arnsberger et al. p. 106.

62 Tax exemption applied to nonprofits means that in most cases the sales tax normally applied to certain sales and purchases is waived for transactions relating to the charity's "charitable mission." See Colorado Department of Revenue. "Sales Tax-Exempt Status for Charitable Organizations: Application Requirements. April 2014." https://www.colorado.gov/pacific/sites/default/files/Sales02.pdf. In some states, exemption from paying sales tax depends on the nature and volume of the sales activities by the nonprofit. In California, for example, the state Tax Service Center advises that "some" sales and purchases by nonprofits are exempt from sales and use taxes. Examples of exempt sales include, but are not limited to, sales of certain food products for human consumption, sales to the government, sales of prescription medicines, and certain vehicle and vessel transfers. A more comprehensive list is available at www.boe.ca.gov/pdf/pub61.pdf. See California Tax Service Center. "Nonprofit/Exempt Organizations." www.taxes.ca.gov/exemptbus.shtml

Part III

5   Turbulent times

While the American voluntary/nonprofit sector had undeniably grown and developed during the 1800s, it was nonetheless in a stage we might call its "adolescence," not quite fully mature and not really prepared for the challenges the 20th century would bring. Yet in less time than it took for the nation to completely shift from a horse-and-buggy world to one of automotive dominance, the nation faced not only two world wars, but also the greatest economic upheaval in its history. All of this was to have a profound impact on the nonprofit arena as it sought to find its place in a rapidly evolving world.

By the early decades of the 20th century, the concept of "relief" and aid to the needy was evolving. Direct charitable aid to the poor was in the process of being slowly replaced by more ambitious philanthropic efforts aimed at the roots and causes of poverty. Such direct aid as was still undertaken was provided via a patchwork network of local providers. The government's response to need was still spotty. In some parts of the country, state government began to assume more responsibility for helping the "worthy poor," a category and distinction that went back to Elizabethan days: by 1926, forty states had established some type of public relief program for mothers with dependent children, and a few states also provided cash assistance to needy elderly residents through old-age pensions.[1] In most places, however, private organizations such as Catholic Charities,[2] the emerging federated Jewish philanthropy movement,[3] the social ministries of many Protestant denominations, and the budding network of Community Chest organizations[4] around the country carried much of the load. The explosion of various national organizations that was to characterize the early 1900s had not yet occurred; so, for the most part, the work of the country's nonprofits was mainly focused on assisting the poor.

But while this was going on at home, the world was changing. . .and the 20th century had not even begun when the nation found itself embroiled in the short but significant conflict that was the Spanish–American War of 1898. That confrontation not only ultimately helped catapult Teddy Roosevelt to the presidency, but also inaugurated the shift that moved the U.S. from being an isolationist, regionally focused nation to a global power.

It was World War I, however, that proved to be the 20th century's first watershed moment, not only for the U.S. as a player on the world stage, but for its charitable sector as well.

World War I

It is one of history's ironies that an event that so profoundly changed the nation, *and* its nonprofit sector, found the country so unprepared at the outset.

To say that the nation was ill-equipped for World War I would be an understatement. The demands of fighting in Cuba and the Philippines during the conflicts of 1898 and 1899–1902, respectively, forced the U.S. to modernize somewhat an army that until then had mostly been involved in limited continental conflicts, and, while becoming a colonial power by virtue of the acquisition of the former Spanish possessions in the Caribbean and Pacific, forced the country to at least peek beyond its borders. However, as the first rumblings of trouble began to echo across the Atlantic from Europe, the U.S. was still mostly rural, mostly agrarian, and mostly locally focused. We not only lacked an army on anything approaching the scale of the Europeans,[5] but our attentions were turned almost entirely inward as the country grappled with changing times in the form of labor conflicts, regulating the railroads, breaking up the trusts, establishing food and drug safety standards, a budding civil rights movement, and women's suffrage. The buffers provided by two oceans and a general isolationism further combined to foster a national complacency regarding international affairs.[6]

At the beginning of the century, this attitude was reflected in the nation's charitable sector, which was still for the most part locally oriented, small scale, and home-grown. The outbreak of hostilities in Europe, however, would change this rapidly and result, in many ways, in a much larger and more confident and ambitious nonprofit arena than we had ever had before.

When the war began, there was only one American civilian organization with any real experience with the demands and realities of large-scale armed conflict, the YMCA (also known as the Y).

As early as November 1861, fifteen YMCA associations had formally gathered to coordinate efforts to alleviate the suffering of the sick and wounded of the Civil War. During the four years that conflict lasted, the Y's United States Christian Commission recruited an estimated five thousand volunteer "delegates" who served without pay in every theater of combat. It was the nation's first large-scale civilian volunteer service corps.

The Red Cross had not yet been created and the military chaplaincy was in its infancy. For these and other reasons, volunteers were recruited by the Commission from a broad range of fields. Some served as surgeons, nurses, chaplains, and chaplains' assistants, while others distributed emergency medical supplies, food, and clothing. They served on the battlefields with horse-drawn canteens, built and operated special-diet kitchens in hospitals, brought books and prefabricated chapels to soldiers, taught enlisted men to read and write, and maintained a hotel for soldiers on furlough and provided free meals.

YMCA prisoner-of-war work also began during the Civil War, with the Y ministering to the needs of Confederate soldiers imprisoned in the north and Union soldiers in the south.

Journal records of the time indicate that the Y distributed some one hundred thousand cases of food, clothing, and medical supplies, and a total of 12 million books, magazines, and pamphlets.[7] Y volunteers also wrote an estimated ninety thousand letters for the sick and wounded, and distributed $1,000 a week in postage for troop correspondence.[8]

None of this expertise, however, was immediately applicable to the situation during the first years of World War I, as the nation sat out the beginning of that conflict. What did become evident, however, was that America had a part to play in the vast humanitarian crisis triggered by the war.

As Europe hunkered down for what would prove to be four long years of trench warfare, famine threatened tiny, German-occupied Belgium, a highly industrialized nation of 7 million people dependent upon imports for three-quarters of its food.

On one side, the German army of occupation refused to take responsibility for feeding the civilian population. *Let Belgium import food from abroad as she had done before the war*, said the Germans. On the other side stood the tightening British naval blockade of Belgian ports. *Let the Germans, as occupiers of Belgium, feed its people*, said the British. Besides, they argued, how could anyone be sure that the Germans wouldn't just seize any imported food for themselves?

Through a combination of circumstances that probably could not be replicated ever again, it fell to future American president Herbert Hoover to coordinate the world's efforts through a novel relief organization, the Commission for Relief in Belgium (CRB).[9] No doubt influenced by British and French propaganda that depicted the Germans as barbarians, a constant flow of private contributions, much of it from the U.S., illustrated the popularity of Belgian relief. Operating with a skeletal, mostly American staff, from its headquarters in occupied Brussels, the CRB coordinated the receipt of more than 2,300 overseas and cross-Channel ships' cargoes, averaging 100,000 tons of bulk foods per month for almost five years, as well as their distribution across occupied Belgium and France.

Here in the U.S., numerous groups were organized to support the work of the Commission.[10] Among the many aid organizations established by Americans to help suffering Europeans was the Fatherless Children of France. Started in October 1915, the group aimed "to maintain the orphaned French children in their own homes, to be brought up by their mothers and fitted for the work of reconstructing the French nation, which will develop upon them."[11] Their efforts were typical of the time, as organizations sprang up across America to provide relief for noncombatants and the wounded across a war zone spreading from the Dardanelles to the North Sea, from the coast of Belgium to the coast of China.

The people of Belgium, France, and other Allied nations, meanwhile, were not the only ones to receive aid from the U.S. Prior to the country's official entry into the war, America's sizable German ethnic population—estimated to be around 30 million at the time—not only pushed back against

Anglo-French propaganda efforts aimed at swaying popular American opinion to the Allied cause, but they also undertook their own relief efforts on behalf of suffering civilians, and "war widows and orphaned babies" of the Central Powers of Europe. Organizations such as Deutschwehr— which was largely funded by German-Americans from Pennsylvania, and which maintained an active soup kitchen in Berlin, as well as providing clothing and food relief—and the Relief Fund of Philadelphia, a German-American charity founded shortly after the beginning of the war which raised funds for civilian war relief in Germany and Austria–Hungary, were quite active.[12] These efforts continued up until the US declared war on Germany.[13]

Figure 5.1 Program of Deutschwehr-Fest, a fund-raiser on behalf of Central Powers troops and civilians. German Society of Pennsylvania. Joseph P. Horner Memorial Library.

When America entered the war, however, a new urgency impacted the nation's voluntary efforts, and a whole new crop of organizations began seeking funds for needs both home and abroad. In 1917 and 1918, "war chests" were organized in hundreds of cities, some of them including appeals for local welfare work as well as for war aims, and many of them relying heavily upon corporate giving.

This was also a period when large, national organizations came into their own.

The YMCA, already having fifty years' experience working with the nation's military, immediately volunteered its support, and President Wilson quickly accepted it. The Y assumed military responsibilities on a scale that had never been attempted by a nonprofit, community-based organization in the history of our nation, and which would never be matched again.

General John Pershing, commander of the American Expeditionary Forces during World War I, publicly recognized the fact that the YMCA conducted 90% of the welfare work among the American forces in Europe. It served not only the 19 million soldiers of the Allied armies, it also extended its activities to over 5 million German, Austrian, and Turkish prisoners of war. Beyond the western, southern, and eastern fronts in Europe, the organization's operations were also conducted in northern and eastern Africa, and in western, southern, and eastern Asia.[14]

Although the YMCA was initially the sole agency authorized to provide war-related services, as America's direct involvement in the conflict got under way, other organizations joined the effort. The National Catholic War Council volunteered its services, first in the U.S. and then with the American Expeditionary Forces overseas. The Jewish Welfare Board expressed a similar interest in serving military personnel of its faith and was also accepted by the War Department. The Young Women's Christian Association (YWCA) offered services for women workers assigned overseas. In addition, the Salvation Army, the American Library Association, and a group of local agencies working together as the War Camp Community Service rounded out the organizations recognized by the federal government for service during the war.

The American Red Cross, although still small and not well known, also played a vital role in the war effort. While America was still neutral, the Red Cross's first major project was to equip a ship with emergency supplies and medical workers. The vessel was the SS *Red Cross*, which became known on both sides of the Atlantic as "the Mercy Ship." It was staffed with 170 surgeons and nurses who were assigned to assist in the medical care of combat casualties no matter what side they had been fighting on.

After America entered the war, the Red Cross began to grow and played an important part in coordinating volunteer efforts. President Woodrow Wilson was appointed the honorary chairman of the Red Cross, and he urged Americans to support the organization and its efforts. The public responded, contributing $400 million in funds and material—by way of example, the organization sponsored a nationwide knitting campaign to produce woolen socks and other warm weather clothing—to support various Red Cross programs, including those for American and Allied forces and civilian refugees. The organization helped staff hospitals and ambulance companies, and recruited twenty thousand registered nurses to serve the military, and also helped to recruit and train ambulance drivers and orderlies at various universities.[15]

But these organizations were not alone. The early years of the 20th century had seen the founding or incorporation of many nonprofits still part of the familiar American landscape. Among these were the American Lung Association, Big Brothers/Big Sisters of America, the Navy-Marine Corps Relief Society in 1904, and the Order Sons of Italy in America and Rotary International in 1905, the same year the Red Cross received its second Congressional Charter. The American Jewish Committee, the Boys & Girls Clubs of America, and the Lighthouse Guild were founded in 1906. Christmas Seals were first sold in 1907, the Federal Council of Churches of Christ was founded in 1908, and the National Association for the Advancement of Colored People in 1909. The Boy Scouts of America and Catholic Charities USA were incorporated in 1910. In 1912, the Better Business Bureau, Jewish Big Sisters, the U.S. Chamber of Commerce, and Girl Scouts USA all came into being. The American Cancer Society was founded in 1913. The Association for the Prevention and Relief of Heart Disease, precursor to the American Heart Association, was formed in 1915. Planned Parenthood was founded in 1916. The American Friends Service Committee and Boys Town were launched in 1917. And all of them wanted to do their bit for the war effort.

The Girl Scouts provide but one example, as girls all over the country tended to victory gardens, volunteered as ambulance drivers for the Red Cross, led local programs on food conservation awareness, relieved overworked nurses during the 1918 Spanish influenza epidemic, sold war bonds, and organized units at Red Cross sewing rooms.

The Salvation Army, meanwhile sent a fact-finding mission to France to assess the needs of American troops. The conclusion reached was that those needs could best be met by canteens/social centers—termed "huts"—that could serve baked goods, provide writing supplies and stamps, and provide a clothes-mending service. Stateside, these huts were established near army training centers. In France, however, the Salvation Army volunteers ran into an unforeseen challenge. Because of the difficulties of providing freshly baked goods from locations established in abandoned buildings near to the front lines, two Salvation Army volunteers came up with the idea of providing doughnuts. These were reported to have been an instant hit, and soon soldiers on both sides of the Atlantic were visiting the Salvation Army huts in search of doughnuts.[16]

Figure 5.2 Salvation Army doughnut girl. Salvation Army National Archives.

Another novel charitable effort was the American Ambulance in Russia initiative in 1917, the goal of which was to organize a volunteer American ambulance company in Russia under the Kerensky government that immediately followed the abdication of Czar Nicholas II.

Figure 5.3 American Ambulance in Russia package tag. Digital Library at Villanova University.

The war's end, meanwhile, did nothing to dampen either America's involvement in overseas relief, or its utilization of nonprofits to accomplish this goal.

Faced with a continent that was in many places starving and most of whose agricultural production had been destroyed by war, America responded with a new wave of private, nonprofit relief agencies. Examples included the National Committee on Food for Small Democracies, the Finnish Relief Fund, the Polish Relief Commission, and the Famine Emergency Committee.

Probably the most important, however, was the European Relief Council (ERC), an American umbrella organization whose members included such private organizations as the American Friends Service Committee, the American Red Cross, the Federal Council of Churches of Christ in America, the Joint Distribution Committee, the Knights of Columbus, the National Catholic Welfare Council, the YMCA, and the YWCA, as well as American Relief Administration (ARA), a government agency formed by Congress in 1919. The purpose of the ERC was to coordinate the fund-raising activities of the many American charitable relief organizations active at the time.

Through its efforts, about $40 million—roughly equivalent to $489 million today—was collected. The funds were turned over to the ARA for distribution in Europe with a mandate focused primarily upon saving children. In 1921, ERC/ARA delivered relief assistance to Albania, Austria, Czechoslovakia, the Danzig city-state, Estonia, Finland, France, Germany, Greece, Hungary, Italy, Latvia, Lithuania, Montenegro, Palestine, Poland, Romania, Russia, Serbia, Turkey, and Yugoslavia. There was an additional special program for Russian refugee children, as well as programs for refugees in Shanghai and Vladivostok.

***

World War I changed the American nonprofit sector in several profound ways.

While the period from about 1908 to the beginning of the war had seen the launch of numerous national organizations, it was the war that brought many of them together in a way they had not imagined before. Their ability to raise money and mobilize resources, particularly when engaging in federated or joint fund-raising efforts, was unprecedented.

The ability of entities like the Red Cross and the YMCA—formed in 1845, but still small and mostly locally focused in spite of its Civil War experience— to undertake the massive overseas efforts they shouldered during the war was a revelation. It began to make people think about what else these organizations could accomplish. It also helped them grow.

As an illustration, by the time the war ended in November 1918, the Red Cross had become a major national humanitarian organization. It had developed a huge membership base with a presence throughout the country, the number of local chapters jumping from 107 in 1914 to 3,864 in 1918, while membership grew from 17,000 to over 20 million adult and 11 million Junior Red Cross participants during the same period of time.

In similar fashion, the Community Chest movement, first launched in Cleveland in 1913, grew to the point that by the end of the war, almost every large city in the nation had a chest. In 1920, chest campaigns in thirty-nine cities raised about $19,000,000—$232.4 million in today's dollars—for local services.[17]

A new level of professionalism that had not previously been seen in charitable endeavors became ever more apparent, as smart young managers began running larger charitable and public benefit organizations as they would a business. The professional fund-raiser became not only a familiar figure in an increasing number of charities, but often a well-off one too.

Perhaps more important, the American public had changed as well. Entering the war as a debtor nation, the U.S. emerged from the conflict a creditor and soon thereafter experienced the boom that led to the Roaring Twenties. Life was good, the car was becoming ever more common, and innovations like the movies and electric appliances were changing people's lives. But during the war, it seems that the American people had been trained through constant and repeated appeals to give "something" no matter what their income. . .and they continued the habit. As an illustration, it has been estimated that total charitable giving grew from an already significant $1,730,600,000[18] in 1921, to $2,330,600,000[19] in 1928. Moreover, the money was going to a wide variety of causes.

A study in New Haven found that contributions to local charities increased from $555,000 in 1900, to $2,239,000 in 1925. Protestant agencies in the city doubled the amount they took in during this period, as did those secular agencies devoted to health and "character building." Jewish agencies in the city experienced a fivefold increase in contributions; Catholic agencies saw a sixfold increase. Local hospitals, meanwhile, saw contributions to their appeals multiply by a factor of eighteen.[20]

It would have seemed that the American nonprofit sector, strong, growing, and having proven itself under the rigors and demands of war, was ready to take a central role in American society.

But then the Depression hit and changed everything.

The Great Depression

Following the great stock market crash of 1929, and as the first waves of unemployed looked for help, the nation's network of voluntary agencies stepped up to meet the challenge. They were confident in both their methods and their ability to meet the need. At the time, in virtually any American city,[21] one could find a fairly standard set of institutions devoted to health, child welfare, recreation, and a variety of other causes. These ranged from assistance for unwed mothers to temporary housing for transient men.[22] Although few private agencies actually wanted to take on the job of direct relief to the unemployed and destitute, many gamely stepped up to do what was necessary.

With the active encouragement of President Hoover, a man who had done perhaps more than any other single person in directing the nation's relief of war-torn Europe, the country's private agencies did their best. Community Chest organizations in a number of cities, including hard-hit Detroit, reached their fund-raising goals in 1930 and in some cases raised larger sums than they had in previous years.[23] The American Red Cross, although this was not its mandate, undertook to relieve 2.5 million people in twenty-three states who were victims of drought as well as the economic downturn, tapping into a $5 million disaster reserve fund and another $10 million raised in a special campaign.[24] The most poignant part of this broad public response was that many who were giving would themselves need help in a very short while.[25]

In spite of their best efforts, however, it became clear by the time of President Franklin Delano Roosevelt's (FDR) election that private agencies, even where their work was augmented by local government, simply were not up to the task of addressing the problem.[26] The national government would have to step in. FDR tapped Harry Hopkins to oversee federal relief efforts. Hopkins quickly issued one of the most influential policies in the history of the nonprofit sector. The first rule Hopkins announced was the prohibition against any federal relief funds going to any private agency. Hopkins' goal was not to hurt the voluntary sector, but to force recalcitrant states and localities to finally make public relief an unquestionably public responsibility. . .not just in its funding, but in its management and administration as well.

Hopkins drove home the distinct roles he had in mind with a second ruling, one that stated that "widows and their dependents, and/or aged persons" would be ineligible for federal relief dollars. No federal relief money was to go to the payment of hospital bills, institutional care, or the "boarding out of children."[27] Those needs, Hopkins thought, could and should be addressed by the voluntary sector.

Many localities had taken to either subsidizing private efforts, or directly funneling public money through private agencies.[28] This was seen as having many benefits, early strains of many of the same arguments that would be heard in the '60s during the Great Society. It was felt that this was a quick and expedient way to deliver relief; that it capitalized on the strengths of the voluntary sector; that, in the absence of public agencies designed and built to take on this task, it preserved the existing structures; and that private agencies were free of the more cumbersome laws and regulations that often hamstrung public agencies.

There were also political considerations, as private agencies were thought to be better able to resist the political favoritism and meddling endemic to nearly any public venture. Utilizing private agencies was also a convenient way to sidestep broad conservative opposition to creating new governmental bureaucracies.

Critics like Hopkins, however, argued that public agencies represented a greater level of stability for the needy. He believed that these efforts were a public responsibility that should not be pawned off on private agencies. For their part, many in the voluntary sector worried that increased or institutionalized public subsidies would lead to a loss of control over their own programs.

They feared that the professionalism they had worked for fifty years to create would ultimately fall victim to both the civil service system and the government's need for a standardization of benefits.

The unfortunate consequence of all this is that it left many voluntary associations out in the cold. Billions of dollars were available to address pressing social needs, but many categories of private voluntary agencies were excluded from accepting them. Many wondered just what they were going to do.

One answer was a "new alignment" that established a dividing line between those who needed "just" economic help, and those who had "underlying issues." According to this new perspective, those who needed money should be the responsibility of public agencies, while those needing the specialized services would be taken care of by the voluntary sector.[29]

This notion got a boost when FDR moved from direct relief to efforts like the Civilian Conservation Corps and the Works Progress Administration. These undertakings sought to create jobs for the nation's millions of unemployed.

The impact, particularly of the Works Progress Administration, was enormous. By the time it was dismantled in 1942, it had spent more than $15 billion, over $200 billion in today's dollars. And while much of this went to the building of roads, parks, and other infrastructure, a vast number of other workers were also employed. They performed a wide array of community services, most of them in conjunction with local nonprofit, voluntary agencies.

The purposes for which these agencies received government money included training thousands of people in citizenship and naturalization classes, vocational education programs, and social science courses taught to industrial workers. The money went to staff nursery schools for underprivileged children, hot lunches for school children, housekeeping and gardening demonstration projects, and training and alternative shelter options for homeless people. There were classes offered in music, art, drama, popular science, and assorted avocational fields. There were even classes for "those who wish to train themselves to think more clearly."[30]

This had three effects. Most of these services were offered through nonprofit voluntary agencies, which made them vital players in a whole new realm of social enterprise. Secondly, it made available to the public an entirely new range of services. . . .and the public *liked* these new offerings. Thirdly, in a seminal shift, it set the sector firmly on the path of providing *services* and not the sort "relief" that had been a central part of its past identity.

There was, however, one other incredibly powerful influence on the fortunes of the American voluntary sector during these years, the spreading conflicts that would result in the conflagration of World War II.

World War II

The nation was still in the grip of the Depression when the first rumbles of impending conflicts around the globe reached our shores. Mussolini had been in power in Italy since 1922. In Japan, a group of junior naval officers and army cadets assassinated Prime Minister Inukai Tsuyoshi in 1932 and were popularly seen as patriots, establishing an atmosphere in which the military was able to act with little restraint. Hitler became chancellor of Germany in 1933.

The Japanese first invaded Manchuria in 1931, attacked Shanghai in 1932, and launched full scale war in 1937. The Spanish Civil War erupted in 1936.

America understandably had a dual reaction to these events.

The first was that, just as during the outbreak of World War I before the U.S. was drawn into the conflict, hostilities spurred the formation of numerous charitable relief efforts aimed at easing the suffering of civilians in the war zones. The Neutrality Act of 1939, adopted shortly after the outbreak of the war in Europe, required charitable agencies that wished to engage in civilian war relief to register with the State Department and submit monthly reports.[31] However, not all obeyed this requirement, and between 1939 and 1941 about seven hundred different American organizations were trying to raise money for the relief of civilians and refugees overseas.[32] The Committee for the Impartial Civilian Relief in Spain was established, and a $1 million relief effort for China was launched by the American Red Cross. . .but both of these were largely disappointments. The problem was that most of these organizations were appealing to the same fairly limited audience, and—while considerable sums *were* raised—overall, America was wary.

Mindful of how Woodrow Wilson's flexible neutrality during World War I had helped draw America into that conflict, many Americans were suspicious of any actions that might put the country in the crosshairs of a belligerent power. We were also still mired in an economic downturn such as the nation had never seen. We had our own problems.

It is also true that it was a minority of Americans who were prepared to see overseas events as our direct concern, or who truly felt for the unknown victims suffering on the far side(s) of the globe.

China and Japan seemed to be a world away, and a long-smoldering American racism toward all Asians acted to dampen what little sympathy the victims of Japanese aggression might have garnered. A never well-hidden anti-Semitism in most of the country worked to stifle any broad-based outcry regarding Hitler's campaign against the Jews.[33] America's mainstream press, meanwhile, largely gave Europe's fascists a pass, failing to recognize until it was too late the threat they posed to humanity. There was also a certain comfort to be found for many Americans in accepting the tempest-in-a-teapot description with which many of the country's leading journalists characterized the developing fascist menace.[34]

The September 1939 German invasion of Poland, therefore, drew a tepid response from the American public. There was a broad feeling among many that the nation's involvement in World War I had been a mistake. There was also, particularly among "old stock" Americans, the persistence of strong isolationist tendencies.[35]

It was only the fall of France in 1940 that began to turn this tide. That same year Congress enacted the Selective Service Act, and service in the military—tarnished by the events surrounding the Bonus Army protests of 1932[36]—once again regained its popularity.

The war effort spurred the formation of a great number of charitable organizations as it seemed that every town and hamlet, every church, business, lodge, and organization of any kind wanted to do its bit for the draftees. The problem was that they all wanted to do it by themselves. The result was bedlam, as by the summer of 1942, the number of organizations—subject to no coordination, supervision, or control—could only be estimated according to a committee reporting to President Roosevelt. "We are fairly tripping over one another," reported one voluntary sector official, "in our efforts to organize, publicize, solicit, and be of service."[37]

It was therefore an exception when, in an unprecedented and landmark move, the YMCA, YWCA, National Catholic Community Service, National Jewish Welfare Board, Salvation Army, and National Travelers Aid Association combined their military service programs *and* the associated fund appeals, and created the United Service Organization for National Defense, more popularly known as the USO, in 1941.[38]

In an attempt to organize the chaos, FDR formed the President's War Relief Control Board in 1942, with the power to control all solicitations for war relief. Only the Red Cross, churches, and other non-war charities remained outside its jurisdiction.

The nation, and certainly the voluntary community, had never seen anything like it before. . .or since.

The Board had the power to license war relief agencies (*and* the power to rescind those licenses), and to force the merger or elimination of organizations it found inefficient or duplicative. It had the authority to schedule fund-raising campaigns and to prevent competing appeals during periods set aside for the Red Cross, the National War Fund, the United Jewish Appeal, and war bond drives.

It sharply scrutinized overhead costs and, finding agencies where overhead costs consumed 50%, 75%, or, in a few extreme cases, 100% of the funds ostensibly raised for charitable purposes, made economy of operation a requisite for continued licensing.[39]

Evidence of the success of this push toward centralization can be found in the National War Fund, a private nonprofit, which was the most ambitious venture in cooperative fund-raising the nation had ever seen. In three national campaigns, in 1943, 1944, and 1945, the Fund combined the appeals of not only the major war-related service and relief agencies, but local non-war charities as well. The three drives collected a combined $750 million, and the local organizations got more than half of the take.

In addition to USO and numerous efforts on behalf of U.S. service personnel at home and abroad, organizations such as British War Relief, American Aid to France, United Service to China, and, after the German invasion of the Soviet Union in June of 1941, U.S. Russian War Relief were all high-visibility, private, nonprofit groups. A slew of alphabet agencies, all federations of individual charitable organizations, also came into being and caught the public's attention. Among these were the Cooperative for American Remittance to Europe (what we today know as CARE), the Council of Relief Agencies Licensed to Operate in Germany (CRALOG), Licensed Agencies for Relief in Asia (LARA), and American Relief for Korea (ARK).

Beyond its growing visibility in the war effort, the charitable sector also received a boost when the military established a special classification for military social work. Functionally, this meant that those who had been providing counseling and other social services prior to the war, if they qualified, could continue this work in the service. Having labored during the preceding decades to professionalize their calling, many who had been working in the field prior to the war welcomed this change.[40]

For these reasons and more, it was with a renewed sense of itself that the voluntary sector looked forward to the end of the war, and peace did little to dampen its ascendency.

Rather, the massive, literally indescribable need the immediate post-war world presented proved to be, in many ways, a boon to the charitable realm as there seemed to be more need than ever for its services. In addition to the roughly $500 million a year ($6.1 billion per year in today's dollars) the U.S. army spent for civilian relief immediately after the war wherever it was stationed, organizations such as CARE, Catholic War Relief Services, and Protestant Church World Services provided additional pipelines through which private contributions could and did flow. In 1946, as just one example, American Jews—numbering fewer than 5 million people at the time—collected $105 million for the United Jewish Appeal, and in 1948 they raised $150 million.

Even though the Korean conflict returned the nation to a limited war footing between 1950 and 1953, overall the nation's nonprofit sector settled into a new, comfortable reality.

With the wholesale entry of the government into the business of relief during the Depression—private agencies never completely abandoned such activity, but had clearly become subordinate to the public sector in this function—both organized philanthropy and the nation's many private charities could focus on pioneering approaches to an assortment of needs, the promotion of research, an improvement of methodologies, and the enrichment of culture.[41]

In addition, wartime prosperity had created an unprecedented if pent-up demand for a new way of life, and the nation's voluntary sector was ready.

In stark contrast to previous decades, during which frugality, scrimping, and making do were lauded as not only necessary but admirable traits, as the generation born before and during the Depression came of age—many of them returning GIs—they found that their earning power created a pocket of wealth and new possibilities their parents had never imagined. This, combined with— as a sad side effect of the war—fewer people around to share the good fortune, and the shifting of America's mighty industrial power to consumer goods, truly meant a whole new world.[42]

As the U.S. settled into the middle-class world of the '50s, the nation's voluntary agencies focused even more on the delivery of services tailored for the country's new sensibilities. . .and concerns. Not only had various forms of therapy and counseling become largely accepted during the '40s, but they seemed especially suited for addressing mounting public worries over the rise in divorce rates, decreased family stability, and a widespread—if inaccurate—impression of rampant juvenile delinquency.

Nonprofits and their growing cadre of allies began to persuade the public that, in addition to the casework these organizations were providing—with decidedly mixed success for poorer clients—they could help address middle-class anxieties *and* their manifestations, such as dysfunction in marriage, sexual problems, and parent–child conflicts. In what was known as the Age of Science, the period that saw the emergence of such wonders as television, the Salk vaccine, and the atom bomb, faith in "experts" soared, and nonprofits of all sorts stepped in to offer their social expertise. It was a massive publicity effort that even saw such popular magazines of the time—*McCall's, Better Homes & Gardens*, and *Today's Woman*—employing columnists with a social work focus.[43]

Desperate never to go back to the days when they were many communities' primary relief agencies, a notable number of nonprofits moved to exclusively offering services. Not only were these offerings tailored for an audience that could pay for them (at least in part), but they also represented a return to the sector's 19th century, Protestant/New-England-inspired heritage of addressing the root causes of social problems, and not, as was the case with relief, merely their symptoms. The developing list of these services often included consultation with social workers on a variety of interpersonal relationship issues, psychiatric consultation, help with debt adjustment, family budget planning, vocational counseling, legal services, and, of course, case work for those requiring a multiplicity of services.[44]

All of these developments "teed up" the sector for the changes in government policy that were to occur during the Kennedy administration and the Great Society.

Kennedy, Johnson, and the 1960s

During his short three-year term, JFK's policy advisors implemented several new approaches that would have substantial impacts on the nonprofit sector. Among these were the ideas that (1) public welfare programs ought to be broadened to include counseling for all sorts of people; (2) casework shouldn't be limited only to the needy;[45] and (3) the revolutionary idea that services, as a preventive measure, should be available to those *likely* to wind up on public assistance. These ideas influenced much of what was to form President Johnson's War on Poverty.

The racial tensions attending the Civil Rights Movement also had an influence. As the face of poverty in America changed, the cultural competency of the voluntary sector had to change as well.

For many years, and certainly since the poverty of the Dust Bowl was captured by Dorothea Lange in her iconic photo of Florence Owens Thompson and her children,[46] the popular national conception of the poor was that they were predominantly white and mostly rural. While the portrait of American poverty had once been the urban slums typified by New York's notorious Five Points,[47] as the nation's overall wealth—*and* its population—shifted from the rural to the urban, it was increasingly the rural that came to be seen as left behind. Bucolic though many of its settings could be, opportunity increasingly lay in the cities' commerce and industry. This impression was only strengthened when JFK, after witnessing first-hand during the Democratic primary campaign of 1960 the impoverished conditions under which some West Virginians lived, initiated a number of legislative measures to address the state's economic and infrastructure problems upon becoming president.[48]

But this was relatively comfortable turf for the voluntary sector. Rural or urban, an impoverished white population could still be addressed with the traditional *If only you'd be more like us* approach, or some variation on that theme, that had been used not only in the urban slums among European immigrants for decades, but also among poorer white populations in the nation's heartland, the accent being on the adoption of middle-class values and mores as a sure way out of poverty.

Figure 5.4 Florence Owens Thompson. Library of Congress.

Meanwhile, poverty among the nation's rural African-Americans was virtually invisible to most of America, as was their daily plight under the Jim Crow laws of the Deep South, while its urban counterpart was mostly confined to neighborhoods underserved by local authorities and ignored and avoided by the majority white population.[49]

Additionally, the overwhelmingly white volunteers and professionals who comprised the sector were often largely clueless regarding black culture and how to address the issues of a people with whom they shared not even the faintest of cultural touchstones.

But all this began to change as the struggles of the nation's urban poor, a largely minority population, began to take center stage in the country's consciousness with the advent of the Civil Rights Movement.

Amid the turbulence of that era, the sector came to realize that it needed an entirely different approach to address the needs of the minority urban poor. For one thing, it turned out that the "needy" of America's inner cities wanted *tangible services*, not just the counseling that had largely sustained the sector through the Truman and Eisenhower years.[50]

By 1958, a significant number of agencies were reporting that they were "desperately struggling for funds." Fund-raising became more important than ever.[51] At the same time, the portion of the sector not directly involved in human services wasn't faring much better. A 1961 Harvard University study looked at fifty-six national voluntary agencies. These included the American Heart Association, the National Tuberculosis League, and the predecessor to the March of Dimes. The study concluded that they were not only spending half of what they raised on fund-raising and administration, but were also "more invested in self-perpetuation than in serving public interests."[52]

Things weren't looking good for the sector. It had largely been the creation of the middle class. It had always, even when serving the poor, demonstrated middle-class sensibilities. The question was whether it should even be attempting to take part in the evolving effort to address not only poverty and the social needs of the disadvantaged, but civil rights, minority community identity, and an expanding concept of social justice.

Several important things, however, began to happen.

By the summer of 1960, JFK had begun using the term "New Frontier" to describe his vision for addressing the "unconquered problems of ignorance and prejudice, [the] unanswered questions of poverty and surplus." It was clear that he intended to bring a national focus to issues that had been largely masked by a combination of racism, segregation, and the nation's post-war prosperity during the Eisenhower years.

Those designing President Kennedy's initial policies regarding poverty turned to a mixture of voluntary sector and public welfare officials to help shape the administration's welfare reform plan in 1961.[53] This drew into the conversation institutions such as the storied Ford Foundation and other important voices of the sector. During his short tenure, JFK saw unemployment benefits expanded, aid made available to cities to improve housing, and a host of other efforts and initiatives launched. With a laudable record of having his legislation passed by Congress— 33 out of 53 bills in 1961, 40 out of 54 bills in 1962, and 35 of 58 in 1963—it was looking as though JFK's vision of a new focus for America was going to come to pass.

But then came Dallas in November.

Prideful and determined to be his own man, the country's new president, Lyndon Baines Johnson (LBJ), was, if anything, more firm than Kennedy in his determination to address poverty. . .which he, *unlike* Kennedy, had directly experienced growing up in Johnson City, Texas, and early in his career as a teacher, when he often had to pay for students' supplies out of his own pocket.

This said, Johnson was also a shrewd politician who was not above invoking the name and myth of this fallen predecessor to further his own aims.

In typical LBJ fashion, he'd continue the work Kennedy had begun, but would do him one better.

Johnson introduced the idea of a "Great Society" during two speeches in 1964, one at Ohio University and one at the University of Michigan. He referred to "a society where no child will go unfed, and no youngster will go unschooled," but he had much broader goals in mind. Johnson literally sought to end economic hardship and privation.

A centerpiece of this "War on Poverty" was the Economic Opportunity Act of 1964, which created an Office of Economic Opportunity to oversee a variety of anti-poverty programs.

To address the most immediate outward symptoms of neglect, federal funds were provided for slum clearance and rebuilding city areas. The overall approach, however, reflected a consensus among Johnson's team of experts that the best way to deal with poverty—*and* to dampen the expected backlash against anything that smacked of simple "hand-outs"—was to help the poor better themselves through education, job training, and community development.

Central to all of this was the idea of "community action," the participation of the poor in framing and administering the programs designed to help them.

Although it took time to find its footing, Johnson's War on Poverty ultimately found new vehicles—Community Action Agencies, and local, community-based organizations among them—for bringing services to their intended beneficiaries while creating a venue for the residents of the targeted areas to be involved in the effort.

The War on Poverty began with a $1 billion appropriation in 1964, spent another $2 billion in the following two years, and resulted in dozens of programs. Among them were the Job Corps, whose purpose was to help disadvantaged youth develop marketable skills, and the Neighborhood Youth Corps, which gave poor urban youths work experience and encouraged them to stay in school. The Volunteers in Service to America program was envisioned as a domestic version of the Peace Corps, and placed volunteers—many of whom turned out to be white and relatively affluent, not much different from the Friendly Visitors of eighty years earlier—with community-based agencies to work with poorer local residents in a variety of ways. Meanwhile, funds provided through the Economic Opportunity Act were used to create avenues through which young people from poor homes could receive job training and higher education.

Yet even as this was happening, still other avenues of potential funding emerged, as when the creation of the National Endowment for the Arts and the National Endowment for the Humanities in 1965 opened up the possibility of government support to even more cause areas and organizations.[54]

This was a rapidly evolving new world, but one for which the American nonprofit arena was largely unprepared for a number of reasons.

One such reason was that the sector, ever since being largely shut out of the government's anti-poverty efforts by Harry Hopkins during the Depression, had focused its fund-raising on private sources, average citizens, and workplace campaigns through Community Chest and similar appeals. While not entirely foreign to the sector, the idea of and expertise in seeking and landing government money had markedly atrophied. With the exception of its wartime efforts, the sector had also been focusing more and more on the private needs of its client base as opposed to public and broad "social" issues as were now being described and addressed in legislation.

Because they had been shifting their focus away from poverty and toward the provision of services such as casework, consultation with social workers, debt adjustment, and vocational counseling,[55] significant portions of the established voluntary sector were offering things that did not at first seem to fit the emerging needs and wants of the newly vocal urban poor and their allies in the government and politics,[56] or the developing strain of social activism that began unfolding within communities targeted by the War on Poverty. Organized and given a new voice by those from their own community, clients were demanding better treatment from welfare and housing agencies. They were coalescing around notions of welfare rights and protests. They were demanding better bus services in their neighborhoods and improved lighting and safety in public housing projects.

The established agencies were increasingly appearing old fashioned, stilted, and out of touch, and once again in danger of slipping into irrelevancy because as this was happening they were, for the most part, not oriented toward what the new realities demanded. The sector at the time, dominated in the popular mind by organizations such as the American Cancer Society, CARE, the Red Cross, and the March of Dimes among others, did not seem to have much to offer to the emerging voice representing the minority poor of the nation's long-neglected inner-city neighborhoods.

In a very real way, it was fortunate for them that it turned out that the new constellation of players in community development, job training, and other areas was not fully prepared for the demands of the task it had taken on. Things like casework, consultation with social workers, debt adjustment, and vocational counseling *were* needed after all, and many of the existing agencies found that at least some of their capabilities were in demand. For example, in Pittsburgh, the local Jewish Family & Children's Service organization began supplying the local Community Action Agency with casework services.[57]

In a complete reversal of the situation that existed under Harry Hopkins, with the 1967 amendment to the Social Security Act, the government opened wide the doors to public assistance agencies paying nonprofits to supply services. Millions of dollars began to flow to the old-line charities as they adapted to the new realities and offered assistance and guidance in many new areas. Organizations as varied as the Catholic Church and Planned Parenthood began to receive federal dollars.

In response to these emerging possibilities, many agencies began to reinvent themselves. Settlement houses, some founded at the turn of the century, began to actively seek out War on Poverty funds. Others were writing proposals for everything from conflict resolution to fatherhood training, and submitting them as new ways to assist the "rehabilitation" of welfare clients. Some organizations simply repackaged old offerings. "Family budgeting" was rechristened "household finances." Familiar services were expanded to include new target populations, like long-term patients recuperating at home. The goal of all these efforts was, to a good extent, to qualify for and access public funding.

At the same time, at least a degree of cultural competency was achieved when community-based efforts were successful in bringing into the fold local residents who could connect with those the programs were supposed to serve. These individuals became the front-line in many instances, buffering the cultural disconnect that existed between many agencies and the minority populations they hoped to serve.

But even as these events were taking place out in the open, there were four tectonic shifts that few recognized taking place beneath the surface.

The first was the slow-but-steady expansion of the sector itself. In 1940 there were only fifteen national and/or regional organizations doing fundraising on the local level. By 1960, there were over one hundred.[58]

There was also a growing competition among organizations. As older entities sought to expand, new groups meantime coalesced around causes ranging from minority rights and specific medical conditions to the environment and the needs of the aged. This put increased financial strain on the entire sector, particularly the financial pressure that many agencies experienced as they tried to maintain salary levels required to safeguard the professionalism they had so long sought to establish within the field. This moved many groups to look to foundation grants, user fees, *and* government funding.

The phenomenon of mission creep also began. Finding creative ways to make it seem as though a government funded service was actually in keeping with their traditional mandate, many organizations began "chasing the money" and applying for the opportunity to provide services never before on their agenda. Even the YMCA began to offer job counseling services.

The flavor of the time was also evident in a fourth development, the birth of a new political constituency of nonprofit contracting agencies themselves. They were committed to the continuation of funding for the services they were providing. Many moved their headquarters to Washington, DC, or at minimum opened an office there. They did so, ostensibly, to "strengthen contacts with federal policy makers." Yet it wasn't long before many in the sector were aggressively promoting the purchase-of-services model to lawmakers.[59] The sector now found itself in a position that went far beyond the consultative and even partner roles it had played for decades. No longer external to "the system," it was now *part* of the system, and was becoming almost irreversibly dependent upon public funding to support an ever-expanding array of efforts. Those efforts, meanwhile, had become so popular with the public that by 1972, from a political standpoint, they could no longer be cut or even seriously curtailed.

While the nation's nonprofits certainly faced challenges through the '40s, '50s, and '60s, their long-standing place in America appeared irrevocable by the close of the 1970s. What has happened since then has all but made that a certainty.

Notes

1 Hansan, J.E. "Origins of the State and Federal Public Welfare Programs." Social Welfare History Project. Virginia Commonwealth University. 2011. http://socialwelfare.library.vcu.edu/public-welfare/origins-of-the-state-federal-public-welfare-programs/. A great deal of the public sector's expenditures for those who could not care for themselves, however, went to those we would today consider to have a mental health condition. For an account of just some of New York State's expenses in this regard, see Stuhler, L. at Chapter 3, Note 33, this volume.
2 Founded 1910.
3 Begun in 1895 with the founding of the Boston Federation.
4 The idea of cooperative fund-raising by local charities in the U.S. began in the late 1800s. One of the first such efforts occurred in New York City, when a committee of citizens organized "Hospital Sunday" on December 28, 1879, in support of ten local hospitals. A little over $25,000—$588,392 in today's dollars—was collected. (See Seeley et al. p. 17.) The forerunner of Community Chest—itself the forerunner of United Way—was organized in Denver in 1887, when four individuals—two ministers, a priest, and a rabbi—brought together a federation of twenty-three local charitable agencies for a common fundraising effort. That first campaign raised $20,000, which is $497,870 in today's dollars.

The concept received a further boost in 1900 when the Committee on Benevolent Associations of the Cleveland Chamber of Commerce assumed the responsibility of endorsing a number of charities seeking funds in the city. The chamber thereafter began an educational program to inform potential contributors of the minimum standards they ought to seek in a charity. The result of this was a set of standards and sanctions which was subsequently adopted in a number of municipalities (Seeley et al. p. 18). Also revolutionary was the chamber's system of allotting funds based upon demonstrated need, rather than the traditional "as much money as possible." (See *The Social Year Book*. [Cleveland, OH: Cleveland Federation for Charity and Philanthropy, 1913] at the Social Welfare History Project. Virginia Commonwealth University Libraries. http://socialwelfare.library.vcu.edu/organizations/state-institutions/cleveland-federation-for-charity-and-philanthropy-1913/.)

Thirteen years later, almost all welfare organizations in Cleveland joined to form the Federation of Charities and Philanthropy, regarded as the nation's first true Community Chest. The concept developed quickly and the numbers increased from 40 nationwide in 1919 to about 350 in 1929, and grew beyond

1,000 by 1948. See Pruszewicz, A. and Vander Hulst, A. "Key Dates and Events in American Philanthropic History 1815 to Present." Learning to Give. https://www.learningtogive.org/resources/key-dates-and-events-american-philanthropic-history-1815-present.

5 In 1914, America's standing army was 128,000 strong, while Germany's boasted 840,000, Austria–Hungary's stood at 415,000, the Ottoman Empire's at 210,000, France's at 823,000, Great Britain's at 247,000, Italy's at 290,000, and that of the Russian Empire a staggering 1.4 million.

6 Several members of American military general staff were issuing warnings, as early as 1915, that if war came the country's defenses were woefully inadequate. See "U.S. Defenses Weak, Capt. Hanna Holds; Former Member of General Staff Says Invasion Would Be Easy in Case of War." *New York Times*. April 9, 1915.

7 Blanchard, R. Capt. USN, Ret. "The History of the YMCA in World War I." Great War Society. Doughboy Center. www.worldwar1.com/dbc/ymca.htm.

8 Such efforts continued during the Spanish–American War when YMCA staff and volunteers were dispatched to Cuba, Puerto Rico, and the Philippines. In fact, YMCA supplies, including medicine and office materials, often reached Cuba before the army's own supplies, testimony to this found in early dispatches from Teddy Roosevelt's Rough Riders, which were written on YMCA stationery. See Blanchard. Op. cit.

9 CRB was a unique organization. Although private, it had its own flag, negotiated "treaties" with the warring European powers, and its leaders met regularly with diplomats and cabinet ministers in several countries. (Nash, G.H. "Herbert Hoover and Belgian Relief in World War I." *Prologue Magazine*. Spring 1989, Vol. 21, No. 1. https://www.archives.gov/publications/prologue/1989/spring/hoover-belgium.html).

10 "To Organize State for Belgian Relief; Dr. John H. Finley Will Be Chairman of Committee, Aided by Mrs. Glynn. Need in France Grows. Campaign for Funds for Belgians and New York's Unemployed Begins Monday." *New York Times*. April 10, 1915.

11 Warner, M. and O'Gan, P. "Americans Who Joined the World War Before Their Country Did." O Say Can You See: Stories from the National Museum of American History. April 5, 2016. http://americanhistory.si.edu/blog/americans-who-joined-world-war-their-country-did.

12 Gen. Kurt von Pfuel, chairman of the central committee of the German Red Cross, wrote a letter to the U.S. State Department expressing his nation's gratitude for the millions of dollars being sent by Americans and American organizations in support of German relief efforts. See "German Thanks to America; Red Cross Acknowledges Generous Gifts from This Country." *New York Times*. April 9, 1915. p. 4, col. 3.

13 As much as $750,000—about $17.5 million in today's dollars—was expected to be raised from a series of charity events held for the "widows and orphans of German, Austrian, Hungarian, and their allied soldiers" at Madison Square Garden. "$750,000 Is Expected at Teutonic Bazaar; Total Receipts of $300,000 up to Yesterday Announced by the Management." *New York Times*. March 14, 1916. p. 9, col. 3.

14 Some statistics covering the YMCA's activities during World War I: the organization had a paid staff of 26,000 men and women during the war years; it had 35,000 volunteers attending to the spiritual and social needs of 4.8 million troops. Eight thousand troop trains were served by YMCA volunteers, and the organization mobilized 1,470 entertainers who were sent overseas to perform for troops. It operated 26 R&R leave centers in France that accommodated 1,944,300 American officers and men, 4,000 "huts" and tents for recreation and religious services, and 1,500 canteens and post exchanges. It maintained 44 factories in Europe for the

production of cookies and candy for the troops. Humanitarian services were provided for more than 5 million prisoners of war in both Allied camps detaining enemy troops and Central Powers camps where Allied troops were imprisoned. The organization suffered 286 casualties, including 6 men and 2 women working under the YMCA banner killed in action. Three hundred nineteen citations and decorations were awarded to YMCA staff and volunteers, including the French Legion d'Honneur, the Order of the British Empire, the Distinguished Service Cross, and the Distinguished Service Medal.

15 American Red Cross. "A Brief History of the American Red Cross." www.redcross. org/local/florida/south-florida/about/history.

16 In honor of this, the Salvation Army still recognizes "National Doughnut Day" on the first Friday of June every year, using the occasion as a special fund-raising event.

17 Seeley. p. 21. Community Chest continued its growth over the next decade, expanding from 39 local Chests in 1919, to 353 ten years later.

18 $23.6 billion in today's money.

19 Over $31.865 billion in 2017 dollars.

20 Seeley. p. 21.

21 But particularly on the East Coast and industrial Midwest.

22 Morris. p. xxxi.

23 Bremner. (1960) p. 145.

24 Ibid.

25 In a sign of things to come, U.S. Steel, General Motors, Ford, and many other large industrial companies announced a 10% wage reduction just as one of the biggest voluntary donation campaigns was about to begin in 1931.

26 It was also true that many of these campaigns had no effect on extremely distressed rural areas, mining villages, and mill towns where there were no public charities and only the most rudimentary provisions for poor relief. If a mining company, for example, decided to close a mine, it simply walked away, at best leaving a few guards to watch over property and equipment. The former employees were left to their own devices.

27 Mohl, J. "The Effect of State Intervention in the Nonprofit Sector: The Case of the New Deal." *Nonprofit and Voluntary Sector Quarterly.* Vol. 25, No. 4. (December 1996) p. 529.

28 As recounted earlier, this practice went back to the early 1800s. To use only New York as an example, in 1875, the state passed the Act to Authorize the Various Associations and Societies Incorporated Under the Laws of the State of New York, For the Purposes of Taking Care of and Protecting Destitute Infant Minor Children, To Bind Out by Indenture Destitute Children Who Are in Their Care and Keeping (Chapter 522, Laws of 1875). In 1889 an act "Incorporating the 'Salvation Army in the United States,' to establish and maintain, subject to the written approval of the State Board of Charities, when established in New York State, hospitals for the sick and convalescent, and homes for children, the aged and fallen women." Appropriations for these efforts followed. Stuhler. Op. cit.

29 Morris. p. 25.

30 Mohl. p. 530.

31 *Except* the Red Cross.

32 Bremner. (1960) pp. 166–167.

33 America's Jews, however, gave unstintingly to the Joint Distribution Committee's efforts to save Europe's persecuted Jewish population. Bremner. (1960) p. 166.

34 The *Saturday Evening Post* serialized Mussolini's autobiography in 1928. Acknowledging that the new "Fascisti movement" was a bit "rough in its methods," papers

ranging from the *New York Tribune* and the *Cleveland Plain Dealer* to the *Chicago Tribune* credited it with saving Italy from the far left and revitalizing its economy. From their perspective, the post-World-War-I surge of anti-capitalism in Europe was a vastly worse threat than fascism.

Regarding Hitler, while some papers viewed him as a buffoon—*Newsweek* called him a "nonsensical screecher whose appearance suggests Charlie Chaplin"—many American press outlets assumed and offered the opinion that he would either be outplayed by more traditional politicians or that he would have to become more moderate. See Broich, J. "How Journalists Covered the Rise of Mussolini and Hitler." *Smithsonian.com*. December 13, 2016. www.smithsonianmag.com/history/how-journalists-covered-rise-mussolini-hitler-180961407/#zDQTSif7vdqIP UiY.99. This blindness to what they were seeing recalls the coverage many in the American press, particularly Walter Duranty and Louis Fischer, gave to Soviet dictator Josef Stalin throughout the '30s.

35   This situation was further complicated by not only divisions among America's sizable population of German and Italian origins, but also the nation's—in fact, *North America's*—own partisans of fascism.

There were Germans who lauded Hitler; there were those who thought him a menace. There were Italians who thought Mussolini a hero (he got the trains running on time), and those who thought him a dangerous buffoon.

Additionally, and largely spurred by the effects of the Depression and the feeling that the rich had brought the worldwide misery down on suffering common people, fascism had a certain allure in this hemisphere just as it did in Europe. In Canada, the Winnipeg-based Canadian Union of Fascists was modelled on the British Union of Fascists. In Québec, the Parti National Social Chrétien, later renamed the Canadian National Socialist Unity Party, was inspired by Nazism. In Mexico, the National Synarchist Union, the Red Shirts and the Gold Shirts, all bore the hallmarks of fascism.

In the U.S., the paramilitary Black Legion, a violent offshoot of the Ku Klux Klan, sought a revolution to establish fascism in the U.S. The Silver Legion of America, the German American Bund, the Friends of New Germany, and the Free Society of Teutonia all looked to Nazism for their inspiration. Father Charles Coughlin, who publicly endorsed fascism, was a firebrand bigot radio personality with a vast audience. Other well-known fascists included the publisher Seward Collins, the broadcaster Robert Henry Best, the inventor Joe McWilliams, and the writer Ezra Pound. The nationwide newspapers of William Randolph Hurst, at this point a fierce opponent of FDR, ran columns without rebuttal by Nazi leader Hermann Göring and Hitler himself, as well as Mussolini and other dictators in Europe and Latin America. Aviation hero Charles Lindbergh, was allied with an isolationist group with Nazi sympathies called America First. Henry Ford, a rabid anti-Semite, continued to do business with Nazi Germany, including the manufacture for Germany of war material, right up until the U.S. and Germany were at war. Indeed, his German operation, *Ford-Werke*, in 1940 requisitioned and received from German officials between one hundred and two hundred French prisoners of war to work as slave laborers, a number which grew as the war expanded.

With a variety of informing ideologies, American fascism was largely nativist, anti-black, anti-Semitic, anti-Roosevelt, against the New Deal, and effectively opposed to liberal democracy itself. An opposition to Marxism also motivated many varieties of American fascists, including those of the All-Russian Fascist Party, who, along with their German-based compatriots in the Russian National Socialist Movement, looked to fascism to reverse the Bolshevik's ascendency in Russia. See Kleen, M. "The Enigma of American Fascism in the 1930s." *Radix Journal*. March 6, 2011.

www.radixjournal.com/altright-archive/altright-archive/main/the-magazine/
the-enigma-of-american-fascism-in-the-1930s; Nasaw, D. *The Chief.* [New York:
Houghton Mifflin Harcourt, 2001] pp. 470–477; Wallace, M. *The American Axis: Henry
Ford, Charles Lindbergh, and the Rise of the Third Reich.* [New York: St. Martin's Press,
2003]; Stephan, J.J. *The Russian Fascists: Tragedy and Farce in Exile 1925–1945.* [New
York: Harper Row, 1978] *passim.*

36 The "Bonus Army" was a group of veterans, their families, and allies who descended
upon Washington in the summer of 1932 to demand cash payments for their World
War I service certificates. Many of the war veterans had been out of work since the
beginning of the Depression. The World War Adjusted Compensation Act of 1924
had awarded them bonuses in the form of certificates they could not redeem until
1945. Each service certificate, issued to a qualified veteran soldier, bore a face value
equal to the soldier's promised payment plus compound interest.

On July 28, U.S. Attorney General William D. Mitchell ordered the veterans
removed from all government property. Washington police met with resistance,
shots were fired and two veterans were wounded and later died. President Herbert
Hoover then ordered the army to clear the veterans' campsite. Army Chief of Staff
General Douglas MacArthur oversaw the infantry and cavalry supported by six
tanks. The Bonus Army marchers with their wives and children were driven out, and
their shelters and belongings burned.

Although Hoover bore most of the blame, the army did not go unscathed.

37 Bremner. (1960) p. 168.
38 Ibid.
39 Ibid. pp. 168–169.
40 Washington, S.L. "The History and Function of Social Work in the Military Service."
(1957). ETD Collection for Atlanta University Center, Robert W. Woodruff Library.
Paper 1201, pp. 14–21. http://digitalcommons.auctr.edu/cgi/viewcontent.cgi?artic
le=2588&context=dissertations
41 Bremner. (1960) p. 154.
42 Heilman, J. Ed. *The Golden Age of Advertising: The 50s.* [New York: Barnes & Noble
Publishing, 2006] p. 4.
43 Morris. pp. 47–50.
44 Morris. p. 123.
45 Morris. p. 88.
46 Although this famous image is popularly associated with the Dust Bowl, in fact it
was taken in 1936 in Nipomo, San Luis Obispo County, California. Thompson and
her first husband, Cleo Leroy Owens, had migrated from Oklahoma in 1925 to flee
the Dust Bowl, and settled in Oroville, CA. Urseny, L. "'Migrant Mother': Iconic
Woman in Dust Bowl Photo Lived in Oroville." *Oroville Mercury Register.* November
16, 2012. www.orovillemr.com/article/ZZ/20121116/NEWS/121117612.
47 Bremner. (1967) pp. 3–10.
48 Ponton, A.W. "John F. Kennedy and West Virginia, 1960–1963," MA thesis, Marshall
University, 2004. Theses, Dissertations and Capstones. Paper 789, pp. 6–7. http://
mds.marshall.edu/cgi/viewcontent.cgi?article=1793&context=etd. This image of
poverty in America was given an added boost when *LIFE Magazine*, at the time
arguably the most influential weekly magazine in the country, ran a series of shots
capturing the poverty of rural Appalachia. See Cosgrove, B. "War on Poverty:
Portraits from an Appalachian Battleground, 1964." *TIME Magazine.* January 7,
2014. http://time.com/3878609/war-on-poverty-appalachia-portraits-1964/.
49 In 1962, social critic Michael Harrington wrote that in spite of the suburban patina
of prosperity, the U.S. was actually a land of between 40 million and 50 million

relatively invisible poor people: the unskilled workers, the migrant farm workers, minorities, people for whom work was sporadic, demeaning, and demoralizing. Harrington, M. *The Other America*. [Baltimore, MD: Penguin, 1971] pp. 1–2, 17.

50 Morris. p. 167.

51 In 1950, only about 26% of Family Services Association of America member organization were charging clients even a modest 2% fee. By 1963 that number had risen to 96%. Moreover, when it was demonstrated that some nonprofits, like the YMCA, could charge fees and thrive, it placed even more pressure on those who could find a way to charge to do so.

52 Hamlin, R. *Voluntary Health and Welfare Agencies in the United States: An Exploratory Study*. [New York: Schoolmasters' Press, 1961] as cited in Morris. p. 154.

53 Morris. p. 159.

54 Hammack. (1998) p. 439. As just one example, the Public Broadcasting Act of 1967 chartered the Corporation for Public Broadcasting (CPB) as a private, nonprofit corporation. The law initiated the practice of federal aid to public broadcasting. The CPB initially collaborated with the pre-existing National Educational Television system, but in 1969 decided to start the Public Broadcasting Service (PBS). A public radio study commissioned by the CPB and the Ford Foundation, and conducted from 1968 to 1969, led to the establishment of National Public Radio, a nonprofit radio network, under the terms of the amended Public Broadcasting Act.

55 Ibid. p. 123.

56 It should be remembered that 1965 was the year that *The Negro Family: The Case for National Action*—also known as *The Moynihan Report*—was released. Moynihan argued that without access to jobs and the means to contribute meaningful support to a family, black men would become systematically alienated from their roles as husbands and fathers, which would cause rates of divorce, child abandonment, and out-of-wedlock births to skyrocket in the black community (a trend that had already begun by the mid-1960s), leading to vast increases in the numbers of households headed by females, and the higher rates of poverty, low educational outcomes, and inflated rates of child abuse that are associated with them. Moynihan made an argument for programs for jobs, vocational training, and educational programs for the black community.

57 Ibid. p. 182.

58 The total number of registered public charities in the U.S. was in the tens of thousands in the 1960s. By 1977, that number had grown to 276,000. In 1992, it was 546,000. In 1998, there were 734,000. The number today is 1.6 million. See Weitzman, M. et al. *Nonprofit Almanac and Desk Reference*. 2002. p. 8., and Urban Institute. "Highlights." *Nonprofit Almanac*. 2012. www.urban.org/center/cnp/almanac/.

59 Morris. p. 202.

Part IV

6   The growth of the nonprofit sector

The Johnson administration, and with it the specific experiment that was the Great Society, came to an end in 1969. Through all of the separate events that followed, there have been a number of trends that have moved inexorably ahead no matter what else might have been going on. These shifts in the bedrock upon which the nonprofit arena is built will, in the long run, have more impact upon how the sector operates, is perceived, and fares over the next decade or so than all the other events combined. These thematic developments are worth examining in some detail.

Of all the changes that have taken place within and around the American nonprofit community in the last forty-something years, none has had the profound impact that the explosive growth of the sector has had.

No one knows for sure, according to Lester Salamon, just how many nonprofit organizations exist in the U.S., since large proportions of the sector are made up of extremely small organizations, and data available on the sector overall are notoriously incomplete.[1] For a variety of reasons, the best we have is some educated guesswork based upon the few numbers we do know.

The U.S. Government Accountability Office (GAO) reported that in 2012 there were an estimated 2.3 *million* nonprofit organizations operating in the U.S. As of 2011, 1.63 million had been recognized as tax-exempt.[2] Of these, an estimated 1.08 million are 501(c)(3) corporations, the "charities" with which most of us are familiar. Of these, however, only 274,000 actually filed a Form 990 with the Internal Revenue Service (IRS), meaning that we really know little or nothing about three-quarters of those the government *thinks* are out there. What we do know, however, is that over 90% of the nonprofit organizations currently in existence were created since 1950,[3] and every year there are more than there were before. By one estimate, in 1940 there were only 12,500 charitable tax-exempt organizations registered with the IRS.[4] By 1980, there were 320,000.[5] Today there are over a million.

Figure 6.1[6] illustrates the dramatic growth in all American nonprofits since 1940. Moreover, the annual rate of that growth has been increasing.

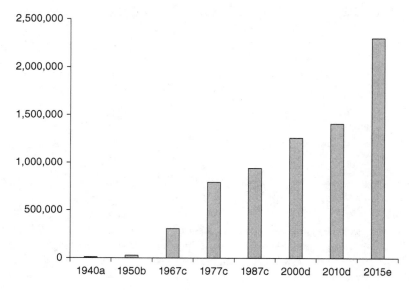

Figure 6.1 Estimated growth in nonprofit sector.

In the early post-World-War-II period, there were about ten thousand new nonprofits per year. In the '60s, the era of the Great Society and marked civil activism, the rate doubled to approximately twenty thousand new entities per year. Between 1977 and 1991, the number of charities registered with the IRS increased 115%. By comparison, new for-profit businesses increased only 78%. Growth was particularly robust among arts and cultural, social service, and health organizations, each of which grew at a rate twice that of the national economy.[7]

Beginning in 1991, however, the rate of increase grew even more sharply. Between 1977 and 1987, fifteen thousand new nonprofits entered the market each year. During the span between 1987 and 1997 that number grew to twenty-seven thousand per year.[8] By 2000 almost fifty thousand new nonprofits were being formed each year.[9]

Moreover, they are increasingly specialized to an amazing degree, comprising an astonishing array of groups, causes, and initiatives.

The single largest set of them operate in the Human Services category, with the picture essentially rounded out by Education; Arts, Culture and Humanities; Public and Social Benefit; Health; "Religion-Related"; and the Environment and Animals.[10] Yet even these classifications only present the view from thirty thousand feet, because the IRS recognizes four hundred different "cause areas," those specific activities or focuses within which organizations may operate and to which people can contribute their tax-deductible support.[11]

One of the remarkable characteristics of this growing diversity in the causes around which charities are being formed is that even today, in the modern world of the 21st century, strains of the old Puritan impulse to make the world better can still be found in the purposes for which many new charities exist.

While Mothers Against Drunk Driving, founded in 1980, seeks to stop drunk driving, support those affected by drunk driving, prevent underage drinking, and works for stricter impaired-driving policies, it has also been part of a larger battle, working to change deep-seated cultural attitudes toward not only drunk driving, but also the abuse of alcohol overall. It must be recalled that less than twenty years before the organization's founding, not only were popular television shows regularly depicting overindulging in alcohol as normal American behavior,[12] but living-room bars were depicted as being a necessity in any upscale home, and several popular performers—Dean Martin and Foster Brooks come to mind as well-known examples—made the theme of constant inebriation part of their act.

In its larger crusade against irresponsible drinking and alcohol abuse, Mothers Against Drunk Driving is literally seeking to change a very strong American social norm,[13] one which saw the abuse of alcohol (although not alcoholism itself) as a generally accepted behavior. In this effort, the sector's DNA of social, behavioral, and attitudinal reform is unmistakable.

Similarly, organizations such as the National Coalition Against Domestic Violence, the Earth Resource Foundation's Campaign Against the Plastic Plague—which seeks to convince Americans to turn away from plastic bags and packaging—and the Brady Campaign to Prevent Gun Violence are all working to change not only public laws, but also private behaviors and attitudes. Here again, the reformist flavor that has inspired much of the sector's history is readily apparent.

Beyond the sector's growth and broadening diversity, also surprising to some is the sector's combined economic power. In 2013, by way of illustration, it is estimated that almost **$2 trillion** flowed into the sector.[14] That same year, the nation's charities reported that they spent $1.63 trillion—money they put back into the economy in one way or another—and that they had over **$3 trillion** in assets.[15] Nonprofits provided 5.4% of the nation's entire Gross Domestic Product (GDP) in 2012,[16] and slightly less, 5.3%, in 2014.[17] That's about **$887.3 billion**.

In 2014, nonprofits also provided 11.4 million jobs, accounting for 10.3% of the country's private-sector workforce, according to the Bureau of Labor Statistics.[18]

Interestingly, at a time when so many other sectors of the economy struggled, between 2000 and 2010, employment in the nonprofit sector grew an estimated 18%, a rate faster than the overall U.S. economy.[19] Moreover, the nonprofit sector continued to add jobs throughout the Recession and into the recovery,[20] with employees of nonprofit organizations accounting for 9.2% of wages paid in the U.S., a total of $587 billion in wages and benefits in 2010.[21]

This growth, moreover, shows little sign of abating. In fact, according to one report, from 2001 to 2011, the number of nonprofits in the U.S. grew 25% while the number of for-profit businesses rose by 0.5%. Over that period, nonprofits also outpaced businesses in their percentage growth in hiring, wages, and contribution to the GDP.[22]

In New York City alone it was reported that the nonprofit sector was the largest private employer across the five boroughs in 2009, employing some 500,000 workers—just over 15% of the total private-sector workforce—and accounting for a combined payroll of over $20 billion.

Perhaps more importantly, the sector added more than fifty thousand jobs between 2000 and 2007 while the rest of the city's private economy lost jobs.[23] By April of 2012, New York's private nonprofit sector employed more than 1.25 *million* workers, accounting for more than 18% of all private-sector jobs in the state.[24] Wages in the sector grew to more than $57 billion.[25]

But New York has not been the only beneficiary of the nonprofit sector's economic power. Rhode Island's number of nonprofit jobs as a proportion of total statewide private employment tops New York's 18%. Meanwhile California boasted 900,800 nonprofit positions, Pennsylvania had 727,200 while Illinois accounted for 497,300 and Ohio reported 482,500.[26]

Colorado provides a good example of the growing power of the sector. It was reported in 2008 that the combination of the paid and full-time volunteer workforce made the state's nonprofit sector the third largest industry in the state in terms of employment. The paid workforce of Colorado nonprofits alone represented 5.6% of the total Colorado workforce (or one out of every eighteen workers), more than the state's banking and insurance industry.

Colorado's charitable nonprofit sector generated $13.1 billion in revenues, spent over $11.9 billion, including over $4.2 billion in wages and compensation, held nearly $23 billion in assets, and accounted for more than 5% of the state's gross state product. During the timeframe examined, the state's nonprofit sector accounted for a greater share of Colorado's gross state product than the transportation, utilities, and agriculture industries combined. Moreover, through the $4.2 billion in wages and compensation that they paid, Colorado's nonprofits generated at least $240 million of sales and income tax revenues for Colorado governments during that period.[27]

There is evidence, moreover, that the economic impact of the sector is moving beyond the larger cities and is increasingly being felt in the suburbs and in rural areas as well.[28] A report by the Johns Hopkins Center for Civil Society, by way of illustration, found that the nonprofit sector in New York's suburban Westchester County employed 53,987 paid workers as of the first quarter of 2013, making it the county's largest industry, employing more people than the construction, finance, and wholesale trade industries combined. This translates to 13.6% of the county's total workforce, putting Westchester well above the national average of 8.4%.[29]

But this growth in the size, diversity, and economic power of the nonprofit community has not happened in a vacuum. Rather, it has been a direct outgrowth of the sector's ever-closer partnership with the government. And that is the second most important trend of the last few decades.

The government/nonprofit partnership

In an ever-widening range of fields, from health care and social services to culture and community development, nonprofit organizations have been the beneficiaries of government support for providing a growing array of services.

With roots in the '50s era orientation which saw them move away from the direct relief that had been their historical calling card and gravitate instead toward the provision of specific services, nonprofits today provide a broad palate of undertakings, everything from aged care to scientific research, that the American public wants but is reluctant to have the government directly provide.[30] In a uniquely American formulation, the government provides the resources while the nonprofit sector provides the knowledge and manpower. More than any other single factor, this government/nonprofit partnership is responsible for the growth of the sector as we currently know it.[31]

What we have today is a nonprofit sector larger and more varied than any of its counterparts anywhere else on the globe, but one that is inexorably tied to the government, a "uniquely American, superficially anti-statist form of big government," whereby the government has expanded its mission but out-sourced its administration.[32]

By way of illustration, one study found that government money paid to nonprofits accounted for 52% of day care costs, 64% of the cost of drug abuse clinics, 59% of legal aid, 65% of the cost of mental health services, and 51% of women's crisis centers.[33] Massachusetts recognizes over two hundred distinct types of social services in the purchase-of-services system it uses with its non-profits. In New York City, some city agencies do not deliver services at all, relying entirely upon nonprofits to discharge their responsibilities.[34]

Moreover, a certain favoritism began to creep into the system, whereby the same agencies received government funding year after year, after year. By way of just one example, one study found that 90% of New York City's funding for Aid to Families with Dependent Children went to only 20% of the city's eligible agencies.

The sector's reliance on public funding was nowhere more evident than in the impact of the 2007–2009 Great Recession on the nonprofit community.

Governmental revenues at all levels suffer during economic downturns as the engine providing those dollars sputters, slows down, and, in some cases, fails altogether. Due to the Recession, by the fourth quarter of 2008, the American GDP had dropped approximately 7%.[35] Some 900,000 jobs were lost. The impact was such that even at the close of 2016, the nation's GDP was still 1.5% lower than what the economy was capable of producing.[36]

This clearly had an impact on the government as tax revenue, so much of it dependent upon the financial exchanges of a healthy economy, dropped. In fact, as bad as the Recession's impact on the overall national job market was, some of the most drastic effects were on local, state, and federal pay-rolls.[37] In this environment, it was not surprising that the government at all levels cut funding for non-essential programs. . .the very efforts mostly carried out by the nonprofit community. By just one estimate, state government funding to the sector dropped 5% in 2009 and 4% in 2010. As of 2011, state governments owed nonprofits over $15 billion in back payments.[38] While corporate donations, government grants, and investment all fell during the Recession, the decrease in government grants was reported as having the most significant impact on the nonprofit organizations.[39] In North Carolina alone, state government cuts were estimated to have impacted 70% of all nonprofit organizations.[40]

According to one study, as a result of this loss of funding in 2009, about 50% of nonprofit organizations reported instituting hiring freezes. While this number dropped, in 2010 and 2011, there was an increase in the percentage of organizations reporting that they were freezing salaries. Almost 52% reported doing so in 2011. That year also brought an increase in the number of organizations reporting that they were reducing service delivery as well as reducing programming. In all three years there was an increase in the percentage of organizations reporting that they were reducing employee benefits. The degree to which the American nonprofit arena has become dependent upon government funding was never so apparent.

The closeness of the government/nonprofit relationship, however, the dependency of much of the sector upon government funding, raised a number of issues with which the sector has not come to terms.

The first, as was just recounted, is that if and when government revenues fall the nonprofit arena suffers. A second issue came into sharp focus several years ago when controversies arose over public funding for the Corporation for Public Broadcasting because of its alleged liberal bias, and for the National Endowment for the Arts and the National Endowment for the Humanities[41] over the kinds of art, research, and other projects they were supporting. The funding became politicized, and the ensuing debates saw allegations of censorship being hurled at those expressing outrage that public funding was going to what they claimed were offensive purposes. As the debate over funding for Planned Parenthood sparked during the 2016 presidential campaign illustrated, at the dawn of the Trump era, with conservative forces ascendant in Congress and controlling thirty-three of ninety-nine state legislative chambers and thirty-three of fifty governorships, it has to be wondered the degree to which other funding streams upon which American nonprofits are dependent might also fall victim to politics.

This closeness between the government and the nation's nonprofit community has also called into question the issue of exactly *whose* voice nonprofits are representing on a variety of political and social issues, whose interests they are actually fighting for in Washington, the state capitals, and city halls around the country. Are they speaking on behalf of what is best for the nation, on behalf of those in need. . .or in their own self-interest as organizations that absolutely need public funding to continue existing?[42] In whose interests are they really speaking, some ask, when they advocate for taxpayer-funded programs from which they themselves benefit?

More to the point, the theme of nonprofits as an "independent sector," one that acts to protect society from the threat of a vast, bureaucratic, and stifling government complex, is one these organizations have been employing since they first stood up against cruel punishments for lawbreakers, against slavery, against the railroads and trusts, against child labor, and against a host of other social ills over the course of the last 175 years. This idea, in fact, has been a consistent basis for the sector's claim to legitimacy. But the question is increasingly asked how the sector can "protect" society from a government from which it draws an overwhelming proportion of its financial support.[43]

Also called into question has been the very nature of these organizations.

Looking at the broad array of entities that currently enjoy not only tax exemption, but that are also eligible for tax-deductible donations—everything from rescue missions and crisis centers to bird sanctuaries and opera companies—there are many people who argue that these are not "charities" at all, and that giving to them doesn't constitute *charity* in any real sense because it does not go toward benefiting the poor.[44] With an eye, perhaps, to the days before organized benevolence in the U.S. took on a wholesale mission of improving society, these critics do not believe that those organizations that are not engaged in primarily and directly serving the poor in some way should be tax-exempt, *or* that donations to them should be tax deductible, arguing that there is something inherently wrong with treating donations to shelters for homeless people and horse rescue ranches as somehow the same.[45] They're saying, in essence, that we need to redefine our national notion of "charity," bringing it back more closely to what it originally was, and that we need to stop rewarding certain nonprofits for their role in denying resources to the people who need them the most.

At least one outgrowth of this perspective has been a challenge to the tax-exempt status of some nonprofits.

In addition to the argument just outlined, a case is made that certain entities now enjoying nonprofit status (specifically opera houses, museums, and prestigious universities) should not be tax-exempt because they are essentially private preserves of the rich.[46]

Some argue further that venues that charge an entrance fee (such as museums and zoos) are charging the public twice. They charge us once, the thinking goes, through the extra taxes we must pay to make up for what they don't pay (since they are tax-exempt), and once more at admission. These critics also maintain that this "double jeopardy" falls hardest upon those who can least afford it.[47]

Other observers suggest that tax exemptions should exist only for nonprofit organizations whose services the government would have to directly supply in their absence.[48]

Finally, there are those who find the present arrangement between the taxpayers and nonprofits to be coercive and to violate free speech. Conservatives complain that they must foot the bill for taxes that groups such as Planned Parenthood don't pay, while liberals share this concern regarding groups like the National Rifle Association.[49]

This thinking also resonates with those who believe that churches and houses of worship should not be tax-exempt.

The practice of sparing religious institutions the burden of taxation, however, is not an American invention. There's evidence, in fact, that it goes back to ancient times.[50] Moreover, it has always been controversial. Presidents Madison and Grant, for example, both opposed the idea.[51] This opposition continues today. There are those who object to it on First Amendment grounds. They contend that it represents indirect government support for religion.[52] At the other end of the belief spectrum are those who think they hold the "one true faith." They argue that by providing a religious tax exemption for all religious entities of all faiths, they're being forced to support what they consider false doctrines.[53]

The impact of tax exemptions on localities is also garnering increased attention. The argument is being made that sizable tracts of property are artificially kept off the local tax rolls because they're owned by nonprofit entities. In some cases these charities are sitting on endowments of billions of dollars. At the same time, their local communities are struggling and could use the tax money represented by the assessments on these facilities. As one observer put it:

> If it's important to the people of Fifth Avenue to have a synagogue like Temple Emanu-El or an Episcopal church like St. Thomas in their midst, they should pay full freight for it.[54] They can afford to, more than the millions of poorer New Yorkers whose tax bills the synagogue and church exemptions are currently inflating.[55]

As a result, some jurisdictions are rethinking the traditional tax exemption of certain types of nonprofits, while other observers are calling for doing away with tax exemptions for *all* nonprofits.

It is difficult to judge where this will end.

The explosion in the number of nonprofits means that a record number are seeking exemptions from property taxes, sales taxes, and numerous other levies. Individually, these exemptions aren't always significant, but cumulatively they are substantial. The Congressional Budget Office estimates that charitable deductions represent $39 billion.[56] Another study, looking only at the value of all religious tax exemptions, arrived at a figure of $71 billion.[57] Additionally, the study found that the states bypass an estimated $26.2 billion per year by not requiring religious institutions to pay property taxes. The capital gains tax exemptions for religious institutions may be as much as $41 million a year, and U.S. clergy may claim as much as $1.2 billion in tax exemptions annually via the parsonage allowance.[58] Add to this other costs that nonprofits of all kinds avoid, everything from the sales taxes they don't collect on their fundraisers,[59] to the sales tax they don't pay on their annual banquet.[60] There is even a special nonprofit rate offered by the U.S. Postal Service.[61]

However, the nonprofit exemption from taxes is not as cut and dried as it seems. The use of special districts allows municipalities to charge for sewers, water, lighting, and fire protection in many localities. Nonprofits are *not* exempt from these. It is also the case that nonprofits pay business privilege taxes and property taxes on lots that they own but that aren't used for a direct charitable purpose. In addition, tax exemption does not absolve nonprofits from all the usual employment-related taxes. They also pay taxes on Unrelated Business Income. Finally, unless they file for a refund, nonprofits pay excise taxes on gasoline and telephone services.[62] So it is not accurate to think that nonprofits escape all public financial obligations. The notion of taxing non-profits will continue to face a number of formidable hurdles. . .

Additionally, and reflecting all these concerns, the explosive growth of the sector, the growing diversity of its constituent organizations, and its close relationship with the government have all added to the complexity of even discussing these entities. While under the tax law all 501(c)(3) organizations are considered "charitable," new ones are being created for new, novel purposes,[63] undertaking activities that seem to go well beyond any conventional conception of charitable, religious, or educational enterprise.[64]

Unfortunately, the only language and concepts available to describe the phenomenon have been terms like "charity" and "philanthropy," even though as far back as the '40s these words were already inadequate to describe tax-exempt organizations that were increasingly drawing their financial sustenance from government grants and contracts, and from the sale of services, rather than from traditional sources like donations and bequests.

The term "philanthropy," meanwhile, had been hijacked by the Carnegies, Rockefellers, and Fords, and the public began to overwhelmingly associate it with large-scale foundations. The term "voluntary sector" was not only out-of-date, but largely inaccurate in the face of the sector's increased professionalism and paid staffing. The name "nonprofit," although it came to be adopted around the world, was also inadequate because in the U.S. it encompassed a wide variety of organizations that existed primarily for the benefit of their members.

Over time, the terms "Third Sector," "Independent Sector," "Public Interest Sector," and "Social Sector" were tried on for size and discarded. Perhaps with an eye toward Europe, where the term "civil society organization" came into use after the fall of Communism, Joel Fleishman has suggested "civic sector,"[65] but he is probably too late to change the widespread (if not entirely accurate) use of the label "nonprofit sector," which may first have been used by the Filer Commission, formed in 1973 to study philanthropy and the role of the private sector in American society. In fact, it was probably only in the '70s that the idea of the nation's many varied nonprofit entities constituting a "sector" unto themselves first gelled.[66] Most people, however, still refer to this vast array of organizations as "charities," and use that term, as well as "nonprofit" and "tax-exempt" interchangeably, no matter that all three refer to distinct classifications. This has only served to further muddy the waters in regard to discussing or revamping our policies toward these groups.

But while the growth of the sector and its dependent relationship with the government have been the most far-reaching developments since the end of the Great Society, they have not been the only broad and influential trends that have impacted that realm. . .

Notes

1 Salamon, L. "The Resilient Sector: The State of Nonprofit America." *The State of Nonprofit America*. Ed. Lester M. Salamon. First Edition. [Washington, DC: Brookings Institution, 2002] p. 7.

2 United States Government Accountability Office. "Report to the Ranking Member, Committee on Homeland Security and Governmental Affairs, U.S. Senate: Tax-Exempt Organizations. Better Compliance Indicators and Data, and More Collaboration with State Regulators Would Strengthen Oversight of Charitable Organizations." GAO–15–164. December 2014. p. 8.

3 Hall. (2010) p. 3.

4 Along with 179,742 religious congregations (which did not have to apply for exemption) and sixty thousand non-charitable nonprofits (such as labor unions and fraternal associations) that enjoyed various tax privileges. See Hall. (2010) p. 18.

5 Ibid.

6 (a) Sealander. p. 363; (b) Hall. (2006) pp. 2–838; (c) Hall. (2006) p. 2–858; (d) Blackwood, A. et al. (2012) p. 2; (e) Government Accountability Office. p. 10.

7 Salamon. (2002) p. 30.

8 Ibid.

9 Jones, M. "The Growth of Nonprofits." *Bridgewater Review*. Vol. 25, Issue 1. (2006) p. 14. http://vc.bridgew.edu/br_rev/vol25/iss1/8. The rate of increase, however, may be dropping. In 2015 tax-exempt applications to the IRS dropped more than 13% after spiking in 2014. This said, the number of applications is still considerably more than 2013 and 2012, when 53,192 and 60,980 were filed, respectively. The drop in applications was across the board among all subsections of 501(c)(3) organizations. Applications for 501(c)(3) charitable organizations was down almost 8%, but as usual made up the bulk of application, about 85%. Other subsections, including 501(c)(4) social welfare organizations, 501(c)(6) business leagues, 501(c)(7) social and recreation clubs, and 501(c)(19) veterans' organization, also were down anywhere from 37 to 52%. See Hrywna, M. "Applications for Tax Exempt Status Drop Again." *Nonprofit Times*. April 7, 2016. www.thenonprofittimes.com/news-articles/applications-tax-exempt-status-drop/.

10 The number of organizations operating in these various arenas by the GAO are: Human Services 105,444; Education 47,928; Arts, Culture and Humanities 27,107, Public and Social Benefit 24,718, and Health 35,267; with the so-called "Religion-Related" category 15,628, and the Environment and Animals 11,763. The remaining organizations reported on by the GAO operate in the areas of International and Foreign Affairs, or were mutual benefit or member benefit organizations. However, GAO's numbers only reflect the 274,000 organizations that filed either the Form 990 or the 990-EZ returns with the IRS. The remainder of the nonprofit entities granted the tax exemption is too small to have to file under IRS rules, or are qualifying religious organizations that are exempt from the filing requirement. For more detailed information on the classifications of tax-exempt organization under Section 501(c) of the tax code, see United States Government Accountability Office at Chapter 6, Note 2, this volume. pp. 47–52. "Appendix II: Tax Benefits and Requirements for Different Types of Tax-Exempt Organizations."

11 The IRS uses a system called the National Taxonomy of Exempt Entities Core Codes, or NTEE-CC, to classify the specific areas of focus within the nonprofit sector. The

original NTEE contained 645 distinct categories; the NTEE-CC, the more "simplified" current version, contains 400. See National Center for Charitable Statistics. "National Taxonomy of Exempt Entities." http://nccs.urban.org/classification/ NTEE.cfm. The major groupings, as reflected in the GAO report cited at Chapter 6, Note 2, this volume, are Arts, Culture, and Humanities; Education; Environment and Animals; Health; Human Services; International, Foreign Affairs; Public, Societal Benefit; Religion-Related; Mutual/Membership Benefit; and the Unknown, Unclassified entities that are unique enough not to fall into any of these other categories. But these are further broken down. "Environment and Animals," for example, is next divided into Group C Environment, and Group D Animal Related. Under C Environment, organizations can be further classified as C01 Alliances & Advocacy, C02 Management & Technical Assistance, C03 Professional Societies & Associations, C05 Research Institutes & Public Policy Analysis, C11 Single Organization Support, C12 Fund Raising & Fund Distribution, C19 Support NEC, C20 Pollution Abatement & Control, C27 Recycling, C30 Natural Resources Conservation & Protection, C32 Water Resources, Wetlands Conservation & Management, and numerous other areas of specialization. See National Center for Charitable Statistics. Search NTEE Definitions. http://nccsweb.urban.org/PubApps/nteeSearch.php?gQ ry=allMajor&codeType=NTEE.

12 The classic *Twilight Zone* episode "Person or Persons Unknown" (episode 27, season 3, originally aired March 23, 1962), by way of example, has as its premise the fact that David Gurney (played by Richard Long) had too much to drink at a party the night before and awakens to a nightmarish world.

13 It is worth noting that while the American liquor industry long observed a voluntary ban on broadcast advertising of liquor products like vodka, Scotch whisky, gin, and tequila—in effect since 1936 for radio and 1948 for television—and while the almost ubiquitous liquor ads that appeared in magazines of the 50s and 60s largely disappeared, they never entirely vanished and the advertising for beer never ended, being a mainstay, for example, of National Football League broadcasts. America's relationship with alcohol, while changing and shifting over the past several generations, has never really ended.

14 Roughly half of this money was earned income from a variety of sources. A great deal of this money went to large educational institutions and medical facilities, but the practice of generating earned income is gaining ever-increased acceptance throughout the sector. See Foster, W. and Bradach, J. "Should Nonprofits Seek Profits?" *Harvard Business Review*. February 2005. https://hbr.org/2005/02/should-nonprofits-seek-profits/ar/1.

15 National Center for Charitable Statistics. "Quick Facts About Nonprofits." www. nccs.urban.org/statistics/quickfacts.cfm.

16 McKeever, B. and Pettijohn, S. "The Nonprofit Sector in Brief 2014: Public Charities, Giving, and Volunteering." Urban Institute. October 2014. www. urban.org/sites/default/files/alfresco/publication-pdfs/413277-The-Nonprofit-Sector-in-Brief--.PDF.

17 United States Bureau of Economic Analysis.

18 Bureau of Labor Statistics. "Commissioner Announcing New Research Data on Jobs and Pay in the Nonprofit Sector." October 17, 2014. http://beta.bls.gov/labs/ blogs/2014/10/17/announcing-new-research-data-on-jobs-and-pay-in-the-non-profit-sector/.

19 Blackwood et al. Op. cit.

20 Bureau of Labor Statistics. Op. cit.

21 Blackwood et al. Op. cit.

22 Bernasek, A. "For Nonprofits, a Bigger Share of the Economy." *New York Times.* March 8, 2014. https://www.nytimes.com/2014/03/09/business/for-nonprofits-a-bigger-share-of-the-economy.html?_r=2.

23 Fiscal Policy Institute. "NYC Nonprofit Sector the Largest Private Employer: A Vital Part of the Safety Net, Source of Jobs for Minorities." April 7, 2009. http://fiscalpolicy.org/new-york-nonprofits.

24 Nearly 90% of private-sector nonprofit jobs in New York State fell in just four sectors in 2010: Health Care, Education, Social Assistance, and Religious, grant-making, civic, professional, and similar organizations. In 2010, health care industries employed 570,600 nonprofit workers in the state. This large sector was responsible for 45% of all nonprofit jobs in the state that year. Three in five nonprofit health care workers (343,000) were employed by hospitals. Another 27% of nonprofit health care employees (154,000) worked at nursing homes and other residential care sites. The remaining 13% of nonprofit health care workers (74,000) were employed in ambulatory health care services. This industry is very broad, and includes the offices of doctors and dentists, outpatient care centers, medical labs, and home health care services. In total, nonprofits employed 57% of private health care workers.

The second-largest nonprofit sector was private education, which employed more than 245,000 New York workers in 2010. Two in three (65%) nonprofit education workers were employed by colleges and universities. Another 28% of nonprofit education jobs were at private grade schools and high schools. Nonprofits comprise 83% of all jobs in private education in the state. This is the highest share of any of the four largest nonprofit sectors in New York.

25 New York State Department of Labor, Division of Research and Statistics. "New York's Nonprofit Sector is Nation's Largest." *Employment in New York State.* April 2012. p. 1. https://labor.ny.gov/stats/PDFs/enys0412.pdf.

26 Ibid.

27 The Johns Hopkins Center for Civil Society Studies, Corona Research, Inc., and the Colorado Nonprofit Association. "Return on Investment: The Economic Impact of the Nonprofit Sector in Colorado." 2008. p. 2. http://ccss.jhu.edu/wp-content/uploads/downloads/2011/09/NED_Bulletin30_CO_2008.pdf.

28 Johns Hopkins Center for Civil Society Studies. "Nonprofit Economic Data Project." http://ccss.jhu.edu/research-projects/nonprofit-economic-data/.

29 Newhouse, C. "Westchester County Nonprofits: A Major Economic Engine." Johns Hopkins Center for Civil Society. Nonprofit Economic Data Project. March 5, 2014. http://ccss.jhu.edu/westchester-county-nonprofits/.

30 Salamon. (2002) p. 5.

31 Ibid.

32 Gerson, M. "Government 'Leviathan by proxy.'" *The Washington Post.* February 16, 2015. www.washingtonpost.com/opinions/taming-big-government-by-proxy/2015/02/16/783792f4-b5ff-11e4-9423-f3d0a1ec335c_story.html. Also see Kamarck, E. "The Government Reform Series: Leviathan by Proxy and the Big Lobotomy." Brooking Institute. January 26, 2015. www.brookings.edu/blogs/fixgov/posts/2015/01/26-government-reform-series-diiulio-kamarck.

33 Wagner, D. *What's Love Got to Do with It?* [New York: The New Press, 2000]. p. 131.

34 Smith, S. and Lipsky, M. *Nonprofits for Hire: The Welfare State and the Age of Contracting.* [Cambridge, MA: Harvard University Press, 1993] p. 4.

35 Center on Budget and Policy Priorities. "Chart Book: The Legacy of the Great Recession." December 2, 2016. www.cbpp.org/research/economy/chart-book-the-legacy-of-the-great-recession.

36 Ibid.

37 Ibid.

38 Morreale, J. "The Impact of the 'Great Recession' on the Financial Resources of Nonprofit Organizations." Wilson Center for Social Entrepreneurship. Paper 5, p. 7. http://digitalcommons.pace.edu/wilson/5.

39 Gassman, J. et al. "A Three Year Study of the Nonprofit Sector's Response to the Economic Challenges in Six Cities Across the Nation." Center for Nonprofit Strategy and Management. Baruch College School of Public Affairs. June 2012. p. 2. www.baruch.cuny.edu/mspia/centers-and-institutes/center-for-nonprofit-strategy-and-management/documents/GassmanetAl_AThreeYearStudyoftheNonprofitSectorsResponstotheEconomicChallengesinSixCitiesAcr.pdf.

40 Hungarland, L. "North Carolina Nonprofits: Coping with Government Budget Cuts." North Carolina Center for Nonprofits. April 20, 2012. http://dukespace.lib.duke.edu/dspace/bitstream/handle/10161/5166/MP%20Final.pdf;sequence=1.

41 Fleishman. p. 22.

42 Albassam, B.A. "The New Role of the Nonprofit Sector." *Mediterranean Journal of Social Sciences*. Vol. 3, No. 1. (January 2012) p. 77.

43 Estes, C. et al. "How the Legitimacy of the Sector Has Eroded." In Hodgkinson et al. p. 23.

44 Reich, Robert. "Rich People's Idea of Charity: Giving to Elite Schools and Operas." Salon.com. December 14, 2013. www.salon.com/2013/12/14/the_wealthy_give_to_charity_elite_schools_and_operas_partner.

45 Quigley, F. "The Limits of Philanthropy: Time to End the Charitable Tax Deduction." *Commonweal*. January 8, 2015. https://www.commonwealmagazine.org/limits-philanthropy.

46 Ibid.

47 Knight, C. "Museum Admission Should Be Free: The State of Art in 2014." *Los Angeles Times*. December 19, 2014. www.latimes.com/entertainment/arts/la-et-cm-ca-knight-art-essay-20141221-column.html.

48 Winston, K. "Study Challenges Tax Exemption for Religious Organizations." *USA Today*. June 16, 2012. http://usatoday30.usatoday.com/news/religion/story/2012-06-15/religious-tax-exemption-challenged/55629908/1.

49 Oppenheimer, M. "The Supreme Court's Ruling on Gay Marriage Makes It Clearer than Ever that the Government Shouldn't Be Subsidizing Religion and Non-Profits." *Time Magazine*. June 28, 2015. http://time.com/3939143/nows-the-time-to-end-tax-exemptions-for-religious-institutions/.

50 The notion of exempting churches from taxation did not begin in the U.S. Medieval Europe, the Roman Empire under Constantine, and even Egypt in Joseph's time exempted church property from taxation. See Shapiro, B. "Government Crusade against Churches Begins with Removal of Non-Profit Status." *Breitbart*. July 2, 2015. www.breitbart.com/big-government/2015/07/02/government-crusade-against-churches-begins-with-removal-of-non-profit-status/.

51 Winston. Op. cit.

52 Gaylor, A.L. "State/Church FAQ: Tax Exemption of Churches." Freedom From Religion Foundation. December 2010. http://ffrf.org/faq/feeds/item/12601-tax-exemption-of-churches.

53 Matthews, D. "You Give Religions More than $82.5 Billion a Year." *The Washington Post*. August 22, 2013. www.washingtonpost.com/news/wonkblog/wp/2013/08/22/you-give-religions-more-than-82-5-billion-a-year/.

54 For the record, St. Patrick's Catholic Cathedral is also located on Fifth Avenue.

55 Oppenheimer. Op. cit.

56 Matthews. Op. cit.

57 Winston. Op. cit.

58 Ibid.

59 Comptroller of Maryland. "Tax Exempt Sales to Nonprofit Organizations." Spotlight on Maryland Taxes. http://taxes.marylandtaxes.com/Business_Taxes/ Business_Tax_Types/Sales_and_Use_Tax/Filing_Information/Tax_Exemptions/ Exemption_Certificates/Sales_to_Nonprofit_Organizations.shtml.

60 These costs to the government, of course, cannot include those levies to which governmental entities are immune.

61 U.S. Postal Service. "Special Prices for Nonprofit Mailers." http://pe.usps.com/ businessmail101/rates/nonprofit.htm.

62 Depending upon whether a nonprofit meets strict criteria, it may be able to have the government reimburse its excise tax expenditures, but the taxes must be paid by the vendors first. If a nonprofit has been paying an excise tax, it can ask for the reimbursement when it files its tax returns. To receive the reimbursement, the organization must file a separate form, indicating the amount paid in excise tax and demonstrating the purchase was used for the nonprofit's mission exclusively. Although telephone tax is an excise tax most nonprofits pay, according to the IRS, it is reimbursable only to educational organizations, governments, and nonprofit hospitals, and the IRS defines an educational organization very narrowly. Depending upon the state of incorporation, a nonprofit may have to fill out multiple forms to recoup the money it spent in taxes. Each state that offers excise tax exemptions on state taxes requires its own separate form, as does the federal government.

63 Berger, K. "The State of Nonprofits: Nudity, Ghosts and Perpetual Indulgence." LinkedIn. March 25, 2014. https://www.linkedin.com/pulse/20140325115534-15445193-state-of-nonprofits-nudity-ghosts-and-perpetual-indulgence.

64 Berger. Op. cit. Also see Tuohy, J. "IRS Dubs First Church of Cannabis a Nonprofit." *Indianapolis Star.* June 2, 2015. USAToday.com. www.usatoday.com/story/news/ politics/2015/06/02/first-church-of-cannabis/28364521/.

65 Fleishman. p. 14.

66 Hall. (2010) p. 3.

7   The growth of advocacy

Of all of the developments within the nonprofit arena that have taken place since the Great Society, perhaps none have been as controversial—and led to as much confusion—as the increased activist role taken by some nonprofit organizations.

This is not to say that an activist or advocacy role is at all new for these organizations. To the contrary, as we have argued, this impulse to make the world a better place has been part of the sector's DNA going back to its earliest eleemosynary days in old New England. As early as the 1820s to the 1840s, the forerunners of today's nonprofits were advocating for penal reform and the amelioration of cruelty to animals; they were pushing measures aimed at addressing the abandonment and mistreatment of children, advocating for the care of the sick and those labeled insane, arguing for better treatment of reformed prostitutes. These voluntary groups opposed drunkenness, dueling, wars and imperialism, the abuse of the poor, press gangs, and injustice generally. They organized and worked to end political corruption and the "seduction and abandonment of women."

And, of course, many worked tirelessly to end both the slave trade and slavery itself.

Later in the century, voluntary groups worked on behalf of compulsory childhood education, temperance, and women's and workers' rights. The efforts of these organizations in continued penal reform were rewarded by such changes as the abolishment of public hangings, floggings, and other cruel punishments in many states.[1]

In the early 20th century, the National Child Labor Committee, organized in 1904, led to the creation of numerous state labor committees and new state laws restricting child labor. As the voluntary sector saw its membership rise in the mid-1920s, several of these groups famously advocated for women's suffrage and against American participation in World War I, to protect the rights of minorities and to restrict immigration. Some worked for workers' rights and others against them. So, advocacy and activism, per se, are *not* a new phenomenon when it comes to the sector.

Two things, however, are fairly new developments, and disturbing to some observers. The first is the *amount* of advocacy undertaken by some nonprofits, and the other is the mixing and blurring of the activity of different *types* of nonprofits since their categorization under the modern tax code.

While charitable organizations have a long tradition of advocating social change, over the last several decades many have expanded both the amount of their advocacy activity and their repertoire of advocacy strategies. These organizations have turned their efforts to raising public awareness, demanding accountability from governmental agencies, and pressing for changes in law and policy. Legal service organizations, which were established to provide direct representation for the indigent, have more recently undertaken law reform efforts in the courts and in the legislative arena in order to challenge the broader, systemic problems that face their clients. Other groups have been created for the express purpose of bringing about social change. Some claim to speak for the general population on issues of broad public concern, such as consumer rights, environmental quality, and nuclear-arms control. Others define their missions as the protection of particularly vulnerable sub-populations. These advocates have demanded recognition of, and respect for, the rights of individual clients within the public arena. They have fought for the recognition of a broad range of rights, while others have waged battles to obtain and maintain the allocation of public resources to programs serving the poor, the old, the young, and the ill. Still others have taken it upon themselves to monitor the performance of the government in its role as provider of social services and promoter of general well-being.[2]

Although this activism may not fit comfortably with what some believe to be the traditional role of a "charitable enterprise," many others believe that the roles of advocate and improver of social systems, empowerer of citizens, and critic and monitor of government policies and programs are among the most crucial functions of the nonprofit sector. To those holding this view, the sector provides countervailing or balancing definitions of reality, morality, perspectives and world views that frequently challenge the prevailing assumptions about what exists and what is good and what should be done in society. Put another way, it is the most likely part of society to say that the emperor has no clothes.[3]

However, as the charitable sector has grown increasingly vocal and articulate about the state of the emperor's wardrobe, its activist role has become the object of mounting scrutiny. While the precise question has varied—depending upon the context in which it has been raised—the issue that has emerged is one of basic definition: does the fact that an organization directs its energies toward system change, rather than direct service delivery, disqualify it for tax-exempt status or render it ineligible to receive contributions which are deductible to the donor? If it is entering the public arena and engaging in the open debate and effective partisanship which surround many contentious issues, does it, *should* it, forfeit the special status it enjoys under the tax laws?[4]

This brings us to another development of recent years that raises questions in the minds of some observers: the blurring of the activity between different types of nonprofits

Although most people, when they think of nonprofits, think of *charities*, the fact is that these familiar organizations are but one of twenty-nine different kinds of tax-exempt entity recognized by the IRS and Section 501(c) of the tax code.[5] But while organizations falling into all of these categories are tax-exempt, only those in the 501(c)(3) group—the charities—are eligible for tax-deductible contributions. This special allowance goes back to 1917. But there was a price to pay for this status, as the degree of political activity in which these organizations could engage was soon challenged.

Early action and the 501(c)(3)s

Questions regarding the kinds of activity in which tax-exempt entities could engage arose very quickly after their status was codified in 1917, primarily because of the purposes for which the organizations we call *charities* were exempted from federal taxation in the first place. Under law they were supposed to be focused upon charitable, religious, scientific, literary, or educational activities, or upon the prevention of cruelty to children or animals. Where, critics (*and* the Tax Bureau) asked, did advocacy and political activity fit into these categories?

But with a century-long tradition of advocacy for and against a broad array of social issues, the nation's voluntary associations were not about to sit on the sidelines as such issues as prohibition, women's suffrage, and civil rights were debated during the turbulent years of Woodrow Wilson's second term as president. It was not long before the sector and the tax laws collided.

In 1919, the Treasury Department took the position that organizations "formed to disseminate controversial or partisan propaganda" were not "educational" for purposes of qualifying for tax-exempt status, even though the organizations themselves saw their role as raising public awareness and "educating" the public. As a result, contributions to these organizations were deemed not deductible under the new federal income tax.[6]

Through the course of various legal challenges, no clear standard emerged from the resultant court decisions. While some courts denied the tax deduction if the organization advocated for *any* type of change in existing laws or policy, others considered "how controversial the advocacy was, or if the organization's actions were intended to influence legislation."[7]

Ultimately, *Slee v. Commissioner*,[8] a 1930 dispute involving contributions to the American Birth Control League, emerged as a leading case on this issue. Mr. Slee had for several years been making contributions to the league and, under the prevailing 1917 statute, taking a deduction for these contributions. This, however, led to trouble with the Bureau of Internal Revenue: it denied the deduction. In 1929 the Board of Tax Appeals denied Mr. Slee's appeal on the grounds that the league was involved in "controversial propaganda."[9]

When it reached his court, however, Judge Learned Hand, writing for the Second Circuit Court of Appeals, crafted a different theory. He ruled that "contributions to [the] organization were not deductible because it did not appear that the [organization's] lobbying was limited to causes that furthered the organization's charitable purposes." It was clear that the league wanted to change the laws regarding the availability of contraception. As such, it advocated and engaged in activism not unlike that of countless voluntary organizations before it: it disseminated information on the relationship between national and world problems and uncontrolled procreation, and sought to repeal anti-contraception laws through direct lobbying. It also operated a clinic to advise women on how to prevent conception.[10] Unfortunately for the league and Mr. Slee, the organization was not operating in the unrestricted environment of the 1800s, but rather in the post-1913 world which featured not only the income tax, but the Revenue Bureau and regulations.

Judge Hand reasoned that the purpose of changing the law would have been permissible if it had been ancillary to the purpose of conducting the clinic. However, it appeared that the purpose of changing the law was regarded by the league and its supporters as an end in itself under the circumstances—if anything, the clinic was ancillary—and was therefore not considered an exempt purpose.

The problem with Judge Hand's decision was that it turned on the issue of whether an organization's lobbying furthered its exempt purpose, while the focus in the Revenue Act seemed to be whether the lobbying was a substantial part of the organization's activities.[11]

It was against these confusing developments that Congress reshuffled the deck with the Revenue Act of 1934.

As enacted, the 1934 lobbying provision includes the concept that is familiar from the current Section 501(c)(3): no "substantial part" of the activities of an exempt organization can be the "carrying on of propaganda" or "attempting to influence legislation." As originally proposed, the Act had included an explicit provision that would have restricted the ability of charities to participate in partisan politics in any way. But there were concerns that this was too broad, so that language was stricken in conference. It would take another two decades before there was additional action on such a restriction.

In 1954 there was a major restructuring of the federal tax code. This was the year that the current Section 501(c) was added. The new Section 501(c)(3) combined several older provisions and covered:

> Corporations, and any community chest, fund, or foundation, organized and operated exclusively for religious, charitable, scientific, testing for public safety, literary, or educational purposes, or to foster national or international amateur sports competition,[12] or for the prevention of cruelty to children or animals.

In addition to ensuring the nonprofit nature of these entities—no part of the net earnings of such organizations could inure to the benefit of any private shareholder or individual—the 1954 legislation stipulated that "no substantial part" of the activities of such organizations would be "carrying on propaganda, or otherwise attempting, to influence legislation." What was completely new was the provision that these entities would *not participate in, or intervene in (including the publishing or distributing of statements), any political campaign on behalf of any candidate for public office*[13] (emphasis added).

Two more changes would follow:

- Section 501(h) of the tax code was enacted in 1976, and allows charities to engage in a limited amount of lobbying subject to a spending cap.[14]
- The Revenue Act of 1987 clarified that political campaign activities may not be conducted in opposition to, or on behalf of, any candidate for public office.

So, as it now stands, 501(c)(3) organizations, the familiar charities that include everything from churches and the Red Cross to the local food bank and opera, are not supposed to engage in lobbying or political activity,[15] the *exceptions*, however, being that they:

- *can* advocate before administrative agencies—presumably those that oversee their areas of operation—either on their own behalf or on behalf of those they serve. In other words, they can advocate for or against administrative policies that would impact their service populations, and they can advocate in their own interest regarding funding and other matters;
- *can* engage in general issue advocacy;
- *can* lobby for or against legislation;
- *can* support or oppose the appointment of individuals to nonelective offices.[16]

However, the separation between charity on the one hand, and partisanship or legislative advocacy on the other, is, in reality, more fig leaf than firewall for a number of reasons, and one of the major of these is that even now it is still not completely clear just how much of what kind of activity, addressing which social issues, will so color the character of an organization that it no longer qualifies for exemption and donor deductibility.[17]

The other reason for questioning the intended separation is that many 501(c)(3) organizations get around it by forming another kind of nonprofit, the 501(c)(4), which allows them to do all the things the law essentially was intended to prevent.

The rise of the c(4)s

In one way, it is odd that Congress should have gone to such lengths to prohibit political activity on the part of 501(c)(3) charities, because in the very next subheading of the tax code, 501(c)(4), it created entities seemingly designed to do almost nothing else. The crucial differences between the two classifications are that the (c)(3) may not engage in any form of political activity,[18] while the (c)(4) can, and while both may accept donations, only those going to a (c)(3) are tax deductible to the donor.

The 501(c)(4), or social welfare organization[19] is the oddest of ducks, created for reasons lost to history, for purposes that have never been entirely clear. What is clear, however, is that it has become a tax-exempt vehicle for virtually unbridled political activity, including that by entities otherwise banned from engaging in such actions.

The background of the (c)(4) is, to say the least, murky. The predecessor of Section 501(c)(4) of the tax code was enacted as part of the Tariff Act of 1913.[20] But the legislative history of the Act contains no reason or explanation for the exemption. The general belief, however, is that the U.S. Chamber of Commerce pushed for the enactment of exemptions for both civic and commercial nonprofit organizations,[21] intending to carve out a tax-free space for entities which could not qualify as charitable, educational, or religious, but whose activities could somehow be interpreted as benefitting the general public.[22] There was nothing in this original formulation regarding political activities; that came later. Originally, these organizations were those that were interpreted as promoting in some way the common good and general welfare of the people of the community, "interpreted" because even the IRS admits that:

> IRC 501(c)(4) remains in some degree a catch-all for presumptively beneficial nonprofit organizations that resist classification under the other exempting provisions of the [Tax] Code. Unfortunately, this condition exists because "social welfare" (the original defining term) is inherently an abstruse concept that continues to defy precise definition.[23]

Examples of those organizations demonstrating "community benefit" and allowed under the Section include:

- an organization that purchases acreage in a stated locality, makes arrangements for water and sewage facilities and enters into arrangements for the erection and sale of dwellings to low and moderate-income individuals;
- a corporation organized for the purpose of rehabilitating and placing unemployed persons over a stated age;
- a corporation formed to provide a school district with a stadium provided that the title to the stadium is to be transferred to the school district after all indebtedness has been liquidated and its capital stock retired, with no profit to the stockholders;
- a corporation formed to cooperate with the parent–teacher association of a local school district, its activity to consist of reviewing the proposals of and designating the insurance company allowed to solicit accident insurance from the students, teachers, and other employees of the school district;

- a corporation organized to aid and promote the purposes of the Area Redevelopment Act by providing loans to purchase or develop lands and facilities to alleviate unemployment in areas classified as "redevelopment areas";
- a memorial association organized to study and develop methods of achieving simplicity and dignity in funeral and memorial services, and to educate and inform its members as well as the public as to the results of such study;
- a junior chamber of commerce operated exclusively for the purpose of rendering civic services for the promotion of the welfare of the community and its citizens (however, ordinary chambers of commerce, which are organized to promote the business interests of a community, instead generally qualify for exemption under IRC 501(c)(6));
- an organization formed to advise, counsel, and assist individuals in solving their financial difficulties by budgeting their income and expenses and effecting an orderly program for the payment of their obligations.[24]

It can readily be seen that none of these organizations or efforts was partisan in nature, and was therefore probably in keeping with the legislation's assumed original intent. So where did the politics enter the equation?

From the best evidence available, it seems that it was the IRS itself that originated the concept in the 1950s in a case involving a "social welfare organization" engaged in the promotion of sound government by means of disseminating literature and occasionally advocating or opposing pending legislation. It was made explicit in regulations adopted in 1959, which assigned the label of "action organization" to any legislatively active nonprofit organization,[25] and stated that "[e]ven though an organization is an 'action organization,' it can qualify as a social welfare organization under Section 501(c)(4)."[26] The IRS then further loosened the rules on political campaign activity in 1981 with another ruling, which stated that "[an] organization may carry on lawful political activities and remain exempt under Section 501(c)(4) as long as it is primarily engaged in activities that promote social welfare,"[27] *social welfare* still very broadly understood.

Functionally, this had two impacts. The first was the unbridled political activity of various kinds of nonprofits engaged in "public education" by virtue of their disseminating information about issues and even candidates. These include organizations such as the National Rifle Association (NRA), which clearly has a position regarding the Second Amendment, its interpretation, and the exercise of rights thereunder, and the Sierra Club, which urged its members to oppose Scott Pruitt's nomination as head of the Environmental Protection Agency.[28]

However, the second impact of all this has been to prompt many nonprofit organizations, but particularly 501(c)(3) charities, to split off their legislative and other advocacy activities and place them in an "action organization" 501(c)(4). This is both why and how Planned Parenthood, by way of illustration, while barred itself from engaging in partisan activity, can have a 501(c)(4), the Planned Parenthood Action Fund, which can and does engage in politics. Meanwhile, 501(c)(4)s, such as the NRA can form "charitable foundations," capable of accepting fully deductible donations. This is the difference, for example, between AARP (American Association of Retired Persons) and the AARP Foundation.[29] AARP advocates and engages in partisan activity; the foundation collects tax-deductible donations.

In these instances, the restrictions applying to the (c)(3) would not apply to the related (c)(4); just as the activities allowed for the (c)(4) could not be undertaken by the (c)(3). What this means is that when someone reads a headline saying that a charity has "endorsed" a candidate or some legislation, it is most likely doing so through its (c)(4) affiliate, and, meanwhile, when we hear of an organization that clearly attempts to influence politics inviting deductible contributions, it is probably doing so through its charitable arm (c)(3). Both actions are completely legal—confusing and seemingly contradictory—but completely legal.

Unfortunately, all of this has led to a lot of confusion, more smoke as opposed to heat or light, as to what actions a group may take, what's legal, what's illegal, which groups are eligible for tax-deductible contributions and which are not.

Among the general public, there is hardly any awareness that there is a difference between 501(c)(3)s and (c)(4)s, or that these classifications even exist. . .most people just assume that they're all "nonprofit," that donations to all of them are deductible, and that none of them are supposed to be involved in political campaigns. Liberals are therefore outraged at the NRA's partisan backing of candidates who support gun owners' rights, and conservatives are similarly furious when they hear of a group like Planned Parenthood supporting certain candidates. What neither group realizes is that the actions of both organizations are perfectly legal given the elastic nature of the (c)(4) category and the ability of even (c)(3)s to have both kinds of entity operating effectively under the same banner.

For their part, (c)(3)s have to be ever-vigilant lest they run afoul of the IRS's often fluid interpretations of actions and boundaries, and/or a complaint lodged by a legislator, "concerned citizen," or other party.[30]

In a broader context, the whole question of the purpose of the (c)(4) designation and its utilization has come under renewed scrutiny in recent years. In addition to confusion over just how many (c)(4)s there are,[31] many observers regard the existing law regarding nonprofits' political activity, one of the two key differences between the (c)(3)s and the (c)(4)s, as fundamentally flawed in both its conception and its application, the limitations on charities' political activities often appearing to be drawn from a mix of historical accident, assorted political pressures, a subjective grab-bag of conclusions about the traditional role of "charity,"[32] as well as the occasional personal whim.[33]

Given all this, it should come as no surprise that some observers have called for a clarification and loosening of the current restrictions on (c)(3)s' advocacy activities,[34] while others advocate for new measures to ensure that the (c)(4) status is not exploited by partisan-oriented political organizations, and a few suggest that the entire (c)(4) classification be done away with entirely.[35] Meanwhile, the number of organizations applying for the (c)(4) status has reportedly more than doubled since 2010.[36]

However this situation is resolved—and it is unlikely to be resolved any time soon—it can be expected to continue to be an arena of important developments impacting the nation's charities. Their activist gene is not likely to go dormant, and it should be expected that the controversy over which advocacy actions they are allowed and which they are not will only grow as these organizations are either drawn into or feel the need to engage in the country's unfolding culture wars.

Notes

1 Feldmeth, G.D. "U.S. History Resources." March 31, 1998. http://home.earthlink. net/~gfeldmeth/USHistory.html.
2 Chisolm, Laura B. "Exempt Organization Advocacy: Matching the Rules to the Rationales." *Indiana Law Journal*. Vol. 63, Issue 2, Article 1. (1988) pp. 204–205. https://www.repository.law.indiana.edu/ilj/vol63/iss2/1/ .
3 Ibid. p. 205.
4 Ibid.
5 Under Section 501(c), the following categories of tax-exempt entity are recognized: 501(c)(1) Corporations Organized Under Act of Congress (including Federal Credit Unions); 501(c)(2) Title Holding Corporation for Exempt Organization; 501(c)(3) Religious, Educational, Charitable, Scientific, Literary, Testing for Public Safety, to Foster National or International Amateur Sports Competition, or Prevention of Cruelty to Children or Animals Organizations; 501(c)(4) Civic Leagues, Social Welfare Organizations, and Local Associations of Employees; 501(c)(5) Labor, Agricultural, and Horticultural Organizations; 501(c)(6) Business Leagues, Chambers of Commerce, Real Estate Boards, etc.; 501(c)(7) Social and Recreational Clubs; 501(c)(8) Fraternal Beneficiary Societies and Associations; 501(c)(9) Voluntary Employee Beneficiary Associations; 501(c)(10) Domestic Fraternal Societies and Associations; 501(c)(11) Teachers' Retirement Fund Associations; 501(c)(12) Benevolent Life Insurance Associations, Mutual Ditch or Irrigation Companies, Mutual or Cooperative Telephone Companies, etc.; 501(c)(13) Cemetery Companies; 501(c)(14) State-Chartered Credit Unions, Mutual Reserve Funds; 501(c)(15) Mutual Insurance Companies or Associations; 501(c)(16) Cooperative Organizations to Finance Crop Operations; 501(c)(17) Supplemental Unemployment Benefit Trusts; 501(c)(18) Employee Funded Pension Trust (created before June 25, 1959); 501(c)(19) Post or Organization of Past or Present Members of the Armed Forces; 501(c)(20) Group Legal Services Plan Organizations; 501(c)(21) Black Lung Benefit Trusts; 501(c)(22) Withdrawal Liability Payment Fund; 501(c)(23) Veterans Organization (those created before 1880); 501(c)(24) Section 4049 ERISA Trusts; 501(c)(25) Title Holding Corporations or Trusts with Multiple Parents; 501(c)(26) State-Sponsored Organization Providing Health Coverage for High-Risk Individuals; 501(c)(27) State-Sponsored Workers' Compensation Reinsurance Organizations; 501(c)(28) National Railroad Retirement Investment Trust; 501(c)(29) Qualified Nonprofit Health Insurance Issuers (created in Section 1322(h)(1) of the Affordable Care Act).
6 Harris, M. and Rosenthal, L. "The Political Ban in 501(c)(3): Its Odd History." The For Purpose Law Group. June 23, 2016. www.forpurposelaw.com/501c3-political-ban-history/.

7 Ibid.
8 *Slee v. Commissioner*, 42 F.2d 184 (2d Cir. 1930).
9 15 B.T.A. 710, 715 (1929).
10 Thomas, W.L. and Fontenrose, R. "Education, Propaganda, and the Methodology Test." Internal Revenue Service. Exempt Organizations Continuing Professional Education text. 1997. p. 85. https://www.irs.gov/pub/irs-tege/eotopich97.pdf.
11 Harris and Rosenthal. Op. cit.
12 But, oddly, only if no part of its activities involved the provision of athletic facilities or equipment.
13 Ibid.
14 Under the 501(h) expenditure test, public charities may spend on Direct Lobbying—defined as an organization attempting to influence legislation by stating a position on specific legislation to legislators or other government employees who participate in the formulation of legislation, or urging its members to do so—20% of the first $500,000 of its exempt purpose expenditures, and 15% of the next $500,000, and so on, up to one million dollars a year...and on Grassroots Lobbying— defined as an attempt to influence legislation by stating a position on specific legislation to the general public and asking the general public to contact legislators or other government employees who participate in the formulation of legislation—5% of the first $500,000 of its exempt purpose expenditures, and 3.75% of the next $500,000, and so on, up to $250,000 a year.
15 The ban on "participating" in a political campaign is generally understood to mean that a 501(c)(3) charity cannot be involved in any campaign, directly or indirectly, on behalf of or in opposition to a candidate. If an organization takes a stand in any campaign, supporting or opposing one or another candidate, it is in violation. Beyond this, some activities that the IRS has found to violate the prohibition on political campaigning include inviting a political candidate to make a campaign speech at an event hosted by the organization; using the organization's funds to publish materials that support (or oppose) a candidate; donating money from the organization to a political candidate; any statements by the organization's executive director, in his or her official capacity, that support a candidate; criticizing or supporting a candidate on the organization's website; inviting one candidate to speak at a well-publicized and well-attended event, and inviting the other candidate to speak at a lesser function; inviting all candidates to speak at an event, but arranging the speaking event or choosing the questions in such a way that it is obvious that the organization favors one candidate over the others; conducting a "get out the vote" telephone drive in a partisan manner by selecting caller responses for further follow-up based on candidate preference; and using the organization's website to link to only one candidate's profile. However, the IRS will evaluate any potential misconduct within the current political climate...meaning that a particular activity might be considered political campaigning two weeks before an election, but not two years before an election. See Fitzpatrick, D. "Limits on Political Campaigning for 501(c)(3) Nonprofits." NOLO. www.nolo.com/legal-encyclopedia/limits-political-campaigning-501c3-nonprofits-29982.html. Also see United States Internal Revenue Service. "The Restriction of Political Campaign Intervention by Section 501(c)(3) Tax-Exempt Organizations." September 13, 2016. https://www.irs.gov/charities-non-profits/charitable-organizations/the-restriction-of-political-campaign-intervention-by-section-501-c-3-tax-exempt-organizations.
16 Lunder, E. "Tax-Exempt Organizations: Political Activity Restrictions and Disclosure Requirements." Congressional Research Service. Library of Congress. April 20, 2006. Updated January 25, 2007. p. 8. http://digital.library.unt.edu/ark:/67531/metacrs9271/m1/1/high_res_d/RL33377_2006Apr20.pdf.

17 Chisolm. p. 207.

18 At this writing, President Trump is vowing to "totally destroy" the restriction pro-hibiting churches from engaging in political activities at the risk of losing their tax-exempt status. See Landler, M. "Trump Vows to 'Destroy' Law Banning Political Activity by Churches." *New York Times.* February 2, 2017, and Note 51, Chapter 4, this volume. It should also be noted that churches that meet the IRS require-ments of Section 501(c)(3) are automatically considered tax-exempt and are not required to apply for and obtain recognition of tax-exempt status from the IRS. See United States Internal Revenue Service. "Tax Guide for Churches & Religious Organizations." Publication 1828 (Rev. 8–2015). Catalog Number 21096G. https://www.irs.gov/pub/irs-pdf/p1828.pdf.

19 Section 501(c)(4) covers, in addition to social welfare organizations, local associa-tions of employees, and some homeowner associations and volunteer fire companies. See United States Internal Revenue Service. "Types of Organizations Exempt under Section 501(c)(4)." October 12, 2016. https://www.irs.gov/charities-non-profits/other-non-profits/types-of-organizations-exempt-under-section-501-c-4.

20 Tariff Act of 1913, Ch. 16, § II (G)(a), 38 Stat. 172.

21 Desiderio, R. *Planning Tax-Exempt Organizations.* [Danvers, MA: Matthew Bender & Company, 2013] § 23.02.

22 Chisolm. p. 291.

23 Reilly, J.F. et al. "IRC 501(c)(4) Organizations." United States Internal Revenue Service. Exempt Organization Technical Instruction Program for FY 2003.2003 EO CPE text. p. I-3.

24 Ibid. pp. I-4, I-5.

25 Chisolm. p. 290 and Treas. Reg. §1.50l(c)(3)-l(c)(3) (1959).

26 Ibid and Treas. Reg. §1.50l(c)(4)-l(a)(2)(ii) (1959).

27 Gersham, J. "The Surprisingly Muddled History of the 501(c)(4) Exemption." *Wall Street Journal.* Law Blog. May 16, 2013. http://blogs.wsj.com/law/2013/05/16/the-surprisingly-muddled-history-of-the-501c4-exemption/.

28 The Sierra Club, while seeking recurring contributions in the form of "monthly gifts," *does* explicitly state that it is a 501(c)(4) and that contributions, dona-tions, gifts, and dues to the club are not tax deductible. See https://sierra.secure.force.com/donate/rc_connect__campaign_designform?id=70131000001Ye8u AAC&formcampaignid=70131000001184AAAQ&ddi=N16JSEGO04&utm_medium=cpc&utm_source=google&utm_campaign=sem_monthly&utm_conten t=exp&gclid=CIrKqOekuNECFQpXDQodfPsJQw#!form=00P3100000dcu0F EAQ. Political Action Committees, meanwhile, although they engage in some simi-lar activities are generally not (c)(4)s, but rather are "527 organizations," organized under Section 527 of the Internal Revenue Code and created primarily to *influence* the selection, nomination, election, appointment or defeat of candidates to federal, state, or local public office. They may not, however, expressly advocate for specific candidates or coordinate with any candidate's campaign. See 26 U.S.C. § 527.

29 Also complicating the situation is that some organizations may differ in their tax status as one moves from the national entity to local chapters. The Boy Scouts of America (BSA) provides a case in point. The national organization, the BSA, is a public charity, tax-exempt under Section 501(c)(3). An IRS group exemption allows it to extend this tax-exempt status to "subordinate organizations," which includes all BSA local councils. Local units, however, Cub Packs, Scout Troops, Sea Scout Ships, and Venture Crews, are not considered either subordinate units, or tax-exempt under the national organization's exemption. Rather, they are chartered to partner organizations such churches, PTAs, and civic groups. Since a unit is "owned"

by its chartering organization, each unit takes its tax status from *that* organization, which may or may not be a 501(c)(3). See National BSA Foundation. "Unit Gifts and Tax-Exempt Status." March 2006. www.capitalscouting.org/capital_docs/bsa_unit_policy_update_2006.pdf.

30 The poster child for this sort of thing occurred in 2004 when the IRS began investigating whether the National Association for the Advancement of Coloured People (NAACP) had violated its 501(c)(3) status because of remarks criticizing President George W. Bush made during the election campaign of that year. During that campaign, NAACP chairperson Julian Bond criticized Bush in a July speech, saying his administration preached racial neutrality and practiced racial division. "They write a new constitution of Iraq and they ignore the Constitution at home," Bond said. This led two members of Congress to call for an IRS investigation and several others to forward complaints and requests for an investigation that came from constituents. After two years, the IRS determined that the organization had not, in fact, violated its status. See Fears, D. "IRS Ends 2-Year Probe of NAACP's Tax Status." *Washington Post*. September 1, 2006. www.washingtonpost.com/wp-dyn/content/article/2006/08/31/AR2006083100737.html. Meanwhile, the IRS itself was accused of improperly delaying and scrutinizing the 501(c)(4) applications of groups some of the IRS's employees thought were conservative in nature. See Goldfarb, Z.A. and Tumulty, K. "IRS Admits Targeting Conservatives for Tax Scrutiny in 2012 Election." *Washington Post*. May 10, 2013. https://www.washingtonpost.com/business/economy/irs-admits-targeting-conservatives-for-tax-scrutiny-in-2012-election/2013/05/10/3b6a0ada-b987-11e2-92f3-f291801936b8_story.html?hpid=z1&tid=a_inl&utm_term=.b9db193483c5. Also see Levine, C. "The Wisconsin Example: A Thin Line between Charitable Purposes and Politics." *Nonprofit Quarterly*. June 2, 2017. https://nonprofitquarterly.org/2017/06/02/wisconsin-example-thin-line-charitable-purposes-politics/?utm_source=Daily+Newswire&utm_campaign=a4951cfd0c-EMAIL_CAMPAIGN_2017_06_02&utm_medium=email&utm_term=0_94063a1d17-a4951cfd0c-12341229 for another example of the blurring line between 501(c)(3)s and politics.

31 The IRS cited 121,170 in a training document in 2003. (See Reilly et al. p. I-1), but an Urban Institute correspondent cited 86,451 "active" 501(c)(4) organizations approved by the IRS as of December 2012. (See Koulish, J. "There Are A Lot of 501(c)(4) Nonprofit Organizations. Most Are Not Political." The Urban Institute. Urban Wire: Nonprofits and Philanthropy. May 24, 2013. www.urban.org/urban-wire/there-are-lot-501c4-nonprofit-organizations-most-are-not-political.)

32 Chisolm. p. 207.

33 A story is told regarding the origin of the 1954 proposal banning charities from taking part in any way in political campaigns. The prohibition, not part of the original legislation, was offered as a floor amendment by then-Senate Minority Leader Lyndon B. Johnson. Although LBJ's motivations for the amendment were never made clear and are absent from the legislative history, it has been suggested that he proposed it as a way to get back at an organization that had supported an opponent. See Lunder. p. 5, and Peters, J.W. "The Johnson Amendment, Which Trump Vows to 'Destroy,' Explained." *New York Times*. February 2, 2017. https://www.nytimes.com/2017/02/02/us/politics/johnson-amendment-trump.html.

34 Chisolm. *Passim*.

35 Colombo, J.D. "The I.R.S. Should Eliminate 501(c)(4) Organizations." *New York Times*. May 15, 2013. www.nytimes.com/roomfordebate/2013/05/15/does-the-irs-scandal-prove-that-501c4s-should-be-eliminated/the-irs-should-eliminate-501c4-organizations.

36 Goldfarb and Tumulty. Op. cit.

8 Dollars and sense

The funding roller-coaster

Rarely have the financial prospects of the nonprofit sector been as open to conflicting interpretations as they are today. While many in the nonprofit community have viewed the election of Donald Trump as an existential threat, others point to a "Trump Bump" in giving, and see him (or opposition to him) as the best spur to donations.

Only time will tell whether either of these visions ultimately matches reality, but the question remains of just how fragile or essentially steady the sector's overall funding base actually is.

With the election of Donald Trump as president and Republican majorities in both the House and Senate in November of 2016, many nonprofits across the land not only feared the worst, but some also began basing fund-raising drives on it. One solicitation went:

> The recent election raised uncertainty—how will this affect the most vulnerable among us? Will it crush the budgets of crucial community services? Are our nonprofits prepared for the challenges ahead? Like me, you are thinking carefully about your charitable giving this year. Maybe you will give more than usual toward advocacy or basic services.[1]

Another nonprofit wrote:

> Many folks who work in our sector were taken by surprise by Donald Trump's victory. Shock, fear, dread and more fear are dominant emotions today among my nonprofit friends, including me. We're worried about what kind of impact will we see.[2]

Some of this may have been genuine. Some may have been hyperbole. Some may just have been smart marketing, striking while the iron was hot and no one knew, really, what a Trump presidency would mean for the sector and the policies and public funding upon which it so largely depends.

But taking a longer view, the question must be asked if the sector's funding is really as precarious as is sometimes implied by these appeals. A number of facts are required to put this question into context.

Perhaps the first and most basic is that the nonprofit sector is not a monolith. . .and neither are its funding sources.

The American nonprofit arena is composed of a broad variety of entities, ranging from the giants with budgets in the billions or hundreds of millions,[3] to small Mom 'n' Pop organizations with budgets barely reaching $10,000. Different organizations also focus upon different issues or policy areas and therefore draw upon different sources of funding. Broadly speaking the nonprofit arena's funding sources include the government, individuals, foundations, and the corporate sector. While the sector *as a whole* gets most of its money from the government, the fact is that while some nonprofits get the majority of their money from the government, far more get very little or none at all. Beyond this, the segmentation of government funding, which includes not only federal funding related to entitlement programs, human services, education, science, and a host of other programs, but often state and local program dollars as well, dictates that no one budget cut will have an equal across-the-board impact on the entire sector. Rather, it takes a combination of cuts across the whole spectrum of funded programs to impact the sector as a whole.

In modern times, the closest to a universal threat to the nonprofit arena's funding came in the guise of the Great Recession that ran from December of 2007 to about 2010. This broad impact was due to the fact that the Recession hit *all* segments of the American economy and therefore offset the traditional tendency of multiple sources being able to provide a basic equilibrium.

It is also true under the American system that the executive branch submits a budget, but the legislative branch passes a budget. In other words, what the president, governor, county executive, or mayor submits to the legislature is his or her *preferred* allocation, often more political statement[4] than serious policy proposal.[5] But it is rarely the one that passes.[6] However, the implied threat is often great for fund-raising.

At the end of May 2017 when the Trump administration submitted its first budget to Congress, a number of public radio stations sent out emails reading something along these lines:

> What if you turned on your radio this morning and there were no familiar voices? What if you couldn't hear [your favorite shows] every afternoon? Unfortunately, the administration's budget eliminates the funding that helps keep these programs on air.
>
> A dangerous proposal to cut essential public media funding is looming. Earlier this week, the president released his Fiscal Year (FY) 2018 budget to Congress, which recommended eliminating public media funding.
>
> Communities could be left without any access to local media. Essential programming and community services that educate, inform and inspire Americans of all ages could be cut.

In this environment, we need your support more than ever. So please consider a donation today.

The two points these appeals neglect to mention are (1) that funding for public broadcasting is routinely recommended for cuts in federal and many state executive budget proposals year in and year out, only to be restored by the legislative branch, and (2) that governmental funding, while not unimportant, generally does not represent the lion's share of most stations' budgets. Quite to the contrary, for many public television stations and many public radio stations, 75–80% of their operating dollars come from individual contributions and nongovernmental grants.[7]

However, this is *not* to say that budget cuts do not happen or that they do not impact nonprofits. By way of illustration, during the 2017 budget cycle, New Hanover County in North Carolina considered a proposed budget that would have cut $135,000 that had been going to ten local nonprofit agencies, some of them located within the city of Wilmington.[8] The city council was outraged because $45,000 of that money would have gone to the city's downtown development agency, and another $11,000 to a local city-based shelter for homeless people and soup kitchen.[9]

Even if these shortfalls were mitigated by the city, there is no doubt that if the county's budget went unchanged that the remaining $79,000 going to the other eight local agencies would be sorely missed. Some might be forced to cut staff and/ or services. It is even possible that one or two might be forced to close.

But this is, unfortunately, the actuality of what happens and who gets hurt during budget cuts. It is the small, nonprofit with a small profile, small constituency, and small donor base—*and* those they serve[10]—that are usually hurt the most, not the biggest organizations and not really the sector as a whole.

But if nonprofit stability *is* tied to government spending, how has the sector fared over the last few decades since the Great Society?

Although a critic of LBJ and his Great Society, President Nixon did not dismantle so much as redirect federal anti-poverty efforts. He did so by promoting legislation that helped the working poor and what America has historically viewed as the "deserving poor," older Americans, people with disabilities, and children. The Nixon administration enacted the Supplemental Security Income program in 1972, which placed Old Age Assistance, Aid to the Blind, and Aid to the Disabled solely under Social Security Administration, and most of the cost for the program was assumed by the federal government. Supplemental Security Income, better known as "SSI," also provided assistance to people with mental and physical disabilities. Nixon also pioneered the use of Revenue Sharing and Block Grants. His program of "General Revenue Sharing" provided federal funds to local government for general operating expenses, while "Special Revenue Sharing" (including Block Grants) contributed federal funds to local government for broad categorical areas.[11]

Examples of Nixon's Special Revenue Sharing were the Comprehensive Employment and Training Act (CETA) and the Housing and Community

Development Act. CETA was a consolidation of job training programs, some of which included public service jobs. The 1974 Housing and Community Development Act contained the Community Development Block Grant Program. These federal grants could be used by local communities for neighborhood improvement.[12]

The nonprofit sector, while perhaps not seeing during these years the amount of money that had flowed during the Johnson administration, nonetheless was the beneficiary of much of this spending.

Jumping forward to the Reagan years, the record shows that President Reagan halted a twenty-year pattern of ever-expanding social spending and programs. The impact was such that by 1986 spending levels had only once again reached those of 1980.[13]

Money flowed once again, however, under President Clinton, as he increased federal funding for Head Start and child care. In 1993, the first year of his administration, federal funding for Head Start totaled $3.3 billion (in constant 2000 dollars). After two major reauthorizations, funding for Head Start grew to $5.3 billion in the year 2000. President Clinton also increased nutritional and housing support for low-income families. Under his watch, Congress noticeably increased federal support for several critical nutritional and housing support programs.[14] Many of these initiatives also benefited the nonprofit sector as it continued to play its role as the government's service-providing partner.

The presidencies of George W. Bush and Barack Obama both were impacted by outside events: 9/11, the focus on national security and the Afghan and Iraqi wars in the case of the former, and the Great Recession in the case of the latter. Both of these, but particularly, as we have seen, the Recession, had an impact upon the fortunes of the American nonprofit sector. In spite of the early concerns, it does remain to be seen what effect a Trump presidency will ultimately have.

But there are several points to be made here.

The first is that the record shows that, no matter who was in the White House, no matter which party controlled Congress, the nonprofit sector has experienced unremitting growth since the end of the Johnson administration. In fact, 1972, a Nixon year, and 2002, a Bush 43 year, saw the two highest annual growth rates in the history of the American nonprofit sector, with about 55,000 new nonprofits, most of them 501(c)(3)s, entering the realm during both of those years. The growth was depressed, but still comparable to the Johnson years, during the administrations of Presidents Ford and Carter. The year of President Reagan's election, 1980, saw the slowest growth in the sector since 1970. But since then, not only has the growth continued (there has never been a net loss year) but the rate of growth has also steadily increased.[15] While there was a significant impact on the sector during the Recession years, the difference was more modest than some had expected. The nonprofit arena regularly experiences a "death" rate of about 4.3% per annum as, for a variety of reasons, some organizations go out of business, outlive their usefulness, or simply close. With the Recession, it might have been expected that this attrition would have surged. . .but it didn't. Rather, in 2012 there were only 5% fewer organizations reporting $50,000 or more (about thirteen thousand) than there had been in 2008. . .not a particularly significant loss given the 4.3% of such organizations that disappear each year. More to the point, however, even given this slight uptick in closures, almost fifty thousand new nonprofit organizations were formed.[16] Even nonprofit employment grew during the Recession, posting gains each year from 2007 to 2012.[17]

This overall growth has happened through good economic years and bad, through periods of boom and bust. . .through both Democrat and Republican administrations and both liberal and conservative philosophies influencing policy. In other words, the nonprofit arena has seen, and survived, up-and-down funding cycles and both philosophical allies and foes in the government before. Funding may have waxed and waned—indeed, the last forty-something years since the Great Society have been something of a funding roller-coaster for the nonprofit world—but through it all it has not only survived, but has continued to expand, grow, and adapt. It has proven that it is, as Lester Salamon has noted, *resilient*.

There is no telling at the dawn of the Trump era what the ultimate impact on the nonprofit realm of his tenure and that of his congressional allies will be. But the historical evidence suggests that the sector will be around, fundamentally strong and probably still growing, long after he is gone.

Moving toward the market

If the demarcation between the American nonprofit arena and the government has become somewhat blurred over the last fifty-odd years, so too, in recent years, has the line between the classic not-for-profit realm and its for-profit cousin. This can be seen in a number of ways. As a general statement, it has been observed that industries like the performing arts and health care, which had been almost entirely for-profit in ownership before 1950, became dominated by nonprofit entities in the course of the next half-century. Meanwhile, industries like elder care, which had been largely nonprofit, have become increasingly for-profit in ownership as government social and medical insurance programs made nursing homes an increasingly profitable enterprise.[18]

As we have seen, after World War II many local nonprofit agencies began offering services to the nation's growing middle class. This was partially an attempt to remain relevant in a world that no longer looked to charitable organizations as the first or even primary response to want and need. The Great Depression had finally moved the government into the forefront of that effort. Needing other avenues for their energies, many charities sought to fill a newly emerging space characterized by such private concerns as family and marriage counseling.

Another consideration influencing this development, however, was that the middle class could pay for these services. This transactional relationship differed greatly from the traditional connection between organization and client, in which the organization expected nothing from the recipients of its help or guidance.

In the decades since the Great Society, as the government increasingly became the one paying for an ever-increasing range of interventions, the fee-for-service model not only survived, but became a major component of many nonprofits' funding stream. The difference, by way of illustration, between a nonprofit offering government-funded youth counseling and a private practice of psychologists and social workers offering the same services but relying upon client payments or private insurance is often difficult to discern.

A similar issue exists regarding nonprofit hospitals.

Many who call for an end to most tax exemptions agree with the idea of continuing nonprofit hospitals' tax-exempt status. They do so under the theory that they "are an indispensable, and noncontroversial, public good,"[19] and that they serve the poorest and those most unable to pay.

Yet some nonprofit hospitals can't demonstrate that they are operating any more charitably than their for-profit counterparts. It's noted that the charity care that these nonprofit hospitals provide (a feature which is supposed to distinguish them) is sometimes no different than that provided by comparable for-profits institutions.[20] In these instances, it appears that the only difference between the two kinds of hospitals is that nonprofits have a strategic business advantage over the for-profits because they don't have to pay taxes.[21]

Moreover, whatever its future and the controversies surrounding it, Obamacare significantly addressed the issue of millions of uninsured people in the U.S. so that by 2015 only 11.4% of the population reported that they had no coverage at all.[22] Arguably, this lessened the central justification for nonprofit hospitals.

Indeed, one study has shown that nonprofit hospitals spend about the same proportion of their budgets as for-profit hospitals for free or subsidized care. Nonprofits were found to dedicate an average of 1.9% of their total operating expenses to free care. For-profit hospitals were spending an average 1.4% for such care. About a third of the nonprofits spent *less than 0.9%* on charity care. The difference between those institutions that pay taxes and those that don't is only 0.5%,[23] causing more than a few observers to wonder just what the difference between the two classes of institutions actually is, particularly in an era when charitable hospital staffing structures have moved away from unpaid or only nominally paid staff to full professionalization.[24]

A second factor in the blurring of the lines between the nonprofit and for-profit realms has been the increased reliance among charities on earned income.

While it may come as a surprise to many, "nonprofit" does not mean that these organizations cannot make a profit. A nonprofit *can* generate income, and many do.[25] What they can't do is distribute profits in the form of dividends or share value to anyone else.

Suggestive of the degree to which this practice is employed, the National Center for Charitable Statistics estimates that nearly 70% of the $1.4 trillion generated by nonprofits in 2008 came from the sale of goods and services.[26] In a 2003 Bridgespan Group survey of American nonprofits' executives, half of the respondents said they believed earned income would play an important or extremely important role in bolstering their organizations' revenue in the future.[27]

The classic example is the Girl Scouts of the USA, synonymous with cookies. The organization generates more than $700 million in revenue each year from its annual cookie sale program.[28]

The way this usually works is that the nonprofit has a valuable asset, product, or expertise upon which it can capitalize in the open market. . .and a customer base willing and able to pay. While large nonprofit educational institutions and medical facilities are the largest beneficiaries of this revenue stream,[29] more common examples include nonprofit animal shelters and humane societies offering reduced-cost spaying and neutering services,[30] the rental of organization facilities to outside parties,[31] and gift shops in museums and other nonprofit sites. Some counseling organizations charge middle-class customers, even as they offer free services to social service clients. More out-of-the-box examples include the Chicago Children's Choir—which runs a singing telegram business *and* a Ben & Jerry's Scoop Shop—and Shelter, Inc., of Contra Costa County, a Californian organization dedicated to serving the homeless, which has launched a property management firm.[32] The National Wildlife Federation, meanwhile, endorses environmentally friendly outdoor products like birdbaths sold by Home Depot and receives a percentage of the product sales.[33]

Opinion has been divided regarding this "move to the marketplace" by nonprofits. Some have seen it as both understandable and necessary in the face of uncertain funding over the last decade or so.

The general enthusiasm for business, which reached a fever pitch during the booming 1990s, had a profound impact on nonprofits and the institutions that support them. Like their counterparts in the commercial world, managers of nonprofits increasingly want to be viewed as active entrepreneurs rather than as passive bureaucrats; many viewed launching a successful commercial venture as one direct route to that goal.

Meanwhile, board members, many of whom are accomplished business leaders, often encourage and reinforce that desire. At the same time, many philanthropic foundations and other funders were urging nonprofits to become financially self-sufficient and aggressively promoted earned income as an avenue toward "sustainability."

As a result, nonprofits increasingly feel compelled to launch earned-income ventures, if only to appear more disciplined, innovative, and businesslike to their stakeholders.[34]

At the same time there are those who point to the inherent dangers in nonprofits' involvement in business ventures,[35] and to the alleged inherent unfairness of market competition when one group of competitors enjoys a government-subsidized competitive advantage, in this case, the tax-exempt status enjoyed by most nonprofit organizations.[36]

The entry of nonprofits into areas heretofore reserved for private enterprise, however, has not been a one-way street. Increasingly, for-profit companies are moving into areas that have traditionally been populated by nonprofits. . .

Privatization

Privatization, or the movement of private enterprises into areas that were previously viewed as not within that domain, has both helped and hurt nonprofits.

Largely sparked in the U.S. by the work of David Osborne and Ted Gaebler,[37] and the stewardship of Vice-President Al Gore during the Clinton years, the "Reinventing Government" movement led to, among other things, an effort to downsize the public-sector workforce. This downsizing, however, did not necessarily mean that the functions previously or potentially carried out by government employees vanished. A good deal of it, particularly in the area of human services, was effectively contracted out to nonprofits. In this, nonprofits were the beneficiaries of privatization.

However, privatization has taken a different turn in recent years, as the government has looked to private, for-profit companies to take on certain functions as a way to save money. Not only have the results been mixed,[38] but there is evidence that for-profits are looking to enter additional arenas traditionally reserved for the nonprofit sector.[39] By way of illustration, according to some reports, for-profit corporations are developing a pattern of buying up or otherwise acquiring nonprofit hospitals in some parts of the country.[40] At the moment, the arenas of social assistance, education, and nursing home care represent the greatest areas of current concern, as for-profit employment in these realms out-paced nonprofit employment during the 2000–2010 decade. Nonprofits in these areas lost considerable market share to their for-profit competition.[41] In addition, the nonprofit share of employment in rehabilitation hospitals fell by 50% between 1982 and 1997, while it was also decreasing 60% within health maintenance agencies, 45% in kidney dialysis centers, 15% in hospices, and 11% in mental health clinics.[42] What is most alarming about this trend is that this loss of market share is showing up even in fields that were traditionally the overwhelming province of nonprofits. For example, as recently as 1997 nonprofits accounted for over 90% of all employment in the sphere of individual and family services, but accounted for only 60% of such employment in 2012.[43]

This dynamic may be of long term concern to the sector for a number of reasons, not the least of which is that human services, education, and health care have traditionally been central areas of nonprofit activity and employment. It has been noted, moreover, that there seems to exist a preference for for-profit providers on the part of some state and local governments, which have increasingly been outsourcing traditional government functions to private entities, particularly in the area of social assistance. As to why governments might prefer for-profit providers, it has been suggested that considerations include the strong political connections that often exist between government officials and for-profit leaders (reinforced through campaign contributions), the higher wage rates paid by nonprofits in some fields, and certain nonprofit practices which result in higher overall service costs.[44]

Should this budding competition continue, it may not bode well for the sector, as for-profit corporations enjoy a number of market advantages—most particularly their access to capital and resultant ability to respond quickly to regulatory and economic changes—generally not shared by nonprofits. It is a trend that definitely bears watching.

Clients as consumers

The traditional model for the charitable sector's relationships with those it served was that of provider and beneficiary: the nonprofit provided services and the beneficiary (most often) gratefully accepted them. For the greatest part of the sector's history, long before the term became either fashionable or widely used, the "clients" of various nonprofit agencies turned to those organizations that served their community. Whether Catholic Charities working in the Taylor Street section of Chicago or in South Boston, the National Jewish Welfare Board working in New York, or the Marquette General Hospital serving Michigan's Upper Peninsula, the idea of those being served as "consumers" was completely foreign.

In most cases, the situation between client and service provider most closely resembled that between taxpayer and government: the individual really had few, if any, choices. If you owned property, for example, you had to deal with the county tax department; there was nowhere else to go to pay your taxes. If you intended to use public transportation, in most cases the government-owned bus and rail lines were your primary (if not only) option.

So it was with many nonprofits. There was usually little (if any) competition for the services they provided in an area. Clients did not "shop around," and there were several structural reasons why they couldn't.

For people with limited access to transportation, utilizing the services of the nonprofit closest to home made the most sense.

Clients were often assigned or referred to specific agencies for services, and by the 1970s, to access those services within the byzantine maze of most cities' social service systems meant going where you were assigned.

But one of the greatest factors was that the money made available for the provision of services, whether by the government, foundations, or other sources, invariably went to the agencies and not the client. Not only were clients generally exempt from paying for the services they received, but they were completely removed from the entire financial process that made the services possible. That relationship was solely between the agency and its funders. But this too has changed.

Beginning in the 1980s, as more conservative forces gained ascendency in Washington and many state capitals, a variety of perspectives prompted a shift away from the traditional provider subsidies whose heyday had been the Great

Society, to consumer subsidies, whereby client/taxpayers became eligible for a variety of financing tools that put money or its equivalent—in other words, the power of choice—into their hands.

Whether loan guarantees, vouchers, or tax credits, channeling aid to consumers of services rather than to the providers of services forced non-profits to have to compete. . .and not just against one another, but against for-profit entities as well. While such mechanisms were not entirely new, the addition or introduction of vehicles such as the child care tax credit, the credit for student loan interest payments, the low-income housing tax credit, and the new market credit significantly altered the nonprofit playing field.[45]

The election of Donald Trump and the Republicans' control of the House and Senate as well as at least half the state governments mean that conservatives' preference for consumer choice—at the expense of large, publicly run or agency-dependent systems—may find fertile ground for expansion. It is conceivable that within the next several years a new array of traditional "nonprofit services," offerings ranging from anger management and day care to pediatric speech therapy and hospice care, will find themselves subject to increasing consumer choice.

This trend has been one of a number of influences impacting the nonprofit arena in recent years, forcing these organizations to plan in ways they have not had to even consider throughout their long history.

Beyond thinking "entrepreneurially" and being forced to come up with ways to make money, they are increasingly having to learn how to market their services to potential customers, while still demonstrating their *value* to potential funders. This shift has not always been easy, and not all nonprofits have been able thus far to manage the challenges of "appealing" to the often contradictory wants and desires of institutional funders, their traditional stakeholders, and new potential individual clients.[46]

It remains to be seen how these trends that are chipping away at the traditional demarcation between the nonprofit and for-profit realms will ultimately play out.

Notes

1 Graham, K. Idealware fund-raising letter via e-mail. December 8, 2016.
2 Perry, G. "How Will a Trump Presidency Impact Nonprofits, Fundraising and Philanthropy?" Gail's Blog. Fired-Up Fundraising. November 9, 2016. https://www.gailperry.com/how-will-trump-presidency-election-impact-fundraising-nonprofit-philanthropy/.
3 Charity Navigator. "10 Super-Sized Charities." https://www.charitynavigator.org/index.cfm?bay=topten.detail&listid=24.
4 It is also often an easy, though cynical, way for a president, governor, or mayor—particularly one facing an upcoming election—to cast him/herself as a tough fiscal watchdog and blame spending (and any new taxes) on a profligate legislature.

5 McCambridge, R. "Disastrous 2018 Presidential Budget Likely DOA." *Nonprofit Quarterly.*May23,2017.https://nonprofitquarterly.org/2017/05/23/disastrous-2018-presidential-budget-likely-doa/?utm_source=Daily+Newswire&utm_campaign=843b37b47f-EMAIL_CAMPAIGN_2017_05_23&utm_medium=email&utm_term=0_94063a1d17-843b37b47f-12341229.

6 On May 2, 2017, the *Nonprofit Quarterly* reported that Congress and the Trump administration had reached agreement on a five-month spending plan that not only retained, but in some cases increased, funding for many of the domestic programs threatened by the president's campaign. It did not, therefore, represent the immediate disaster for nonprofits many were predicting. The $18 billion in domestic spending reductions the administration sought were not forthcoming. Some notable programs remained virtually untouched: no cuts to Planned Parenthood, the National Institutes of Health (which got a $2 billion increase instead of the $1.2 billion cut that was requested by the administration), the Legal Services Corporation, the National Endowment of the Arts, the National Endowment for the Humanities, or the Corporation for Public Broadcasting. Additionally, the proposed border wall was not funded, and the Environmental Protection Agency retains 99% of its budget despite threats of a 40% cut. While the first formal budget presented by the administration did contain substantial cuts, the earlier agreement on the five-month plan illustrated the frequent difference between what an executive might propose and what a legislature ultimately approves. See McCambridge, R. and Wyland, M. "A Spending Bill Summary for Nonprofits: Trump Gets Warned and Threatened Cuts Don't Materialize." *Nonprofit Quarterly.* May 2, 2017. https://nonprofitquarterly.org/2017/05/02/victory-through-not-losing-spending-bill-nonprofit-spending-bill/?utm_source=Daily+Newswire&utm_campaign=a989b5ae14-EMAIL_CAMPAIGN_2017_05_02&utm_medium=email&utm_term=0_94063a1d17-a989b5ae14-12341229.

7 Winke, Chris. Vice President for Radio. WMHT Educational Telecommunications. Telephone Interview. April 10, 2014.

8 The city of Wilmington, NC, lies completely within New Hanover County.

9 In response, the city considered making up at least part of the possible shortfall in the development agency's budget by increasing its own contribution. See Buckland, T. "City Blasts County Nonprofit Cuts." *Star-News.* May 27, 2017. p. A2.

10 Levine, M. "Trump's 2018 Budget Proposal Would Eviscerate Food Programs." *Nonprofit Quarterly.* May, 23, 2017. https://nonprofitquarterly.org/2017/05/23/trumps-2018-budget-proposal-eviscerate-food-programs/?utm_source=Daily+Newswire&utm_campaign=843b37b47f-EMAIL_CAMPAIGN_2017_05_23&utm_medium=email&utm_term=0_94063a1d17-843b37b47f-12341229.

11 Marx, J. "American Social Policy in the 1960's and 1970's." Social Welfare History Project. Virginia Commonwealth University. http://socialwelfare.library.vcu.edu/war-on-poverty/american-social-policy-in-the-60s-and-70s/.

12 Ibid.

13 Salamon in Hodgkinson et al. p. 45.

14 Center for American Progress. "The Power of Progressive Economics: The Clinton Years." October 28, 2011. https://www.americanprogress.org/issues/economy/reports/2011/10/28/10405/power-of-progressive-economics-the-clinton-years/.

15 Jones. pp. 14–15.

16 Brown, M.S. et al. "The Impact of the Great Recession on the Number of Charities." Urban Institute. July 2013. www.urban.org/sites/default/files/publication/24046/412924-The-Impact-of-the-Great-Recession-on-the-Number-of-Charities.PDF.

17 Couch, R. "Nonprofit Employment Actually Grew During the Recession: Report." *Huffington Post Impact*. January 7, 2015. www.huffingtonpost.com/2015/01/07/ nonprofit-sector-growth_n_6424428.html; Philanthropy News Digest. "Nonprofit Jobs Increased Throughout Great Recession, Data Show." March 7, 2016. http:// philanthropynewsdigest.org/news/nonprofit-jobs-increased-throughout-great-recession-data-show.

18 Hall. (2010) p. 19.

19 Oppenheimer. Op. cit.

20 Chronicle of Philanthropy. "Study: Nonprofits and Non-Profits Spend about the Same for Charity Care." August 4, 2015. https://philanthropy.com/article/Study-Nonprofits-and/232149?cid=pt&utm_source=pt&utm_medium=en.

21 Berger. Op. cit.

22 Obamacarefacts. "Obamacare Enrollment Numbers." August 12, 2015. http:// obamacarefacts.com/sign-ups/obamacare-enrollment-numbers/.

23 This has moved some to suggest that tax breaks to nonprofit hospitals contribute far less to community benefits than they do to higher executive salaries. See Chronicle of Philanthropy. Op. cit.

24 The Catholic Church is to this day the nation's largest private provider of health care, accounting for a total of about one in every six hospital beds. Through various dioceses and religious orders, the church operates 566 hospitals, many of them founded by congregations of nuns. (Neibur, G. "The Health Care Debate: The Catholic Church; Catholic Leaders' Dilemma: Abortion vs. Universal Care." *New York Times*. August 25, 1994. www.nytimes.com/1994/08/25/us/health-care-debate-catholic-church-catholic-leaders-dilemma-abortion-vs.html?pagewanted=all&src=pm.) St. Vincent's Hospital in New York, by way of illustration, was opened by four members of the Daughters of Charity religious order in 1849. Several orders of nuns—the Sisters of Mercy, for example, which still serve six health systems in the U.S.—founded and traditionally ran numerous hospitals in the U.S. However, as vocations have diminished and these hospitals have been acquired by larger secular medical corporations, the sisters' involvement—and often minimal pay—has also largely disappeared from the scene.

25 The IRS categorizes earned income into two categories: related and unrelated. A public charity generally does not pay taxes on related income, but it does pay taxes on unrelated business income at the corporate rate, also called the unrelated business income tax. The IRS determines whether earned income is related or unrelated using a three-part analysis. The general rule is that income is treated as unrelated if it is a trade or business, regularly carried on, and not substantially related to the organization's exempt purpose. See Chan, E. "The Profitable Side of Nonprofits—Part I: Earned Income." Nonprofit Law Blog. May 6, 2011. www.nonprofitlawblog.com/ the-profitable-side-of-nonprofits-part-i-earned-income/.

26 Lapowsky, I. "The Social Entrepreneurship Spectrum: Nonprofits with Earned Income." *Inc. Magazine*. May 2011. www.inc.com/magazine/20110501/the-social-entrepreneurship-spectrum-nonprofits-with-earned-income.html.

27 Foster, W. and Bradach, J. "Should Nonprofits Seek Profits?" *Harvard Business Review*. February 2005. https://hbr.org/2005/02/should-nonprofits-seek-profits/ar/1.

28 Lapowsky. Op. cit.

29 As one example of nonprofit entrepreneurship, picturesque Fordham University in the Bronx, with its classic Gothic look, has long leant its campus and facilities, for a fee, as the backdrop for not only Hollywood movies ranging from *The Exorcist* to *A Beautiful Mind*, but also commercials for the U.S. Army and other organizations. See Schreifels, J.K. "Filmed at Fordham." *The Ram Realm*. October 18, 2013. www. theramrealm.com/2013/10/18/filmed-at-fordham/.

30 Ibid.

31 The Hebron Academy in Maine, in fact, went to court to defend its nonprofit status in the face of town attempts to make it pay property taxes. The town of Hebron was challenging the school's exemption on two grounds, the second being that it wasn't utilizing its grounds "solely for its own purposes" because it was generating about $130,000 per year by renting some of its facilities on a short-term basis to outside individuals and organizations.

32 Foster and Bradach. Op. cit.

33 Ibid.

34 Ibid.

35 Critics note that, overall, nonprofits are not making large profits from their business ventures, with 71% of the organizations responding to a recent survey reporting that their ventures were unprofitable, 24% believing that they were profitable, and 5% stating that they were breaking even. Of those that claimed they were profitable, half did not fully account for indirect costs such as allocations of general overheads or senior management time. Simply put, there is every reason to believe that the lion's share of earned-income ventures does not succeed at generating revenues beyond their costs. (See Foster and Bradach. Op. cit.). Beyond this, there is the danger that a for-profit venture intended to provide an earned-income revenue stream for a nonprofit could actually trigger its downfall. Perhaps the most notorious example in recent years was the unexpected collapse of New York City's 80-year-old and venerated Federation Employment & Guidance Service (FEGS). Founded in 1934 "to help Jewish men and women and others to identify, prepare for, and find jobs and careers; and to fight workplace discrimination for all people," eventually the agency expanded its mission to help poor people and those with disabilities in New York City find jobs, adequate housing, and proper healthcare. FEGS' latest numbers showed $202 million in multiple-year contracts with the city and the state. With 2,000-plus employees, FEGS served over 135,000 people in the New York metropolitan region annually. However, with no warning it shut all of its programs, leaving city and state officials scrambling to find new providers of job placement, housing, mental health care, and other services for tens of thousands of vulnerable New Yorkers as it grappled with a $19 million budgetary shortfall. While numerous reasons were cited by critics—30% of FEGS's budget went toward administrative costs, including salaries, which is considerably higher than most watchdog groups recommend—many blamed the massive amounts of money the agency was paying out to its for-profit subsidiary, AllSector Technology Group. FEGS created the corporation in 1998 to be a source of revenue for the non-profit, but by 2011 FEGS was paying *it* money, reportedly $9.1 million that year alone. (Swarns, R. "With Little Warning, Agency Aiding New York's Most Vulnerable Crumbles." *New York Times.* February 8, 2015. www.nytimes.com/2015/02/09/nyregion/with-little-warning-agency-aiding-new-york-citys-most-vulnerable-crumbles.html?_r=0;Stanley,J."The Troubling Downfall of a New York City Safety Net." Next City. April 1, 2015. https://nextcity.org/daily/entry/fegs-new-york-city-social-services-nonprofit-closed; Nathan-Kazis, J. "Why Did FEGS Funnel Millions to For-Profit Tech Subsidiary?" *The Forward.* March 6, 2015. http://forward.com/news/215978/why-did-fegs-funnel-millions-to-for-profit-tech-su/.)

36 Gomes, G. and Owens, J.M. "Commercial Nonprofits, Untaxed Entrepreneurialism, And 'Unfair Competition.'" *Journal of Small Business Management.* April 1988. pp. 8–16. *Passim.* www.csuchico.edu/mgmt/gomes/JSBMVol26No2.pdf.

37 Osborne, D. and Gaebler, T. *Reinventing Government: How the Entrepreneurial Spirit Is Transforming the Public Sector.* [Reading, MA: Addison-Wesley Pub. Co., 1992] *passim.*

38 Chicago's mayor, Rahm Emanuel, privatized janitorial services in 2014 in the Chicago Public Schools, contracting with two firms: Aramark for $260 million, and SodexoMagic, partly owned by basketball superstar Magic Johnson, for $80 million.

The deal turned out to be actually more expensive than originally estimated, as the city has had to pledge another $7 million to Aramark because it miscounted the number of schools Aramark's staff would have to clean. After Aramark's dismissal of hundreds of janitors at the schools as a means of saving costs, exacerbating the dirt and grime in many, teachers at Oriole Park elementary school filed a grievance to force Chicago Public Schools to hire back the dismissed janitors.

The U.S. Senate is also reportedly considering a proposal to privatize the operations of commissaries on military bases, but the idea drew opposition from a number of sources, including the Obama administration. (Cohen, R. "Nonprofit Conundrum: Support Government Privatization or Not?" *Nonprofit Quarterly*. June 5, 2015. https://nonprofitquarterly.org/2015/06/05/nonprofit-conundrum-support-government-privatization-or-not/.) Traditional public functions from the management of airports to the Veterans Administration have been suggested as targets of privatization. Meanwhile, a 2009 analysis of water and sewer utilities by Food and Water Watch found that private companies charge up to 80% more than municipal entities for water and 100% more for sewer services. A more recent study confirms that privatization will generally "increase the long-term costs borne by the public." Privatization is "shortsighted, irresponsible and costly."

Numerous examples of water privatization abuses or failures have been documented in California, Georgia, Illinois, Indiana, Massachusetts, New Jersey, Rhode Island and Texas—just about anywhere it's been tried. Meanwhile, corporations have been making outrageous profits on a commodity that should be almost free. Nestle buys water for about 1/100 of a penny per gallon, and sells it back for ten dollars. (Bucheir, P. "8 Ways Privatization Has Failed America." Common Dreams. August 5, 2013. www.commondreams.org/views/2013/08/05/8-ways-privatization-has-failed-america.) Perhaps the most controversial privatizations, however, have been among America's jails. According to the American Civil Liberties Union, for-profit companies are responsible for approximately 6% of state prisoners, 16% of federal prisoners, and inmates in local jails in Texas, Louisiana, and a handful of other states (American Civil Liberties Union. "Private Prisons." https://www.aclu.org/issues/mass-incarceration/privatization-criminal-justice/private-prisons), leading to conditions and situations some critics find intolerable. (Corrections Project. "Prison Privatization." www.correctionsproject.com/corrections/pris_priv.htm.)

39 Shapiro, S. "Privatizing Social Welfare Hurts." *Arutz Sheva*. June, 30, 2011. www.israelnationalnews.com/Articles/Article.aspx/10367; Chung, Y. "The Impact of Privatization on Museum Admission Charges: A Case Study from Taiwan." *International Journal of Arts Management*.Vol. 7, No. 2. (2005); Stephens, Simon. "Union to Oppose National Gallery Privatization Plan." *Museums Journal*. The Museums Association (UK). July 8, 2014. www.museumsassociation.org/museums-journal/news/08072014-national-gallery-privatisation; Kenny, H. "Privately Operated Zoos Now Considered the Standard." The Reason Foundation. May 29, 2012. http://reason.org/news/show/zoo-privatization-2011.

40 Edgar, J. "For-Profits Gobbling Up Community Hospitals in Michigan." *The Bridge*. The Center for Michigan. March 18, 2014. http://bridgemi.com/2014/03/for-profits-gobbling-up-community-hospitals-in-michigan/.

41 While nonprofit employment in social assistance grew by an average annual rate of 2.2% between 2000 and 2010, for-profit employment in this field grew by an average of 5.4% over the same period. Other fields in which for-profit growth outpaced nonprofit growth include education (4.4% vs. 2.6%) and nursing home care (2.3% vs. 1.3%). See Salamon, L. et al. "Holding the Fort: Nonprofit Employment

during a Decade of Turmoil." *Nonprofit Employment Bulletin No. 39.* Johns Hopkins Center for Civil Society. January 2012. p. 8. http://ccss.jhu.edu/wp-content/uploads/downloads/2012/01/NED_National_2012.pdf.

42 Salamon, L. (2105) p. 40.
43 Ibid.
44 Ibid. p. 9.
45 Ibid. pp. 34–38.
46 By way of an example, one nonprofit that had been founded for the purpose of offering special services to very severely disabled children found that its publicly available information on that subject—including brochures and its website—as well as its historic association with that mission were actually turning off parents who might have selected it for speech therapy for their otherwise fully-abled children.

9 The Outcomes Movement and performance measurement

Of all the developments since the Great Society, few match the potential of Results and Performance Measurement for bringing about dramatic changes in the way the nonprofit arena operates.

For most of its history, the nonprofit sector did not have to prove that it was having the impact its constituent organizations claimed to be having...or, for that matter, that it was having *any* positive impact at all.[1] While several reasons could be cited as an explanation for this, perhaps the most basic is that almost no one asked. The sector was therefore able to almost exclusively couch its appeals and justify its existence in terms of problems and activity. Moreover, this lack of true accountability is not limited just to the charities that comprise the sector, but to its foundations as well. Joel Fleishman, in perhaps the most thorough book yet written on American philanthropic foundations, has listed their virtually complete lack of accountability to anyone as among their greatest failings.[2]

It is also interesting to note that this phenomenon has not been restricted to the U.S. Most Americans, having seen or read at least one version of this oft told tale, are familiar with Dickens' *A Christmas Carol*. It may be recalled that at one point early in the story, two gentlemen stop in on Scrooge seeking a donation for the relief of the poor. Their appeal is based upon two facts: it's the "festive season of the year," and there are "poor and destitute who suffer greatly at the present time."

"Many thousands," they point out, "are in want of common necessities," and "*hundreds of thousands* are in want of common comforts"[3] (emphasis added).

These gentlemen are presenting an irrefutable statement of a problem, and asking for a positive reaction in the form of a donation or pledge. They pointedly do not mention exactly how Scrooge's donation would be put to use, or the results that they claim his contribution will make possible. They merely present a problem.

Dickens wrote this passage in 1843 and presented a scene with which his audience, both in the UK and the U.S., was quite familiar. What this suggests is that not only was this "problem approach" being used well over 170 years ago, but also it was already quite common by that time.

It is still used today.

In countless appeals made by an equally uncounted number of organizations, donors are presented with images or descriptions of need. *Won't You Help?* is the common closing refrain. . .and one to which most of us respond. Whether it is our sympathy, empathy, anger at the situation, or guilt that is triggered by these appeals, we respond. Few of us ever ask whether our contributions *or* the organizations' activities are making real, measurable, sustainable progress toward fixing whatever problem is being presented.

When pressed, however, to account for what they are doing with the donations they receive, the vast majority of nonprofits fall back upon activity accounts.

Traditionally, most social service nonprofits (and many of their funders) focus on what the agency is doing and how many people it has served. The questions they ask include: How many meals were cooked and served in the soup kitchen, to how many people? How many middle schoolers attended the after-school program, and in what kinds of activities did they engage? How many newly released felons participated in the community re-entry program? How many unemployed people visited the job center and used the computers? How many job seekers took work-readiness classes?[4]

With this as their focus, they tell us how many they have served, the number of communities in which they operate. They tell us how many training classes they have held, how many reports they have issued, how many times they have testified at hearings, and how many bologna sandwiches they have delivered.

The question this approach misses, however, is *Once the meal is eaten, what has changed?*

While of course it is necessary for children to have safe havens, is that enough to set them on course for successful living? Once the felon has finished his or her coursework, what difference has this made? And if one prepares for a job but can't get it, or gets a job but can't keep it, where is the benefit?[5]

Put another way, for all the things nonprofits generally do tell us, what they don't generally tell us is what any of this effort is doing to improve the actual circumstances of those the organizations exist to serve. In many cases, it has historically been difficult to tell whether our support and their actions were having any impact whatsoever. Perhaps worse are those situations where not only has no coherent strategy for dealing with a problem been arrived at—in some cases such a strategy, according to Joel Fleishman, may be "inconceivable, inappropriate, or premature"[6]—but money has been and often still is thrown at a problem anyway, with no real hope of any positive and meaningful expected outcomes. Such situations only make worse the tendency to focus on problems and activities.

But to be fair, a great deal of all this stemmed from the times in which the voluntary sector developed and came of age. It would take developments in both the for-profit, corporate world and the public/nonprofit realm to eventually open the door to changes in this situation. . .

The nonprofit side of measurement

While the organized social work of charities and religious institutions had begun to take modern recognizable form by the second third of the 19th century, there was effectively no thought given to assessing the impact of those efforts. No one, for example, thought to examine whether the Friendly Visitors were actually changing the thinking or behavior of those they visited in Five Points. Rather, the social change and benevolence activists of the time took such victories as the end of the pillory and stock in Massachusetts as evidence of their effectiveness.

For its part, the government, too, largely failed to make any meaningful effort to track the efficacy of such policies and programs as existed at the time. Although Massachusetts formed a Board of State Charities in 1864 with a mandate to inspect, report upon, and make recommendations for the improvement of both public welfare institutions and private ones receiving state aid or support—and within a decade a number of other states had followed suit[7]—these bodies were not looking at the effectiveness of the entities it examined. Rather they were looking at finances and other practices to determine whether they were humane, exercised proper control over their charges, and in particular, were not doing anything that might prove embarrassing.[8]

As for the federal government, it was not particularly active in the area we would today call human services, and was doing little.[9]

But with the onset of large-scale immigration and the crowded slum conditions to which it contributed in cities such as Boston, New York, and Philadelphia, growing concerns with public health in 1874 led to the first concerted efforts at collecting programmatic information regarding the effectiveness of public policies in the U.S. By 1907 the New York City Bureau of Municipal Research was collecting data on social conditions.

But the collection of data did not mean that analysis necessarily followed. Evaluation, assessment, and performance measurement of either government or private efforts were not thought to be necessary.[10] Instead, for over a century there existed such faith in the effectiveness of these programs that little or no "proof" was required.[11] By way of illustration, a 1970s study of over sixty years of social science writing did not find evidence that there existed within early research efforts any question about the effectiveness of social interventions. To the contrary, there seems to have been an implicit assumption that, armed with a proper understanding of social problems, social work professionals would have no trouble changing negative conditions through the right combination of policies and direct intervention.[12]

It should also be added that the government further contributed to this perspective when it based its own estimation of success upon such activity accounts as the miles of electric line the Tennessee Valley Authority strung,[13] the number of applicants to the Social Security program, or the number of college enrollees the GI Bill had produced.

This is not to say, however, that no one suggested the idea of determining whether social interventions were working. In 1926, a prescient Edgar

Syndenstricker was already writing that for either social policies or their assessment to be successful, objectives and methods both needed to be clearly defined.[14]

Andie Knutson, in 1955, similarly argued the importance of defining program objectives more specifically, calling for a hierarchy of objectives, and the identification of intervening conditions that might be necessary for the achievement of the ultimate objective.[15] And in 1960, Antonio Ciocco, perhaps mindful of the developing reliance upon strict measurement in the corporate field of management theory, began stressing the importance of using indices of "known reliability and validity" in looking at social work.[16]

As late as 1969, the same year the Urban Institute completed an extensive study of the evaluation of federally sponsored programs and concluded that such evaluation was "almost non-existent,"[17] Edward Suchman would also observe that "what passes for evaluative research [today] is. . .a mixed bag at best, and chaos at worst." Too many program objectives, Suchman complained, "are grandiose, but usually vague statements of intent and procedure. . .based upon largely untested or even unsound assumptions whose validity rests primarily upon tradition or common sense and not upon proven effectiveness."[18] To address this problem, Suchman suggested an essential "test of the validity of the 'cause–effect hypotheses' in social action."[19]

By the mid-1970s, Joseph Wholey and a team of Urban Institute researchers were asking some basic questions about the public and private programs they saw around them. Effectively, what they asked was *Why can't we know whether any of these things actually worked?*

Developing a concept of "Program Evaluability," Wholey would argue that many programs were not actually designed to be meaningfully assessed. He suggested at least two reasons:

- A lack of definition: the target problems, actual program interventions, expected outcomes, and desired impacts were often not sufficiently defined as to be measurable. The problems addressed by many social programs, Wholey concluded, were almost never stated so that institutions, people, or relevant conditions could be classified according to the degree to which they are affected.[20] Adding to this was the common practice of describing programs in an "elegant but elusive language" that often amounted to little more than "vaporous wishes."[21]
- A lack of clear program logic: the logic of assumptions linking an expenditure of resources, the implementation of an intervention, the anticipated outcomes, and the predicted impacts were often not specified or understood clearly enough to permit effective testing. Echoing Suchman, Wholey and his team asked *what*, beyond wishful thinking, really linked A to B in these programs?

The understanding that Wholey and others were coming to was that if we are to evaluate or assess social initiatives to any degree of success and validity, we must plan along lines that make assessment and evaluation possible and meaningful.

These few voices aside, however, overall there was roughly a century—from the 1870s through the 1970s—when the efforts of reformers, whether working through the government or the benevolent philanthropies and emerging organized charities, were largely characterized by well-intentioned activity, with precious few resources devoted to even thinking about how to ascertain if social improvement measures were actually having their hoped-for effect.

The dawning realization that this approach was insufficient, it is important to add, was not cropping up exclusively, or even primarily, in the field of social change. Rather, from medicine to mental hygiene, practitioners and theorists in a variety of disciplines were beginning to look beyond the activity of various interventions, and instead were asking the seminal question of why they should or might not work. In this, they had several developing examples over in the corporate world that could act as their guide.

The management genome

Management guru Peter F. Drucker has argued that nonprofit institutions need management no less than do for-profit entities, that they must learn to use it as their tool, and that it is *necessary* if they are to successfully concentrate upon their missions.[22]

In a historical sense, the earliest forms of management focused on "work," largely because manual labor described the tasks at hand for the greatest part of human history. This manual labor, even if it was skilled, comprised the vast majority of work in agrarian, pre-industrial, and even industrial societies. The "management" of people working in a farm, a shop, or even a factory was largely the management of the work those people did. Evidence of this is to be found in the focus on inputs, labor, and raw materials that was long a dominant theme in American industry.[23]

Frederick Taylor's "scientific management" in the early years of the last century was perhaps the first real effort to analyze work[24] in an attempt to bring about something unprecedented: increased worker productivity.[25] Until that time, the only way to increase worker output (the word *productivity* was not even used in English until 1898 to refer to work[26]) was for workers to work longer or harder. The only recognized differences between workers at the time were between "lazy" ones and "hard-working" ones, and between physically strong ones and physically weak ones. But Taylor did not agree. His insight was that there might be something about the *work* itself that could be improved upon. Within a decade of Taylor's initial efforts, the productivity of the manual laborer began its first real rise in history, and continues to rise to this day.[27] Henry Ford's legendary assembly line was merely an extension of Taylor's principles, Ford's contribution being the limitation of one constituent task (continually repeated) per worker along the line.

The next important evolutionary step in this chain came about as the post-industrial economy evolved. More and more "work" in this new economy involved less and less physical labor. Slowly, the accent of management shifted from "work" to "performance."[28] To be sure, manufacturing processes that required manual labor still required and received the attention of management thinkers, but the accent had shifted from simply "more" (more flour milled, more yards of textile produced, more widgets made) to "quality."

For this shift to be complete, however, the starting point had to be a new definition of "quality," for it was that *quality*—effectively the *results* of the work—and not the work itself that now had to be managed.[29] In other words, if we want "better," we must first define what "better" is. But we should recognize at this point that these "results" were not the same results with which modern performance measurement is familiar; it was still too early for those insights to have taken root. Rather, this early notion of results referred more to the characteristics of the output: *Did it work? Did it fit? Did it last?*

With this developing shift in perspective, W. Edwards Deming began to supply the answer to the question of "better" with his concept of Total Quality Management (TQM). Initially, Deming followed Taylor's analysis model. But around 1940 he added an underlying statistical theory[30] and the result was a philosophy of management rooted in an understanding of the power and pervasiveness of variation, and how it affects processes.[31]

All systems, Deming suggested, are subject to an amount of variation, which leads to an eventual erosion of process and product. For quality to be maintained, Deming insisted, variation must be reduced. It was soon recognized that a central facet of any reduction in variation was *measurement* and what became known as Management-By-Fact.

This evolving accent on measurement led to a number of new approaches and theories in corporate management. Among them were the Baldrige System—developed by the man many consider to be the world's foremost authority on management[32]—as well as such innovations as TQM, the Japanese "Quality Circle," and the internationally acclaimed Six Sigma.[33] These developments could not long be ignored in the nonprofit world. When the "Reinventing Government" movement led to the passage of the Government Performance and Results Act (GPRA) during the Clinton administration, the die was cast for a new approach in assessing nonprofit performance.

The modern Outcomes Movement

By the late 1980s, a number of disparate forces began to coalesce around the concept of real performance measurement for nonprofits and the government alike.

Dr. Len Bickman made a powerful contribution when he narrowed the discussion around the need for program theory. "All too commonly," he would write, "programs seem to grow from notions and ideas," rather than from a sound, testable theory. In fact, he would add, "many programs [completely] lack an explicit theory, or the theory they espouse [is] implausible."[34]

Instead of this vacuum, Bickman urged the adoption of program theory that would be "the construction of a plausible and sensible model of how a program is supposed to work."[35]

At about the same time, Hal Williams and his colleagues, Art Webb and Bill Phillips at the Rensselaerville Institute, a think-tank near Albany, NY, published a book, *Outcome Funding*, which posed the revolutionary question of why the government was paying for promises instead of performance. Examining the familiar Request for Proposals system used by the government to find recipient nonprofit agencies to carry out the work the government wants done, Williams and company found that the resultant proposals were "incredibly weak" devices for enabling public-sector investors to understand either what it is they are buying, or the likelihood of getting it.[36] Meanwhile, they added, for the agency seeking government money, the proposal might be a good way to get it, but it was seldom an effective road map for spending it.

Reflecting the activity focus that was still dominant among both nonprofits and their investors at the time, Williams and his co-authors noted that "our eyes are on the wrong target" when we count the number of actions rather than whether those activities had any appreciable impact on the situation they were supposed to address.[37]

But this situation was about to change.

Spurred by taxpayer revolts and, particularly at the state level, legislative movements that demanded an accounting of just where public money was going, two realizations gelled. The first was that governments were not merely "funding" social intervention initiatives; they were actually *buying* services. The second was that how these efforts were managed should be questioned.[38]

The Reinventing Government movement was the catalyst for the passage of the federal Government Performance and Results Act (GPRA) of 1993. With GPRA requirements beginning in 1994, by the year 2000 performance standards—and the outcomes/results focus they required—were a fact of life, not only for most nonprofits that accepted federal governmental money,[39] but also for state governments that received funding through revenue sharing and other pipelines. This in turn prompted many states and localities to adopt rules and standards similar to GPRA governing the grants they made to local nonprofits.

In response to this change in atmosphere, a number of new voices joined Williams and others in suggesting systems nonprofits could utilize to understand, manage toward, and report their results:

- In 1994, Claude Bennett and Kay Rockwell introduced their TOP model (Targeting Outcomes of Programs),[40] of results management. Initially geared toward Cooperative Extension services, the model was at first primarily used and became known in rural areas of the country, but was later utilized in program planning and development by other agencies and organizations in such diverse fields as education, social services, environmental management, and nursing.
- In 1996, United Way of America introduced its handbook on outcomes based upon an idea known as The Logic Model.[41] In 1998, with the

publication of its *Evaluation Handbook*, the Kellogg Foundation added its endorsement of the model, citing multiple benefits to be derived from its use.[42]

- That same year, Kaplan and Norton would improve upon a widely used French outcome management system called the Tableau de Bord[43] and publish their Balanced Scorecard.[44] Initially intended for business, it was thereafter adapted to government and nonprofit work.[45]

- In 2001, Dr. Matt Chinman and his colleagues at the University of South Carolina introduced the Getting to Outcomes (GTO) model.[46] Since then widely promoted by the RAND Corporation,[47] the program leads agency managers and planners through ten questions, each built around a specific focus, that are intended to incorporate the basic elements of program planning, implementation, evaluation, and sustainability.[48]

These efforts were joined by those of Mark Friedman, who created the Results-Based Accountability system,[49] and Barry Kibel, whose work on Results Mapping and other systems offered nonprofits still more ways to address the requirements of results management.

In 2011 President Obama signed the Government Performance and Results Modernization Act of 2010. This legislation updated some aspects of the original Act of 1993, placing a new emphasis on setting priorities, cross-organizational collaboration to achieve shared goals, and the use and analysis of goals and measures to improve outcomes of federally funded programs.[50] The new Act extended the original GPRA's scope to include the requirement that agencies must articulate operational frameworks and plans for monitoring performance.[51] The legislation was also an attempt to correct an unintended consequence of the first GPRA.[52] That legislation's use of the term "performance measurement" had obscured the fact that far more than just measurement is needed for the success of programs, and that measurement is, in fact, only part of a larger requirement of *performance management*: merely measuring performance, if efforts and resources are not managed toward the achievement of desired outcomes, can often result in little more than the documentation of failure.[53]

More recently, a group of the foremost thinkers in the sector have banded together as the Leap of Reason Ambassadors[54] and offered nonprofits a workable, practical guide to higher performance across a range of critical areas ranging from organizational leadership to mission effectiveness.[55] Two volumes have come out of this effort: Mario Morino's *Leap of Reason*, and Dr. David Hunter's *Working Hard & Working Well*.[56] The first is a powerful argument for the implementation of a performance basis in the work of nonprofit organizations, and a guide to how it can be done. The second is an intensive and invaluable guide to broad performance management.

All of these efforts had one central aim: to get nonprofits to stop relying upon the existence of problems and accounts of activity to justify themselves, and to begin to focus on their performance and how well they are keeping their promises to those who support them and those they serve. Far more important than activity, the thinkers behind these efforts maintained, is the question of *whether the organization is actually doing any good, actually helping improve people's lives and life prospects, actually creating social value.*[57]

The sector's response to all this has been mixed, at best.

While most thought leaders and many practitioners embraced this new approach, a good number of those in the field had qualms about it, arguing that, as theoretically laudable as the outcomes/results/performance approach might be, it would effectively only add to the burdens already being shouldered by a generally under-resourced sector.[58]

Others argued that the problems nonprofits work on are not susceptible to simple measurement,[59] and that the entire discussion was a distraction from "the work that needs to be done." [60]

It also must be said, however, that the funder community, those institutions the sector relies upon for its financial sustenance, bears a significant part of the responsibility for this response on the part of some nonprofit practitioners. Most simply put, while funders, from foundations and corporations to the government, increasingly ask nonprofits for outcomes and results measures, they have largely failed to make available the resources required for nonprofits to learn how to use documented performance as the basis of their work.

It is unlikely that the outcomes genie will at this point ever be put completely back in the bottle. But what *is* at question is the degree to which the sector will, as a whole, embrace outcomes and the calls for higher performance.

Problems and activity have a long pedigree within the nonprofit realm. They're also, frankly, easier. And the push for performance and results assessment, in spite of its undeniable intellectual appeal, still does have to prove itself to many as being worth the effort. It also has to be added that, in all honesty, individual American donors are not helping the situation. In spite of saying that performance is the most important thing they look for in a nonprofit—90% responding to a landmark study made this claim—they don't really live up to that standard. Instead, the fact is that only 35% of them said that they actually ever did any research whatsoever before giving, while 65% of those surveyed stated that they never researched before making a donation. The minimal research that is done appears to be a review of facts and figures. Only a 15% minority say that they read any in-depth reports.[61]

Instead, most Americans continue to give on an emotional basis, their empathy, sympathy, anger, or civic pride being the primary spur to donating when they are presented with an image or information regarding a problem or challenge to their beliefs. Moreover, many are quite content with this approach, taking it on faith that their donations are doing some good. This tendency is only exacerbated by today's instant communication via the Internet and charities' developing savvy at using it.[62]

It is therefore an open question as to whether a more data-driven approach will be adopted by the majority of the nonprofit sector.

Abraham Lincoln famously observed that a house divided against itself cannot stand. In that vein, it could be suggested that the nonprofit sector won't thrive with one portion of its membership working with and basing its existential justification upon meaningful, measurable, and sustainable results while the other part continues to rely upon pointing to problems and offering activity accounts as a means of garnering support. But in this case, Lincoln may have been wrong.

As long as emotion-based appeals continue to work, as long as people respond to accounts of injustice and pictures of homeless puppies with donations, there is little incentive to change. It is entirely possible, therefore, that those nonprofits relying heavily upon institutional funding may have to adopt at least some performance measures, but that those whose finances are predominantly underwritten by individuals or local for-profit contributions may not have to. They may be able to continue doing what they have done for so long and simply rely upon people's notions of what is fair, just, necessary, or desirable to prompt giving. This might not be the best thing for those whom these organizations ultimately exist to serve. But given the history of the sector and how these organizations developed, the accent on problems and activity may ultimately prove to be the unchangeable nature of the arena.

Only time will tell. . .

Notes

1 In an article that challenged the nonprofit sector to its very foundations, Dr. David Hunter argued that because of their tradition of simply ignoring the question, there is virtually no credible evidence that most nonprofit organizations actually produce any social value at all. See Hunter, D. "The End of Charity: How to Fix the Nonprofit Sector through Effective Social Investing." *Social Innovations Journal*. September 25, 2009. www.socialinnovationsjournal.org/74-what-works-what-doesn-t/524-the-end-of-charity-how-to-fix-the-nonprofit-sector-through-effective-social-investing.
2 Fleishman. pp. 149–156.
3 Dickens, C. *A Christmas Carol*. [New York: Simon & Schuster, 1983] pp. 15–16.
4 Hunter. Op. cit.
5 Ibid.
6 Fleishman. p. 4.
7 Massachusetts actually had several such boards after the Civil War: the Board of State Charities, 1864–1878, the Board of Lunacy and Charity, 1886–1898, and the Board of Charity, 1899–1919. Other notable late-19th-century state agencies in the field were concentrated in the Northeast and Midwest.
      In the Northeast they included New York (Board of State Commissioners of Public Charities, 1867–1872; State Board of Charities, 1873–1929), Rhode Island (Board of State Charities and Corrections, 1869–1915), and Pennsylvania (Board of Public Charities, 1876–1917).
      In the Midwest they included Ohio (Board of State Charities, 1868–1921; Ohio Welfare Conference, 1896–1922), Illinois (Board of State Commissioners of Public Charities, 1870–1909; Board of Administration, 1910–1916), Wisconsin (State Board of Charities and Reform, 1871–1890; State Board of Supervision of Wisconsin Charitable, Reformatory, and Penal Institutions, 1881–1890; Board of Control, 1891–1936), Michigan (Board of State Commissioners for the General Supervision of Charitable, Penal, Pauper, and Reformatory Institutions, 1873–1879; State Board of Corrections and Charities, 1879–1920), Minnesota (State Board of Corrections

and Charities, 1884–1900; State Board of Control, 1900–1938), and Indiana (Board of State Charities, 1889–1943).

An exception to the generally slow creation of states welfare agencies in the south was North Carolina (Board of Public Charities, 1870–1916; State Board of Charities and Public Welfare, 1918–1944).

These agencies usually focused on institutions run by their states but included reports on private institutions as well. See Hammack. (2002) p. 1653.

8   See Chapter 2, Note 58, this volume.

9   The broadest initiative of the time being the treatment of sick mariners authorized by the 1798 Act for the Relief of Sick and Disabled Seamen, which created the first Marine Hospitals, and the federal quarantining of ships with sick crew members under the National Quarantine Act of 1878. It wasn't until 1891 that the national government moved further into this area when it assumed responsibility for the medical inspection of arriving immigrants from the states.

10 Suchman, Edward. *Evaluative Research.* [New York: Russell Sage Foundation, 1967] p. 14.

11 Ibid. p. 4.

12 Zimbalist, S.E. *Historic Themes and Landmarks in Social Welfare Research.* [New York: Harper and Row, 1977] as cited in Mullen, E.J. "Evidence-Based Social Work—Theory & Practice: Historical and Reflective Perspective." Fourth International Conference on Evaluation for Practice. University of Tampere, Tampere, Finland, July 4–6, 2002. www.uta.fi/laitokset/sospol/eval2002/CampbellContext.PDF.

13 The electrification of the rural southeast under the Tennessee Valley Authority (TVA) provides an example of how this approach misled reformers. Miles and miles of electric line were strung by the TVA, and countless small homes and farms were hooked up to the grid. The program, seen from that activity-based perspective, was a success. Electrification, however, failed to achieve the goals cited as its original justification: improving the standard of living and the economic competitiveness of the family farm, halting the continuing migration of rural people from the country to the city; stopping the decline in the total number of family farms; and ending the attendant issues of rural poverty such as illiteracy, domestic abuse, abandoned families, and limited economic prospects. (See New Deal Network. "TVA: Electricity for All." http://newdeal.feri.org/tva/tva10.htm.) A secondary flaw was the misinterpretation of significant, though essentially cosmetic alterations, in the circumstances of those "served." To again cite the example of rural electrification, while it is true that through the program many rural residents had electric lights and other conveniences, the underlying circumstances of their lives were not changed. They were still subject to weather and economic forces they could not control; they were still mostly isolated from the larger culture developing in the cities; they and their families still lacked the educational opportunities available elsewhere; and although no longer illuminated merely by candles or kerosene lamps, their culture had not changed.

14 Syndenstricker, Edgar. "The Measurement of Results in Public Health Work." Annual Report of the Milbank Memorial Fund New York. 1926.

15 Knutson, A. "Evaluation Program Progress." *Public Health Reports.* Vol. 70. (March 1955) pp. 305–310.

16 Ciocco, A. "On Indices for the Appraisal of Health Department Activities." *Journal of Chronic Diseases.* Vol. 11. (May 1960) pp. 509–522.

17 Horst, P. et al. "Program Management and the Federal Evaluator." *Public Administration Review.* Vol. 34, No. 4. (1974) p. 300.

18 Suchman. p. 16.

19 Ibid. p. 70.

20 Waller, J. and Scanlon, J. *Plan for the Design of an Evaluation*. [Washington, DC: The Urban Institute, 1973] *passim*.

21 Horst. p. 302.

22 Drucker, Peter. *Managing the Nonprofit Organization*. [New York: Harper Collins, 1990] pp. xiv-xv.

23 Creech, Bill. *The Five Pillars of TQM*. [New York: Truman Tally Books/Dutton, 1994] *passim*.

24 Drucker also gives tremendous credit to early management scholar Mary Parker Follett (1886–1933), who espoused the theory that business was a social institution. However, for various reasons, her work had little impact during her life and was largely forgotten for several decades until its rediscovery in recent years. For more information, see Drucker, P.F. *Mary Parker Follet: Prophet of Management*. [Boston: Harvard Business School Press, 1995]. Also see Micklethwait, J. and Woolridge, A. *The Witchdoctors: Making Sense of the Management Gurus*. [New York: Times Books, 1996] pp. 68–73 for an extensive review of early management works.

25 Drucker, P. *Management Challenges for the 21st Century*. [New York: Harper Business, 1999] pp. 135–141.

26 Compact Edition of the *Oxford English Dictionary* [New York: Oxford University Press, 1971] Vol. II, p. 2315.

27 Drucker. (1999) p. 136.

28 Ibid. p. 21.

29 Ibid.

30 Ibid. p. 139.

31 Gabor, A. *The Man Who Invented Quality*. [New York: Times Books, 1990] *passim*.

32 George, S. and Weimerskirch, A. *Total Quality Management*. [New York: Wiley & Sons, 1994]. p. 7.

33 Six Sigma holds that there is a strong inverse relationship between variation and yield, reliability and cost, such that, as variation goes up, the value of these other variables goes down. See Harry, Mikel. *The Vision of Six Sigma*. Fourth Edition. [Phoenix: Sigma Publishing Company, 1994] *passim*.

34 Bickman, L. "Functions of Program Theory." *Using Program Theory in Evaluation*. Ed. L. Bickman [San Francisco: Jossey-Bass, 1987] p. 6.

35 Ibid. p. 5.

36 Williams, H. et al. *Outcome Funding*. Fourth Edition. [Rensselaerville, NY: The Rensselaerville Institute, 1996]. p. v.

37 Ibid.

38 Micklethwait and Woolridge. p. 8.

39 GPRA required that beginning in FY 1994, there were to be among federally funded programs at least ten 3-year pilot projects in program performance goal setting, measurement, and reporting, and at least five 2-year pilot projects in greater managerial flexibility in return for commitments to greater program performance. In 1997, the Office of Management and Budget and the General Accounting Office were to report on the results of the pilot projects. By FY 1998, the requirements of the Act for five-year strategic planning, annual program performance plans, and annual program performance reports were scheduled to come into force government-wide.

40 Bennett, C. and Rockwell, K. *Targeting Outcomes of Programs (TOP): An Integrated Approach to Planning and Evaluation*. Unpublished manuscript. [Lincoln, NE: University of Nebraska, 1995] *passim*.

41 United Way of America. *Measuring Program Outcomes: A Practical Approach*. [Arlington, VA: United Way of America; 1996] *passim*.

42 W.K. Kellogg Foundation. *W.K. Kellogg Foundation Evaluation Handbook*. [Battle Creek, MI: The W.K. Kellogg Foundation; 1998] *passim*.

43 Lebas, M. "Managerial Accounting in France." *European Accounting Review*. Vol. 3, No. 3. (1994) pp. 471–487.

44 The Balanced Scorecard traces its roots to a study undertaken by the Norton Institute in the mid-1990s. The study was motivated by a belief that existing performance measures, relying as they did primarily upon financial accounting, were becoming obsolete. It was thought that in an increasingly complex operating environment, these traditional measures were in fact hindering business organizations' ability to create future economic value. The problem, Kaplan and Norton suggested, lay in the fact that even though there were a variety of measures available to corporate managers, ROI, ROCE, P/R, and others among them, they all essentially focused upon dollars. They were, in other words, a variety of ways to look at the same variable. Worse still, they were all measures of past performance, and gave little guidance for future action or growth. See Kaplan, R. and Norton, D. *The Balanced Scorecard*. [Boston: Harvard Business School Press, 1996].

45 See Moullin, M. Various works. http://publicsectorscorecard.academia.edu/MaxMoullin.

46 Chinman, M. et al. "Using the Getting To Outcomes (GTO) Model in a Statewide Prevention Initiative." *Health Promotion Practice*. Vol. 2, No. 4, Supp. 277. (October 2001) pp. 302–307.

47 Wiseman, S. et al. *Getting to Outcomes™ 2004: Promoting Accountability through Methods and Tools for Planning, Implementation, and Evaluation*. [Santa Monica, CA: The RAND Corporation, 2007]. www.rand.org/pubs/technical_reports/TR101z2.html.

48 These are: (1) Needs/Resources. What underlying needs and resources must be addressed? (2) Goals. What are the goals, target population, and objectives (i.e., desired outcomes)? (3) Best Practice. Which science (evidence) based models and best practice programs can be useful in reaching the goals? (4) Fit. What actions need to be taken so the selected program "fits" the community context? (5) Capacities. What organizational capacities are needed to implement the program? (6) Planning. What is the plan for this program? (7) Process Evaluation. Does the program have high implementation fidelity? (8) Outcome Evaluation. How well is the program working? (9) Quality Improvements. How will continuous quality improvement strategies be included? (10) Sustainability. If the program is successful, how will it be sustained?

49 Clear Impact. "What Is Results-Based Accountability™?" https://clearimpact.com/results-based-accountability/.

50 See Substance Abuse and Mental Health Services Administration. "GPRA Modernization Act of 2010 Tools." https://www.samhsa.gov/grants/gpra-measurement-tools.

51 Hunter, D. *Working Hard & Working Well*. [Hamden, CT: Hunter Consulting, 2013] p. 12.

52 Ibid. p. 10.

53 Ibid.

54 Leap of Reason. "The Leap Ambassadors Community." http://leapofreason.org/performance-imperative/leap-ambassadors-community/.

55 Leap of Reason. "The Performance Imperative Campaign." http://leapofreason.org/performance-imperative/.

56 Complimentary copies of both volumes are available at http://leapofreason.org/get-the-books/.

57 Hunter. (2009).

58 Berger, K. and Penna, R. "Points of Contention: Ken Berger Defends Impact Measurement." *Nonprofit Quarterly*. March 2, 2011. https://nonprofitquarterly. org/2011/03/02/points-of-contention-ken-berger-defends-impact-measurement/.

59 Lawry, S. "When Too Much Rigor Leads to Rigor Mortis: Valuing Experience, Judgment and Intuition in Nonprofit Management." *Nonprofit Quarterly*. February 17, 2011. https://nonprofitquarterly.org/2011/02/17/when-too-much-rigor-leads-to-rigor-mortis-valuing-experience-judgment-and-intuition-in-nonprofit-management/.

60 Gottlieb, H. "Armchair Change Agents." October 20, 2009. http://hildygottlieb. com/2009/10/20/armchair-change-agents/.

61 But it turns out that those who say they do research are far more than those who actually do. The best information we have suggests that less than 2% of donors actually research meaningful information on results of a charity's performance. See Hope Consulting. "Money for Good." May, 2010. http://hopeconsulting.us/pdf/ Money%20for%20Good_Final.pdf.

62 McCambridge, R. "A New Form of Donor Motivation: Rage Donating!" *Nonprofit Quarterly*. November 15, 2016. https://nonprofitquarterly.org/2016/11/15/new-form-donor-motivation-rage-donating/.

10 Demographics and technology

Whatever other changes in the environment may be facing nonprofits, there are two that can't be influenced by policy adjustments at the federal or state levels, won't be altered by any shifts the sector makes in how it manages itself, and are completely unavoidable. These are the relentless succession of generations and the rapidly accelerating march of technology. Moreover, while these two forces have always had an impact on society, today they are inexorably connected as the younger generations become more and more reliant upon and comfortable with new technological possibilities.

Age impacts giving

It has long been known that older members of society consistently give more than the young. Older women, in fact, give the most.

Researchers have found that individuals over 60 years of age are twice as likely as those under 30 to give to charity.[1] One explanation for this dichotomy is that older people, having had the opportunity to acquire more material wealth, have more to give, both absolutely and proportionately. Given this, it comes as little surprise that of the four generational cadres counted among the nation's adults—the "Traditionals,"[2] the "Boomers," Gen X, and Gen Y[3]—roughly 60% of Gen X and Gen Y respondents said they had given to charity in 2013, compared with 72% of Boomers and 88% of Traditionals.[4] Older people are also more likely to have wills and make charitable bequests. Many are also devoting their retirement years to various forms of activism and community service.[5]

Another variable in this equation is that older people are often more invested in their community than are the young, many of whom move from area to area with considerable frequency. Among the elements included in the concept of "sense of community" is *personal investment*; that is the individual sees for him/herself a gain or loss corresponding to the fortunes of the community with which he or she identifies.[6] The strongest predictor of this sense of community is the length of residency and the amount of social bonding one has with people who share ties to that community during that period.[7] Such bonds clearly take time to develop, so it is not surprising that those who have been in a place the longest will feel the greatest and broadest stake in its welfare and that of their neighbors. This is a powerful inducement to charity.

This is not to say, however, that younger people are not part of America's giving or volunteering patterns. They are. But in addition to giving less, their focus is different than that of the generations that preceded them, and seems to be still evolving. One primary example of the difference in their attitudes toward charity can be found in the significant division between older and younger American adults as regards the issue of donating money versus donating time.

The evidence suggests that money matters most to the older generations, but declines in importance with those who are younger. Traditionals and Boomers feel they make the biggest difference through the money they contribute. While 45% of Boomers say their financial contributions are key to making a difference, only 36% of Gen Xers and 25% of Gen Ys think this way. Instead, they believe that volunteering and—perhaps because they're more adept at social media—"spreading the word" is more impactful.[8]

Traditionals, the parents of the Boomers, volunteered a lot, but in primarily local or neighborhood capacities through organizations such as the Mothers March of Dimes, the PTA, or the Red Cross. They served out of a sense of personal responsibility or civic duty, a desire to make a difference, perhaps as an extension of their religious convictions, which were stronger than those of succeeding generations.[9] Probably reflective of the differences in their life experiences—particularly those who were working during a period in our nation that was characterized by a large industrial economy—and their attitudes toward organizations and hierarchies, Traditionals were more likely than subsequent generations to respond to appeals made in the workplace or union hall, and to efforts by Community Chest and other large organizations.

Boomers were different from their parents from the start, volunteering and becoming involved in a wider range of activities, and more likely overall to be attracted to macro issues such as world peace and hunger in the developing world, to volunteer to be with people they enjoy and whose values they share, and less likely to mention that they volunteered out of a sense of civic duty or religious commitment.[10]

Both Traditionals and Boomers are driven to address the basic needs of the community and give the poor a way to help themselves, as is evident in their support of local social and human services. Both groups share a keen sense of responsibility regarding helping those who have less. Gen Xers, meanwhile, have a strong desire to make the community better, while the Millennials seem to focus on making the *world* a better place.[11]

After Boomers, Gen X individuals volunteer the next most often.[12] Their focus is on the ability of small groups to make a difference for their communities.[13] They think locally and act locally, and they have more than doubled their volunteer rate between 1989 and the present day.[14]

For Gen Y, the pattern is reversed. Perhaps because they came of age at a time which brought to prominence a host of public issues that they feel specifically affect younger people and future generations, things such as environmental sustainability and global health concerns,[15] they're prone to think locally, but act globally.

They're also highly tech savvy, were weaned on diversity, and grew up in the emerging global village. The early indications are that they are drawn to international efforts of a wide variety. As opposed to previous generations, they don't hope for social responsibility on the part of society and corporations; they expect it. They are far more likely to demand accountability and transparency than older donors,[16] and are the least likely of all four cohorts to support local organizations.[17] Evidence also suggests that they like to think of their support as an *investment*, rather than the "donation" that motivated the Traditionals and Boomers.[18] In terms of their donations to charity, about 60% of Gen Y and 50% of Gen X say the ability to see the direct impact of their donation has a significant bearing on their decision to give. Only 37% of Boomers, by contrast, feel that way, even though they account for 43% of all giving, donating almost twice as much to charities as the younger generations.[19]

But it also appears that, in an attitude reminiscent of their view of other established institutions,[20] many within this young age cadre are distrustful of established charities, viewing many of them as "black holes" into which money goes but nothing comes out.[21] Also worth noting are the facts that two significant variables long associated with sustained giving, religiosity and being married, are considerably lower among this age cadre.[22] In fact, several of the traditional spurs to giving—among them an impulse to give back, religious duty, social obligation—are becoming diluted within this age bracket.[23] Possibly counterbalancing this, some evidence suggests that ideological conservatism, a characteristic frequently associated with higher rates of giving,[24] may be somewhat higher among Millennials overall than it was among either Gen Xers or Baby Boomers at the same age.[25]

The different generations also give to different things:

- Correlating with data indicating a marked reduction in religious interest and affiliation across generations as one moves forward in time, Traditionals are the most likely to support religion, while Gen Y is the least likely to do so.
- Older donors (both Boomers and Traditionals) are considerably more likely to support veterans' causes.
- Gen Y is less likely to support local social services than Gen X, Boomers, and Traditionals.
- Younger donors (Gen X and Gen Y) are more likely to support children's charities.
- Gen X and Gen Y are more likely to support human rights and international development causes.
- Gen Y donors are markedly less likely to support organized environmental causes.[26]

Below is a breakdown of the reported priorities of each cohort.[27]

Table 10.1 Breakdown of priorities

Cause	Traditionals (%)	Boomers (%)	Gen X (%)	Gen Y (%)
Local social service	37	36	29	19
Place of worship	46	38	36	22
Health charities	23	19	24	20
Children's charities	20	22	28	29
Education	20	14	16	17
Emergency relief	19	11	18	11
Animal rescue/ protection	11	18	21	16
Troops/veterans	22	15	10	6
Environmental	9	9	10	4
First responders	9	10	8	6
Arts and related	14	6	7	4
Advocacy	10	5	4	6
Human rights/ international development	6	4	10	12
Crime/abuse victims	4	3	3	7

What is unclear at the moment is whether individuals in Gen X and Gen Y will maintain the priorities they have now, or change them to more closely match those of their elders as they themselves mature. But for all this, one thing *is* clear: technology will play an ever more important part in their giving and the giving of tomorrow.

The tick-tock of tech

Time marches on. . .and so does technology, at a rate unprecedented in history.

It is hard to imagine that it was only back in 1977 that Tandy helped usher in the personal computer era when the company introduced its bulky, clunky, and slooooow TRS-80, possessing less computing power than today's simplest child's toy, but revolutionary nonetheless. Improvements since then have only cascaded upon one another. The impact of this can be seen in the Gen Y/Millennials, those who represent the first human generation to have grown up with the Internet, cable TV, and cell phones. They never knew a world without space travel, color television, color photography, remote controls, practically instant access to almost anywhere in the world, and information on command. It has been said that because of this, technology is baked into every Millennial's DNA.[28] When asked by the Nielsen Company what makes their generation unique, these young people ranked "Technology Use" first.[29] They are not only comfortable with tech, however; they seem naturally fluent in it and, beyond a decided comfort level, rely upon it to a degree never before seen. The nonprofit of the future will *have to* utilize technology if it is to reach these potential donors in the years to come. It is still an open question how this will play out ten, fifteen, or twenty years from now, but some clues might be gleaned from how technology has already altered the giving landscape.

Mirroring the social patterns of the time,[30] for most of the 20th century, fund-raising by American charities was done on a person-to-person basis. There were far fewer charities in those days and vastly fewer national nonprofits. Most appeals were local. On a larger scale, organizations such as Easter Seals and the Mothers March of Dimes pioneered neighbor-to-neighbor campaigns, still used today, whereby a local volunteer would send requests to neighbors, usually on the same street, if not on the same block. Local volunteers also canvassed the neighborhood, calling on people they knew and asking for donations.

Workplace campaigns in support of local Community Chest organizations,[31] and later United Way, not only mirrored, but often piggy-backed on bond and other war effort appeals during both World War I and World War II.[32] In the post-war U.S., their popularity continued, particularly in the vast industrial sector of the era, when local companies often competed against one another for the honor of having raised the most.

But all of this began to change in the 1980s when the first really targeted mail became possible. The earliest mail campaigns were fairly crude, based largely upon geography, who was living where, and the type of dwellings in an area. If an area, or an entire community for that matter, was regarded as "upscale," it was assumed that its residents had a certain amount of disposable income. These areas would then become the target for a variety of solicitations, both commercial and charitable.[33] Additionally, subscriptions to magazines resulted in a database of names and addresses that told marketers something about the people purchasing those subscriptions.

But with the dawn of the computer age and the earliest data mining, by the late '80s it was possible to target no longer just households, but Democrats or Republicans, men or women, mothers of school-age children, senior citizens, and even (with occasionally comical results) ethnicities. This allowed marketers, including charities, to target their appeals even more narrowly to those they thought would respond.

This, however, brought what we might call "the Age of the Impersonal Appeal." No longer were requests for support coming to your mailbox because of who you were, but because of your profile. Credit cards, for example, became the source of marketing databases. They not only provided names and addresses, but the financial information with which they were associated was very valuable because it indicated who had disposable income. With the increased sophistication of the algorithms behind the appeals, people were soon targeted based upon not only everything from the catalogs they received to the magazines they subscribed to, but also their credit card buying patterns. Marketers, *including charities*, also soon realized the value of their own mailing lists, selling them to others interested in reaching the people they were reaching. And this was all pre-Internet.

This is not to say that face-to-face appeals died out entirely. Not only do groups like the Lions Club®, the Knights of Columbus, and the Girl Scouts still collect face-to-face outside of supermarkets, but supermarkets themselves have gotten in on the act, many sponsoring appeals for a variety of causes during the year via which shoppers are asked to add a donation to their grocery bill.[34]

With the dawn of the 21st century, however, things changed yet again. . .

The closest things to the old-fashioned general appeals of yesteryear are the television ads that organizations like the American Red Cross, the American Heart Association, Autism Speaks, and The Partnership at Drugfree.org still sponsor to spur giving. However, the new twist is that some of these ads, particularly those tied to a specific disaster,[35] feature a text-to-donate option, instructing donors to use their cell phones to text a keyword to a five-digit shortcode. Those who participate instantly receive a text message linking directly to a donation form that collects full donor data right from their mobile phone. This combination of well-crafted messages and instant access to a giving opportunity is a powerful tool in the effort to increase impulse giving,[36] and nothing could be more tailor-made for the Millennials, a generation of digital natives which has inherently understood that donating is always possible thanks to mobile phones and tablets.[37]

This has had a number of results. One is that online giving has never been more popular. The total number of groups raising money online grew by 20% in 2012, and by another 13% in 2013, one organization, the Leukemia & Lymphoma Society, bringing more than $98 million in Internet gifts that year.[38] Since then this revenue stream has continued to gain strength. Between June 2016 and June 2017, by way of illustration, 1,349,194 online donors had been recorded, making 2,307,352 contributions, a figure which clearly suggests that once a person has donated online, he or she is apt to do it again. Those contributions, moreover, brought in $282,848,736 and went to 34,753 organizations. This represented a 39% increase in donors, a 37.3% increase in the number of donations, a 17.6% increase in the amount donated, and a 4.8% increase in the number of participating nonprofits during the course of a year.[39] And according to the experts, online giving has not yet hit anything approaching its potential stride.[40]

Online giving has a number of other benefits as well. The ease of giving, a major consideration for donors according to one major study,[41] is clearly also working to the advantage of participating nonprofits when their appeals reach tech savvy donors. It also largely obviates the perennial issue of people getting an appeal in the mail, wanting to "think about it," and laying the request down in a pile with other mail where it often gets lost. The immediacy of online giving is certainly a plus when The Ask hits the right person. . .and that person is increasingly a Millennial.

Millennials are heavier Internet users than any of their older counterparts, and the caricature of them walking around glued to their cell phones is not entirely fanciful. Facebook is the platform of choice for 72% of the generation,[42] and 62% of them say they tend to learn about charities through their social networks.[43]

The ALS Ice Bucket Challenge—which began as a Facebook post—offers compelling proof that Millennials are more likely to support a cause when members of their personal network do the same.

Online appeals, particularly those spread through users' individual social networks, also free many charities, in a way never really before possible, from the geographic constraints that long tethered their fund-raising to a given place. Virtual communities cross all sorts of boundaries. Through social media, therefore, a person in Albuquerque can alert her friends to a local charity she is supporting. They, in turn, with a simple mouse click, can send that information on to a literally infinite number of people anywhere, each representing a possible donation for that charity.

Facebook, the world's largest and most powerful social networking platform, presents a particularly attractive opportunity for charitable fund-raising.

Most people do not think about the amount of information they make available on Facebook and other social media sites. It begins with your name, and although your name may not be seen by viewers on a site, you still need to give the site's operators that name to open an account. Then come such vital statistics as your age and gender, followed by places you have lived, where you went to school (thereby telling them how much education you have), and where you work. . .all the basic stuff most of us put into our profile.

Facebook uses all this information in powerful algorithms to make its pages valuable to advertisers. . .including charities. Put simply, almost everything you do on Facebook opens you to sponsored ads and content from someone, again including charities. Moreover, there is evidence that Facebook can even track what you do on the Web away from its page.[44]

The opportunities all this opens for charities are incalculable. By utilizing the information Facebook, Amazon, Google, AOL, Yahoo, and other platforms have on their users, charities can not only select potential donors with incredible specificity (someone, for example, who likes cats, as opposed to simply animals), but also repeatedly place ads within a person's online experience in the hopes of prompting a response in the form of a donation. Moreover, with the consumer-friendly design of many of these ads, it is easier than ever to make that donation. . .and all of this speaks to the culture and behaviors Millennials have embraced.

All this said, there is a downside. The available information indicates that most people,[45] and specifically most Millennials,[46] want to see measurable results as a return on their charitable investment. Researching those results, however, finding out which organizations are actually making a meaningful change in the situations they exist to address, generally takes time.

Online giving, on the other hand, works against this by encouraging both impulse and follow-the-crowd giving. Whether it's the Ice Bucket Challenge, Giving Tuesday, or any of a number of other Web-based appeals, the evidence suggests that while they do motivate people who've never given before to make a contribution—and sometimes can prompt a lapsed donor—they also frequently tend to result in one-time donations because it is *participation* in the event, rather than a commitment to the cause, that underlies the contribution.

There is little indication, for example, that once a person participated in the Ice Bucket Challenge, he or she would repeat that action—how many times are you going to dump a bucket of ice water over your head?—or would follow up with subsequent donations to the ALS Association. Similarly, the RageDonate website, which allows instant donations to a variety of organizations in response to actions and statements by President Trump,[47] may be a useful psychological and emotional outlet for people strongly opposed to him, his policies, and his presidency. But it does not constitute informed giving if the donor knows nothing about the recipient organizations other than that they symbolize opposition to the president.

***

While American giving appears to be strong, the nonprofit sector will have to come to grips with the facts of technological and generational change. The former represents an unprecedented opportunity, as it is increasingly possible to know more and more about potential donors and to reach them through an increasing array of appeals on their various electronic devices. While the nonprofit sector might be slower than commercial enterprises to capitalize upon this, there is no doubt, given the available evidence, that this is the wave of the future. It is within the second development, generational change, that the true challenge lies.

For well over one hundred years American charity was based upon a relatively small set of variables. A person's religiosity, marital status, job longevity, length of residency in a particular place, local relationships, geographically-based sense of community—and, in the second half of the 20th century, even his or her television viewing habits and magazine subscriptions—were all strong predictors of giving and were factors charities could use in honing an appeal. But Millennials are turning a great deal of this on its head. They are less religious and less apt to be married. They stay with a particular job for less time, and move around more. They are tied to virtual communities at least as much as they may be to the physical community in which they (for the moment) happen to live. They stream their entertainment on demand and pick and choose their informational sources. They are not only a still-developing target, they are a moving one as well.

The question is not simply whether the nonprofit sector will master new techniques to reach and appeal to this cadre. The easy and safe bet answer to that is yes.

The more important question, however, is whether Gen Y (and Gen Z behind them) will represent a fundamental change in things that traditionally made people give. While we can expect that such factors as human empathy, a sense of justice, and even guilt and anger will remain as personal spurs to charitable action, the broader variables upon which the sector has for so long relied are in flux.

How the sector responds to those changes may be the greatest challenge it faces.

Notes

1 Sedghi, A. "Charitable Giving—How Does It Differ by Age?" *The Guardian.* September 25, 2012. www.theguardian.com/news/datablog/2012/sep/25/charitable-giving-generation-gap-age.

2 This cohort is also called "The Silent Generation," and "The Matures," depending upon the source and author.

3 While there is no strict definition of, or demarcation between the birth years of these different cohorts, the Traditionals are thought to be those born roughly from 1926–1945, the Boomers are those born 1946–1964, and Gen X is accepted to be those born between 1965 and the early 1980s. Gen Y is thought to be those born between the mid-1980s and the turn of the century, while the term Millennial, originally thought of an alternate name for Gen Y, has increasingly come to mean those born closer to the turn of the century.

4 Rovner, M. et al. "The Next Generation of American Giving: The Charitable Habits of Generations Y, X, Baby Boomers, and Matures." Blackbaud. August 2013. p. 6. http://npengage.uberflip.com/i/147711-american-giving.

5 Hannon, K. "Golden Age of Giving." *Seattle Times.* April 12, 2016. www.seattletimes.com/nwshowcase/active-living/golden-age-of-giving/.

6 We speak here of "community" in its traditional, geographic sense; and not of the "borderless communities" of interest characterized either by affinity groups or possibly today through the Internet.

7 McMillan, D.W. and Chavis, D.M. "Sense of Community: A Definition and Theory." *Journal of Community Psychology.* Vol. 14, No. 1. (1986) p. 6.

8 Hartnett, B. and Matan, R. *Generational Differences in Philanthropic Giving.* Sobel & Co., LLC. Fall 2014. p. 3. http://sobel-cpa.com/sites/default/files/NFP%20Fall%20 2014%20Whitepaper.pdf.

9 One measure of religious conviction is affiliation with a faith tradition. Among Traditionals this number was somewhere around 93–95%. It fell to about 85–90% among Boomers, but is only between 70–80% within Gen X and Gen Y. See Putman, R.H. and Campbell, D.E. *American Grace.* [New York: Simon & Schuster, 2010] p. 123.

10 Jones, S. et al. "Characterizing the Propensity to Volunteer in America." American Statistical Association. *JSM Proceedings.* 2008. p. 3015. https://www.amstat.org/sections/srms/proceedings/y2008/Files/301912.pdf.

11 Hartnett and Matan. Op. cit. While such generalizations are always dicey because of differences between the way two different survey instruments might be worded, etc., according to a September 2017 report by the Case Foundation and Achieve, civil rights and racial discrimination topped the list of causes or issues in which Millennials were interested, outpacing employment and health care, both of which could be interpreted as having more immediate community impacts. See Dubb, S. "The Kids Are Alright: Millennial Generalizations Are Getting Old." *Nonprofit Quarterly.* September 20, 2017. https://nonprofitquarterly.org/2017/09/20/kids-alright-can-keep-broad-generalizations-check/?utm_source=Daily+Newswire&utm_campaign=8d0dff4a18-EMAIL_CAMPAIGN_2017_9_20&utm_medium=email&utm_term=0_94063a1d17-8d0dff4a18-12341229.

12 Ibid.

13 Keene, D. and Handrich, R. "Generation X Members Are 'Active, Balanced and Happy.' Seriously?" *The Jury Expert.* Vol. 23, No. 6. (November 2011). www.thejuryexpert.com/2011/11/gen-x-members-are-active-balanced-and-happy/.

14 Ausland, A. "Generation X and Volunteerism—Nuancing the 'Hero' Status." Web blog post. Staying for Tea. August 13, 2011. https://stayingfortea.org/2011/08/13/generation-x-and-volunteerism-nuancing-the-hero-status/.

15 Farmakis, E. "Millennials and Giving." *Huffpost*. November 25, 2014. www.huffington post.com/epaminondas-farmakis/millennials-and-giving_b_5881434.html.
16 Rovner. p. 5.
17 Hartnett and Matan. p. 3.
18 Hu, E. "How Millennials Are Reshaping Charity and Online Giving." National Public Radio. All Tech Considered. October 13, 2014. www.npr.org/sections/alltechconsidered/2014/10/13/338295367/how-millennials-are-reshaping-charity-and-online-giving.
19 Rovner. p. 6.
20 According to one study, most established institutions of American life fare poorly in the eyes of Millennials. When asked how much confidence they had in an array of institutions, Millennials gave the federal government only a 22% positive rating, the news media 21%, corporate America 20%, organized religion 25%, the criminal justice system 27%, and banks 29%. See Economic Innovation Group. "Millennials & Institutions." http://eig.org/wp-content/uploads/2016/09/Millennials-Institutions.pdf.
21 Hu. Op. cit.
22 Religiosity has long been associated with giving. The more important religion is to a person, the more likely that person is to give to a charity of any kind. About 75% of people who frequently attend religious services gave to congregations, and 60% gave to religious charities or nonreligious ones. By comparison, fewer than half of people who said they didn't attend faith services regularly supported any charity, even a secular one. (Daniels, A. "Religious Americans Give More, New Study Finds." *Chronicle of Philanthropy*. November 25, 2013. https://www.philanthropy.com/article/Religious-Americans-Give-More/153973.) Millennials, meanwhile, are considerably less religious than older Americans, and may be among the least religious generation in American history. (Pew Research Center. "Religion among the Millennials." February 17, 2010. http://www.pewforum.org/2010/02/17/religion-among-the-millennials/; Cooper-White, M. "Millennials Are the Least Religious Generation Yet, and Here's the Surprising Reason Why." *Huffpost Science*. May 27, 2015. www.huffingtonpost.com/2015/05/27/millennials-less-religious_n_7452998.html.)
    Married people are more likely to be donors and give more than twice as much as singles. They're more likely to give than single men, and give more than three times as much as single men. They are also more likely than single women to be donors and give almost twice as much as single females. (Mesch, D. et al. "The Effects of Race, Gender, and Marital Status on Giving and Volunteering in Indiana." *Nonprofit and Voluntary Sector Quarterly*. Vol. 35, No. 4. (December 2006) p. 578.) However, Millennials are waiting longer to marry or are shying away from the institution of marriage entirely. Only 26% of Millennials aged 18 to 32 are married, when at the same age, 36% of Gen Xers, 48% of Boomers and 65% of Traditionals were already married. (Sharpe Group. "Millennial Donors Rising?" October 1, 2014. http://sharpenet.com/give-take/millennial-donors-rising/.)
23 Ibid.
24 Will, G. "Conservatives More Liberal Givers." *The New York Times*. March 27, 2008. www.realclearpolitics.com/articles/2008/03/conservatives_more_liberal_giv.html.
25 Howard, J. "Millennials More Conservative than You May Think." *CNN*. September 7, 2016. www.cnn.com/2016/09/07/health/millennials-conservative-generations/index.html. According to survey data by the Case Foundation and Achieve, Donald Trump outpolled Hilary Clinton among white Millennials by a margin of 46% to 41%. See Dubb at Chapter 10, Note 11, this volume.

26 Ibid. p. 10.

27 Ibid. p. 11.

28 The Nielsen Company. "Millennials: Technology = Social Connection." *Nielsen Newswire.* February 26, 2014. www.nielsen.com/us/en/insights/news/2014/ millennials-technology-social-connection.html.

29 Ibid.

30 Putman, R.D. *Bowling Alone.* [New York: Simon & Schuster; 2000] *passim.*

31 The idea of cooperative fund-raising by local charities in the U.S. dates to 1887 in Denver. The first truly successful implementation of the concept took place in Cleveland in 1900 when the Cleveland Chamber of Commerce assumed responsibility for endorsing a number of agencies seeking funds. Thirteen years later, almost all welfare organizations in Cleveland joined to form the Cleveland Welfare Council, regarded as the nation's first true Community Chest. The concept developed quickly and the numbers increased from 40 nationwide in 1919 to about 350 in 1929, and grew beyond 1,000 by 1948. (See Pruszewicz, A. and Vander Hulst, A. "Key Dates and Events in American Philanthropic History 1815 to Present." Learning to Give. https://www. learningtogive.org/resources/key-dates-and-events-american-philanthropic-history-1815-present.) In the post-war era the concept was so popular and so identified with Americana that Community Chest was promoted on several old-time radio shows, including the H.J. Heinz-sponsored *Adventures of Ozzie and Harriet*, the S.C. Johnson & Son-sponsored *Fibber McGee and Molly*, and the Chevron-sponsored *Let George Do It* show.

32 Bookman, C.M. "The Community Chest Movement—An Interpretation." National Conference of Social Work. Toronto, Ontario, June 25-July 2, 1924. Social Welfare History Project. http://socialwelfare.library.vcu.edu/organizations/state-institutions/ community-chest-movement-an-interpretation/.

33 Retail pioneer Aaron Montgomery Ward is generally credited with originating the idea of direct marketing through the mail. In 1872, Ward produced the first mail-order catalog for his Montgomery Ward mail-order business. Testimony to the success of the idea, the Direct Mail Advertising Association was first established in 1917. The third-class bulk-mail postage rates, which made it all financially feasible, were established in 1928.

34 Supermarkets, of course, are not the only businesses that do this. Companies such as the Rite-Aid drugstore chain participate in a number of these campaigns each year, and Regal Theaters still periodically passes the popcorn bucket on behalf of a number of charities.

35 At this writing, the Red Cross had already, within days of the event, set up a way to make a $10 donation to Louisiana flood relief by texting the word "LAFLOODS" to 90999. See Chillag, A. "How to Help Louisiana Flood Victims." *CNN.* August 15, 2016. www.cnn.com/2016/08/14/us/iyw-louisiana-flooding-victims-help/index.html.

36 Immediately after the earthquake in Haiti in 2010, the Red Cross launched a donate-by-text program, promoted heavily by the U.S. State Department and the mainstream media. Relief agencies collected $43 million in donations via text after the Haiti quake, sent $10 at a time by texting the word "HAITI" to the shortcode 90999. In 2012 the Pew Internet and American Life Project released an in-depth study based on interviews with 863 people who sent donations to Haiti via text message. Pew found that most of these donations were made on impulse as an immediate response to television coverage of the disaster. For three-quarters of those donors, it was the first time they'd ever donated via text message. By and large, these donors did not research this donation beforehand. Their interest in Haiti's recovery also waned quickly: more than half of the donors interviewed reported

that they did not follow Haitian relief and reconstruction efforts much or at all since making their donation. And only a third of them made additional text donations to Haitian earthquake relief. See Gahran, A. "Donating to Charity by Text Message: Lessons from Haiti." *CNN Tech.* January 12, 2012. www.cnn.com/2012/01/12/tech/mobile/charity-donations-text-messages/index.html.

37 Farmakis. Op. cit.
38 Daniels, A. and Narayanswamy, A. "Online Fundraising Goes Mainstream." *Chronicle of Philanthropy.* May 18, 2014. https://www.philanthropy.com/article/Online-Fundraising-Goes/150539.
39 Myers, B. et al. "Online Giving Trends." *Chronicle of Philanthropy.* https://www.philanthropy.com/interactives/online-giving-dashboard.
40 While many charities increasingly believe that success is tied to their Web presence, the facts do not necessarily support this notion.

The concept is that those organizations that have a robust website—particularly if it is working in support of an already high public profile—will find that traffic to their site is high and online giving will be a meaningful factor. It is interesting to note, however, that the charities with the most popular websites are not, in fact, those with the largest budgets…suggesting that a high online presence does not necessarily translate into a proportionate level of donations, nor does it apparently outweigh other sources of income.

Among the most popular charity websites are those of UNICEF, Human Rights Watch, the Museum of Modern Art, the Human Rights Campaign, Do Something (a Millennial-oriented charity aggregator site), the ACLU, Doctors Without Borders, Kiva (a site via which people donate to make loans to those in developing regions), the Rotary Foundation of Rotary International, and the Sierra Club. The largest charities by budget, meanwhile, are the American Red Cross (number 14 on the website popularity list), Feeding America (12), City of Hope (not on the list of the top 100 at all), the Smithsonian Institution (23), the Dana-Farber Cancer Institute (not on list), Food for the Poor (not on list), ALSAC-St. Jude's Research Hospital (24), World Vision (68), Americares (not on list), and Catholic Relief Services (not on list). In fact, several very well-known charities do not do all that well in this report. While National Public Radio comes in at 11, and the American Red Cross as 14, Save the Children is 33, the Make-A-Wish Foundation ranks 42, the Planned Parenthood Federation is 51, Oxfam International comes in at 55, and the Susan G. Komen Breast Cancer Foundation comes in at 73 in popularity.

Charity Navigator provides a list of the "10 Super-Sized Charities" at https://www.charitynavigator.org/index.cfm?bay=topten.detail&listid=24, and the list of the one hundred most popular charitable websites was compiled by Top Nonprofits and can be found at https://topnonprofits.com/lists/best-nonprofits-on-the-web/, along with an explanation of the metrics used in the rankings.

41 See Chapter 9, Note 2, this volume.
42 The Nielsen Company. Op. cit.
43 Farmakis. Op. cit.
44 Cubrilovic, N. "Logging Out of Facebook Is Not Enough." Nikcub.com. September 25, 2011. https://www.nikcub.com/posts/logging-out-of-facebook-is-not-enough/.
45 See Chapter 9, Note 2, this volume.
46 Farmakis. Op. cit.
47 McCambridge, R. "A New Form of Donor Motivation: Rage Donating!" *Nonprofit Quarterly.* November 15, 2016. https://nonprofitquarterly.org/2016/11/15/new-form-donor-motivation-rage-donating/.

Conclusion

The nonprofit sector has come a long way from its humble and uniquely American beginnings as citizens coming together to meet a local need, sometimes in the face of inadequate government capacity, and sometimes to promote a new vision of society. Its roots in the Puritan notion of a better world are long forgotten. The state-by-state fight for the right to incorporate and create lasting organizations has been relegated to a dusty corner of history. No one alive remembers the Friendly Visitors. There are few if any witnesses left to the days before the nonprofit community had to concern itself with such things as tax status. So much has changed.

Yet the missionary zeal of the 19th-century reformers is still there, written in the faces of those who fight to protect the environment, burning in the eyes of those working for social justice in the inner cities, in the Appalachian highlands, and on Native American reservations in the Dakotas. We can clearly see it animating the steps of those who run, bike, or hike to raise money to fight disease.

Responding to influences, laws, and crises, the sector has adapted, evolved, and changed as circumstances dictated. It has come full circle from where it was at the time of the landmark Dartmouth Supreme Court case in 1819, when the nation's infant eleemosynaries won their independence from the dictates of government. It found its voice, it *created* a voice, and became an unquestionable element in the social and political development of the nation. . .particularly from the antebellum period of 1850 through the Great Society of the 1960s.

And while there have been alterations and adjustments since the Johnson era, these have not significantly changed the *course* of the sector. Rather, it has largely continued on the path laid out in the 1960s, building up steam and momentum, growing and becoming an ever more permanent fixture of the American social and political landscape. Today the sector is not only the government's "partner," but also its dependant, with about three-quarters of the sector's financial support in 2013 coming from a broad assortment public-sector revenue streams.

At the same time, there have been profound changes. The image, for example, that many Americans have of nonprofits, the picture of the small neighborhood church group, the local shelter for homeless people, or the volunteer-friendly, visit-the-elderly program, is fast becoming more myth than reality.[1] Yes, these groups do still exist. But they exist in the shadow of phenomenally larger entities that boast budgets in the tens of millions (and higher) and bureaucratic staffs that would rival those of many a corporation.

Although once known as the "voluntary sector," the American nonprofit arena is today overwhelmingly a world of professionals, from the accountants and lawyers who work for the large foundations, to the credentialed health care and social work specialists who provide services upon which so many depend.

Beyond this, the larger world in which the sector operates is changing. The old constants, the population's religiosity, connection to a physical community, the accepted notion that all charities should be tax-exempt, are in flux. New technology is opening new doors, even as generational succession threatens to unravel many of the assumptions upon which decades of charitable appeals were based.

The American nonprofit sector has grown, developed, adapted, and survived a lot of challenges over the course of the nation's history. There is little doubt that it will continue to adapt and will still be a significant fixture of the American landscape in the decades to come.

Exactly what it will look like, we can't say. Yogi Berra was correct when he noted that predictions, especially about the future, are hard.

But however it evolves, we believe that its past is important. It not only provides context for the challenges of today, but also, within the braided threads of long-ago events, offers lessons in resilience. The American nonprofit sector was not always organized, did not always speak with a unified voice. At times it was distrusted and disliked, and at times teetered on the edge of irrelevancy.

But each time, it came back, stronger than before. That lesson alone is one worth remembering.

It is also valuable to recognize that the sector's 21st-century complexity is both a product and reflective of its multifaceted historical roots.

One of the reasons why America's broad enterprise of social consciousness is referred to as the "nonprofit" sector is that, even though that term is inexact, we have not come up with anything better to describe the collective presence that encompasses activity on behalf of the needy, the disabled, the marginalized, the disenfranchised, one that acts to protect the environment, animals, our historical and cultural heritage, and an expansive array of other concerns.

American charity began with a religiously based concern for one's neighbors. But even as the most ardent supporters of that perspective landed on the rocky, barren shores of this continent, their understanding of charity's place in society had already been profoundly impacted by the thoughts of a German prelate and the actions of an English queen. The former, by untethering charitable acts from the formula for spiritual salvation, opened people to the suggestion that an essential human morality mandated a concern for things beyond ourselves. The latter broadened that notion to include concerns that could best be described as "the public good," actions and undertakings that went beyond help for individuals and were somehow of value to society as a whole.

The very setting in which our unique experiment in social action developed also played a part. The absence of many of the social structures familiar in Europe at the time—an aristocracy, and the bureaucracy and capacity of a long-standing unitary national government—all but forced people to come together in common purpose in a way never seen before. Similarly, the sometimes stumbling, sometimes erratic development of a truly *American* form of government, one with novel characteristics such as a separation of church and state and an independent judiciary that could and would disagree with and countermand the dictates of legislative or executive power, also had a role. The diffusion of power that was unique to America from the 1600s to the 1800s meant that the development of cause-based, organized citizen action that occurred here could not and did not happen elsewhere.

The result was a perspective that, rather than seeing the role of "charitable endeavors" as limited, saw it as virtually boundless. It could, would, and did take on not only relief of need, but also changes in law and policy. It sought not simply to relieve negative conditions, but to go to the root causes of those conditions and address them too. This consciousness–reflected–in–action involved itself in child labor laws, the condition of workers, the treatment of the ill and disabled, and the abolition of slavery. It moved art and culture, in Europe largely the province of aristocracy, into the public realm, benefitting the people and not merely royal patrons. It saw the environment as a heritage common to all and sought, in a way the government was initially unprepared to do, to protect it from the depredations of despoilers who recognized only profit or convenience as guiding principles.

It looked to what people needed, what *society* needed, and sought to provide for those needs, often acting not only ahead of the government, but sometimes in place of it. Later, it became the government's partner.

If there is one overriding lesson a review and appreciation of the sector's history provides, it is that, yes, it *is* and has been resilient. . .it has had to respond to changes in society and in law. It had to survive a civil war, dramatic shifts in popular attitudes, and the worst economic crisis the modern world has ever seen. But more than that, it has gone beyond being just adaptive and has, instead, been innovative, envisioning both possibilities and solutions that are often beyond the cumbersome mechanics of the public sphere, or the self-interested ones of the corporate world.

This is not to say that our nonprofit sector is perfect, always does everything correctly, or is without challenges. It has been and will always be subject to influences beyond its boundaries. It still needs to address important shortcomings in the way it operates. It needs to demonstrate, in a way heretofore unprecedented, that it is not simply *trying*, but is **accomplishing**. In coming years, it will need to accommodate and find a way to create support within a generation accustomed to almost unlimited sources of information, one with completely new concepts of community, one over whom traditional appeals hold ever diminishing sway. . .and one both unaccustomed to and impatient with the incrementalism that for so long has been accepted as natural and unavoidable.

There will no doubt be still more changes in coming years. A decade from now, the rules under which the sector operates, and the *way* it operates will likely be different than they are today. . .possibly quite different. But even if that proves to be the case, it is a virtual certainty that the sector *will* still be operating. Far from having outlived its usefulness, the American nonprofit sector has proven over the nation's history that it has a place in our culture and our society. It continues to grow not of its own accord, but because we want it to and make it able it to.

If the past is any guide to the future, if the history we have recounted within these pages has demonstrated anything, it is that this is an arena that has never accepted the idea of limits, it has never looked at where it is or what it is doing and said, *Good enough.* For tomorrow's nonprofit leaders, that is admittedly a challenge, but also ought to be an inspiration. The American nonprofit sector, for all its bumps, warts, and shortcomings, can do what neither the public nor corporate arenas are designed to do. It is vital, it is valuable, and still has a very significant role to play.

And that is why we have told this story.

Note

1 Wagner. p. 121.

Index

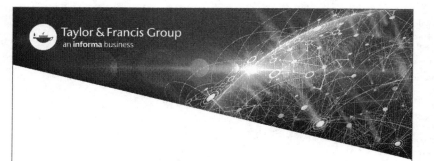